INTERACTIVE HUMAN RESOURCE MANAGEMENT AND STRATEGIC PLANNING

Interactive Human Resource Management and Strategic Planning

CYNTHIA A. LENGNICK-HALL
AND
MARK L. LENGNICK-HALL

Q

QUORUM BOOKS

New York • Westport, Connecticut • London

Library of Congress Cataloging-in-Publication Data

Lengnick-Hall, Cynthia A.
  Interactive human resource management and strategic planning /
Cynthia A. Lengnick-Hall and Mark L. Lengnick-Hall.
    p.   cm.
  Includes bibliographical references and index.
  ISBN 0–89930–502–4 (lib. bdg. : alk. paper)
  1. Personnel management.   2. Strategic planning.   I. Lengnick-
Hall, Mark L.   II. Title.
HF5549.L4614   1990
658.3′01—dc20   90–8959

British Library Cataloguing in Publication Data is available.

Library of Congress Catalog Card Number: 90–8959
ISBN: 0–89930–502–4

First published in 1990

Quorum Books, 88 Post Road West, Westport, CT   06881
An imprint of Greenwood Publishing Group, Inc.

Printed in the United States of America

The paper used in this book complies with the
Permanent Paper Standard issued by the National
Information Standards Organization (Z39.48–1984).

10 9 8 7 6 5 4 3 2 1

To Rebecca and Amanda: Our favorite human resources

Contents

Acknowledgments

The ideas presented in this book took a number of years to germinate and take their present shape. We would like to acknowledge and thank our friends and colleagues at Purdue University who were instrumental in providing the opportunities and scholarly climate that facilitated this process. In particular we would like to extend our thanks to Carolyn Woo, Arnie Cooper, Dan Schendel, and Gary Willard in the strategic management area. We would also like to thank John Cotton, Chris Berger, and Don King in the organization behavior and human resource management group. Each of these individuals in one way or another provided support, encouragement, intellectual challenge, and outstanding examples of scholarship. Finally we would like to thank those students who critiqued our ideas at early stages of development and, thus, helped us clarify our thinking: Lee Burke, Karel Cool, Mary Correa, and Kirk Froggatt.

The theoretical model upon which this book is based was initially published in the *Academy of Management Review*. For this we would like to extend our appreciation to Chuck Behling. Without his encouragement and assistance, the initial publication would not have been possible.

1

Defining Strategic Human Resource Management

Strategic human resource management is gaining increasing attention among strategic planners and human resource managers in both large and small organizations. Strategic human resource management has been described in a variety of ways by different authors reflecting different assumptions about the nature of strategic planning and the composition of human resource management practices. Moreover, efforts at achieving strategic human resource management have been comprised of diverse mixes of activities and intentions across different companies. Therefore, a description of how we envision strategic human resource management is provided in this first chapter. The rationale underlying a need for strategic human resource management is explained along with organizational examples of how strategic human resource management works in practice. Several of the more common approaches to strategic human resource management are compared and contrasted with traditional views. This comparison juxtaposes strategic human resource management with classical models, behavioral models, and other contingency models.

A NEW AGENDA FOR HUMAN RESOURCE MANAGERS

According to *Business Week* a strategic focus in the human resource area is one of the most dramatic changes in a managerial function since financial executives rose to power in the conglomerate era of the 1960s:

At a time when companies are constantly acquiring, merging, and spinning off divisions, entering new businesses and getting out of old ones, management must base strategic decisions more than ever on HR [human resources] considerations—

matching skills with jobs, keeping key personnel after a merger, and solving human problems that arise from introducing new technology or closing a plant.[1]

Recent interviews with seventy-one chief executive officers (CEOs) revealed an interesting shift in perspective.[2] No longer is a human resource department charged with the sole responsibility for managing people. Selecting, motivating, developing, and evaluating employees is now a part of every manager's job. Perhaps even more importantly, a firm's employees are seen as assets, not just as costs. Employees are often acknowledged as a primary facet in securing a firm's competitive position. This is quite different from seeing employee-related expenses as a line item to be kept as small as possible, or from viewing employee expenses as a cost to be contrasted with capital expenditures. Increasingly, CEOs see human resource management as one of the key links in generating a competitive edge.

Michael Porter argues that human resources can help a firm obtain an improved competitive position in a variety of ways.[3] Effective strategic human resource management practices can lower the costs of manufacturing, enhance product development, and upgrade marketing or any other functional area activity. Unique talents among employees, including flexibility, innovation, superior performance, high productivity, and personal customer service, are all cited as ways employees provide a critical ingredient in developing a firm's competitive position. People can provide a significant source of product or service quality or distinctiveness that cannot be duplicated by even the most sophisticated machines.

People can provide the key to managing pivotal interdependencies across functional activities. Likewise, people can manage crucial relationships among important external constituencies. Moreover, a competitive advantage that stems from the management and talents of individuals is much more difficult for competitors to duplicate than a competitive edge derived from product features, manufacturing processes, or marketing practices. It has been estimated that it takes approximately seven years to duplicate a competitive edge obtained from human resources, if such an advantage can be imitated at all.[4] However, achieving a competitive advantage through people requires that human resource activities be managed from a strategic perspective. This presents both a change and a challenge for traditional human resource managers and other corporate officers as well.

Using the human resource management function most effectively as a corporate resource requires that top management implement several important practices.[5] First, the human resource department's responsibility should be defined as the maximization of corporate profits through the better management and use of people. This appropriately focuses the unit's attention on corporate-wide objectives. Moreover, this statement of purpose directs activities toward results, not just toward processes or activities. How often has a traditional training session been evaluated in terms of whether or not participants enjoyed the experience rather than in terms of improved productivity, better competitive positioning, or enhanced product quality? A strategically oriented definition provides an appropriate context for interpreting and evaluating human resource management actions and contributions.

Second, the senior human resource executive should report directly to the CEO. Top-level reporting enables two important network relationships. First, top-level reporting ensures top-level attention to human resource concerns. This encourages corporate officers to consider human resource issues up front when making strategic plans, rather than plugging in people after the critical decisions have been made. Second, top-level reporting supports direct accountability of the human resource professional to the competitive interests of the firm. Neither other corporate officers nor a human resource manager can view the human resource manager's role as anything but directly responsible for making a recognizable contribution to the competitive position of the firm. At this hierarchical level, a human resource manager is unable to hide behind excuses of low influence or supporting role responsibilities. Finance officers, manufacturing vice presidents, marketing directors, and other members of the corporate coalition are likewise unable to discount the expertise of human resource professionals arbitrarily.

Third, the human resource management unit should not be encumbered with unrelated activities. In the past, human resource managers often found themselves functioning as the "default option" when any activity fell outside the direct purview of other functional areas. If a company picnic or a corporate officer's retreat is not expected to contribute either directly or indirectly to an improved competitive position, why should such activities take place? If the events are strictly for enjoyment, they should viewed as social activities, not as part of the human resource manager's operating activities. This dumping-ground approach dilutes the energies and the direction of human resource professionals. Such wasted time and effort can seriously undermine the human resource operation's primary contribution to corporate productivity.

Fourth, human resource executives should be experienced business people. The importance of finance, marketing, production, and other functional areas of expertise for the human resource professional cannot be stressed too strongly. Human resource executives must be perceived as equals by their counterparts in other functional units. This is unlikely to happen unless a human resource manager demonstrates a thorough understanding of the competitive climate, product options, cost constraints, marketing characteristics, and all other aspects of productivity and profitability affecting the firm. Human resource managers must be able to provide pro forma cost-benefit estimates to accompany their recommen-dations.[6] Moreover, human resource professionals must be expected to understand, predict, and be held accountable for the direct and indirect contribution their performance makes to the bottom line. Even though precise bottom-line figures may be difficult to devise, it is essential that human resource managers continually think in financial outcome and bot-tom-line terms. The following are a few examples of this type of thinking:

- "Here's what we did for you in recruiting, here's what it cost, and here's what you would have done without us and what it would have cost you."
- "Here's how much money we saved you by changing insurers in our benefits package."
- "Here's an idea that workers developed in a training program we were leading. It's now working and saving the firm $50,000 per year."
- "You used to have an unhappy person doing this job for $40,000 per year. As a result of our job redesign, you now have a motivated person doing the same work for $20,000."
- "In working with the union on a new contract, we found a new way to reduce grievances by 30 percent, saving the company 6,429 hours per year in manage-ment time."[7]

"The perception used to be that human resource managers thought about the happiness of employees and line managers thought about costs. Now both realize that the overriding concern is the yield from employ-ees."[8] Yield concentrates on the intricate web of costs and benefits that result from investing in and focusing a firm's human resources toward a certain set of activities and away from other behaviors and actions. Yield recognizes both trade-offs and choices. Yield depends on shared respon-sibilities and collaboration across functional units and hierarchical levels.

THREATS, OPPORTUNITIES, AND HUMAN RESOURCE MANAGEMENT

An underlying premise of this book is that human resource management should be an integral part of the strategic planning processes of a firm. The primary rationale underlying strategic human resource management is the concept of competitive advantage. Competitive advantage is the essence of competitive strategy. Competitive advantage encompasses those capabilities, resources, relationships, and decisions that permit a firm to capitalize on opportunities in the marketplace and to avoid threats to a firm's desired competitive position.

Opportunities and threats are environmental events, trends, or potential actions that occur within a firm's primary industry or in ancillary industries comprised of important customers, suppliers, or producers of substitute goods or services. Examples include new technologies, raw material short-ages, consolidation of distribution channels, new marketing techniques, packaging innovations, changes in consumer demand, and the entry or exit of competitive companies within an industry. Whether these events constitute an opportunity or a threat depends on the firm's current competitive position, its goals and aspirations, and the internal strengths and weaknesses that influence its ability to react to the challenge presented.

Opportunities and threats are not restricted to events or interactions among industry and ancillary participants. Opportunities and threats also include more general environmental characteristics such as shifts in the economy or changes in demographics. Think for a moment how the evolutionary, yet far reaching, changes in the structure and behavior of American families is contributing to significant shifts in the workplace, and to corresponding alterations in career paths and work options. Expanding this illustration, changes in family structure have offered exciting business opportunities for some companies (e.g., child care providers, convenience foods, shopper services) and posed significant threats for other businesses (e.g., fabric stores and home sewing machines, volunteer organizations).

According to the Bureau of National Affairs (BNA), less than 10 percent of the population now lives in the "Ozzie and Harriet" two-parent family, where the father is the sole provider of financial support and the mother is primarily responsible for homemaking.[9] Over 70 percent of women with children between the ages of six and seventeen were in the work force by the end of 1987. The number of working women with children under the age of one has increased by 67 percent over the past decade. These trends suggest a number of important individual consequences. For example, women are gaining increased equal opportunity in stress-related physical disorders (accompanied by threats and opportunities for the medical community, insurance companies, and their employing organizations). A recent *Wall Street Journal* article describes how some men are redefining fatherhood and consequently experiencing increased career-family stress, (with accompanying threats and opportunities for health care, physical fitness centers, and how-to publications). Other men are using their spouse's economic contribution as a rationale for abandoning all parental responsibilities (meanwhile providing threats and opportunities for government agencies, social services, and the legal system).

Organizations are also faced with new internal realities as a result of shifts in the family. Many of the individual consequences have both direct and indirect organizational consequences. In the 1950s, organizations could expect employees to attend early morning meetings, work long hours, and to travel and relocate to meet the needs of the corporation. These expectations assumed employees were single wage earners, who needed to maximize economic outcomes and who could delegate responsibility for maintaining a home and raising children to someone else. Such expectations are facing increasing resistance among dual-career couples, single parents, and families with responsibilities that include caring for elderly parents. From a different perspective, organizational commitment is frequently offered as a means for improving productivity and enhancing excellence in the workplace. However, current demographic patterns suggest that organizational involvement and commitment must compete for an employee's attention, energy, and emotion with an ever-widening range of family responsibilities and personal interests.

Clearly, a new diversity in mainstream family structures provides opportunities as well as threats related to product demand, service preferences, sources of competitive advantage and disadvantage, and the ways in which organizations can be organized and managed. Changes in technology, variations in monetary trends, political systems modifications, and shifts in social values and preferences have equally far-reaching and multidimensional consequences that provide opportunities for some firms and introduce threats for others. The more adept a firm is at anticipating, recognizing, and responding to the threats and opportunities it encounters, the better its competitive position. This book is based on the premise that a firm's human resources can offer a key element in this endeavor.

The concept of competitive advantage will be discussed more fully in Chapter 2, but it is important to understand at the outset that human resources can provide an important and substantial competitive edge if they are managed with strategic goals in mind.

STRATEGY CHOICE AND HUMAN RESOURCE MANAGEMENT PRACTICE

There is increasing evidence that while market and cost considerations constrain a firm's avenues for gaining competitive advantage, the limitation is more a matter of degree than of fate or determinism. Managerial values and preferences, corporate cultures, political and ideological issues, and a firm's human resources practices often have as influential an effect on a firm's selection of a competitive approach as do marketplace characteristics. We believe this influence ought to be deliberate, intentional, and analytically based, rather than accidental or the result of neglect or ignorance.

Randall Schuler and Susan Jackson provide an excellent discussion of ways in which specific personnel practices either facilitate or hinder the implementation of particular competitive strategies.[10] They argue that firms seeking competitive advantage based on innovation should invest heavily in their human resources and adopt human resource management practices that enable selection of highly skilled individuals, promote employee discretion, rely on minimal controls, and encourage experimentation. Moreover such firms should develop performance appraisal and compensation systems that permit failure and enhance personal feelings of control. Firms relying on innovation to compete must develop human resource management practices that enable people to work differently.

In contrast, firms that base competitive advantage on low price must develop human resource management practices that enable employees to work harder. These firms rely on continuous, incremental cost reductions per unit of output. Human resource management in cost leader organizations relies on job analyses that enable repetitive and predictable behaviors, facilitate autonomous and individual activities, encourage output quantity, and discourage risk taking among employees. Staffing choices, appraisal systems, compensation alternatives, and training and development practices within firms competing on cost leadership are quite different than these same activities in firms that rely on innovation for a strong competitive position or seek competitive advantage from high quality.

In firms dependent on quality for competitive advantage, employees must be encouraged to work smarter. In quality-oriented firms, human resource practices ensure that appropriate feedback systems are in place, facilitate team building among employees, and develop systems for maintaining flexible job classifications and role expectations.

While the need for different human resource management practices and activities reflecting different strategic objectives and tactics is becoming increasingly obvious, the reciprocity inherent in this relationship has been largely ignored. If a firm identifies and puts in place people and practices to facilitate the accomplishment of specific strategic objectives, it is only reasonable to expect that these same people and practices will serve as a screening device for identifying and selecting subsequent strategic moves. We argue that this iterative and reciprocal relationship should be more fully explored, better understood, and intentionally exploited. This book provides a roadmap for such an exploration, understanding, and action.

COSTS OF STRATEGIC HUMAN RESOURCE MANAGEMENT

The potential benefits of strategic human resource management have captured the attention of managers and researchers alike. Many academicians and practicing managers have examined the broad scope and implications of human resource strategies.[11] These researchers note that the strategic management of human resources is a multidimensional process with multiple effects. They further point out that while strategic human resource management is beneficial, significant costs must be considered as well. Both direct and indirect costs are important to acknowledge.

Direct expenses include such items as skill development, team building, recruiting expenses, carefully constructed reward systems, and accepting higher selection standards for hiring. Many traditional strategic human resource management approaches rely on cross-training and group inter- actions to build a highly flexible pool of human talent in the organization. Such an approach means that at any point in time, available skills may go untapped. While we contend that enhanced flexibility is only one of several different avenues by which human resources can contribute to a firm's strategic objectives, any use of human resources will by necessity entail costs. These costs should be assessed along with the expected benefits to fully evaluate the merits of a particular strategic human re- source management approach.

Indirect costs can have an even larger impact on a cost-benefit equation, simply because they often go unrecognized, and thereby unmanaged. Some of the important indirect costs of strategic human resource man- agement stem from additional information requirements. Information-re- lated costs include increased decision complexity and a greater potential for information overload.

Other indirect costs arise from the raised level of expectations among employees. Expectation-related costs accrue largely because of increased commitment by employees to an organization, and an increased commit- ment by an organization to employee welfare often goes hand-in-hand with an increased strategic focus to human resource management. This heightened mutual interdependence can lead to a number of problems. Consider what is involved with an expansion of existing human resource practices to include strategic concerns. Job requirements for many, if not all, employees take on added dimensions related to a firm's overall strat- egy. Employees not only need to learn new skills, they need to be able to expand their communication network so that entire workflows are examined. Employees may be expected to continue to perform specialized jobs, but to understand and control the effect of job performance on the bottom-line and competitive position of the firm as a whole. It is not surprising that employees expect additional compensation to accompany the additional work requirements. Initially this is accommodated through increased productivity that yields increased profitability. However, ex- pectations of continued organizational growth are often a premise under- lying bonus pay, job rotation, promotion, and other organizational rewards. Yet, continual rapid growth is often incompatible with mature industry conditions. This generally means that, at some point, reality conflicts with expectations.

Expanded performance expectations also often lead to commitments to employees regarding job security and work rules. These commitments, too, can lead to either unmet expectations or to heavy competitive costs. Inflexible work rules can inhibit the adoption of new technology or the use of state-of-the-art production techniques. Job security means that current employees must be retrained to meet changing conditions and production techniques. This investment in developing existing employees rather than purchasing new employees with the needed skills can create timing disadvantages that may undermine effective strategic planning.

Finally, the various types of commitment that frequently accompany strategic human resource management can lead to allocating a disproportionate amount of a firm's financial resources to human resource activities. This overcommitment is often coupled with an unbalanced concern about employee reactions to strategic choices at the expense of concerns with marketplace realities.

DILEMMAS OF COST-BENEFIT ASSESSMENT

An accurate evaluation of costs as well as benefits is rarely presented by proponents of specific strategic human resource management practices. As a result, it is difficult to compare approaches. Further, problems arise in trying to compare strategic human resource management approaches with more traditional approaches to either human resource management or to strategic management. It is difficult to evaluate strategic solutions to human resource problems or assess human resource solutions to strategic problems, relative to the more traditional approach of using human resource management-based solutions to human resource problems and strategic solutions to competitive issues.

The computer industry provides a useful example of using human resources to solve a strategic problem. One of the forces that increases competitive pressure in the computer industry is low costs associated with switching from one supplier to another. In other words, customers face few prohibitive expenses or difficulties in changing from one manufacturer to another supplier with compatible equipment. Schuler and MacMillan describe how IBM was able to counteract this trend and introduce switching costs for their products alone through the creative use of human resources.[12] IBM has for many years taught programming skills to customers' employees. As a result, the loyalty and commitment of these programmers is high toward both IBM and their host firms. Customers gain a stronger tie with IBM, which raises the potential costs of switching to a different manufacturer. Meanwhile, IBM gains programmers who are intimately aware of their own and the customers needs and can thereby provide valuable information regarding upcoming demand. The programmer understands the corporate climate in his or her host organization and can therefore be instrumental in introducing new products or systems through the most effective channels. IBM and the customer mutually benefit from the state-of-the-art skills of the programmer, in that the host firm receives competitive and operational benefits, while

IBM benefits from the probability that IBM equipment will be used to its full capabilities, thus improving the odds that the quality of the equipment will be realized by the customer.

It should also be noted, however, that there is a cost associated with this approach. The stronger tie may also increase the customer's expectation of responsiveness from IBM. Over time, this responsiveness or customization may become more difficult or more expensive for IBM to provide. In addition, an important human resource precedent is set. Programmers are hired from outside the organization and certain career paths are blocked for existing IBM employees. Clearly, the short-term outcome is beneficial to both firms. Equally clearly, the long-term evaluation is uncertain. Therefore, while integration between human resource management and competitive strategy is often proposed as an attractive option, this example illustrates the complex repercussions of such an interaction. One point becomes obvious: integration of competitive strategy and human resource management should not be a unidirectional process from either perspective if undesirable consequences are to be minimized.

AN ARGUMENT IN SUPPORT OF STRATEGIC HUMAN RESOURCE MANAGEMENT

Why is it desirable to integrate human resource management and strategic choice despite these difficulties? First, integration provides a broader range of solutions for solving complex organizational problems. Second, integration ensures that human as well as financial, technological, and information resources are considered in setting goals, assessing implementation capabilities, and evaluating organizational potential. Third, integration recognizes that organizations should explicitly consider their employees, who must not only implement organizational policies but experience the consequences of organizational choices. Finally, reciprocity in integrating human resource management and strategic concerns limits the subordination of strategic considerations to human resource preferences. Likewise, reciprocity reduces the probability that human resources will be neglected as a vital source of organizational competence and competitive advantage. These two factors reduce a potential source of suboptimization that has unwittingly plagued many firms.

THE ROADMAP OFFERED IN THIS BOOK

This book guides strategists who wish to make better competitive use of their firm's human resources and human resource managers who hope to enhance their human resource function's contribution to the strategic objectives of their firm. We do not review or critique human resource management practices in general but rather explore how human resource management activities might be considered in light of a firm's strategic objectives and competitive position. This means that organizations will consider their employees "as important resources to be invested in prudently, to be used productively, and from whom a return can be expected—a return that should be monitored as carefully as is the return on any other business investment."[13] Likewise this book does not evaluate strategy formulation, implementation techniques, or alternatives from a general activity stance. Instead we propose a typology that guides managers in their consideration of human resources as a way to improve their firms' competitive position.

NOTES

1. See Human resource managers aren't corporate nobodies anymore. *Business Week* (December 2, 1985): 58–59, for complete quotation. Additional insights can be gained from D. Briscoe, Human resource management has come of age, *Personnel Administrator* (November 1982) 26: 75–83.

2. See Chapter 2 of W. F. Cascio, *Managing Human Resources, Productivity, Quality of Work Life, Profits*. 2d ed. (New York: McGraw-Hill, 1989).

3. See M. Porter, *Competitive Strategy* (New York: Free Press, 1980) and M. Porter, *Competitive Advantage* (New York: Free Press, 1985). Both books address concepts related to this discussion in great detail.

4. See R. S. Schuler, Human resource management practice choices. In *Readings in Personnel and Human Resource Management*. 3d ed. Eds. R. S. Schuler, S. A. Youngblood, and V. L. Huber. (St Paul: West, 1988).

5. For additional arguments, see Cascio, *Managing Human Resources* (New York: McGraw-Hill, 1989).

6. For a good discussion of methods for determining the financial impact of human resource management activities, see Wayne Cascio, *Costing Human Resources* (Boston: PWS Kent, 1987).

7. For a complete discussion see G. M. Bellman, Doing more with less. In *Personnel Administrator* 31 (July 1986:) 46–52.

8. For additional examples see W. Keichel, Living with human resources. *Fortune* (August 18, 1987): 99–100.

9. The demographic data was cited in a 1988 advertisement for the National Report on Work and Family.

10. For an excellent discussion of employee role behaviors related to competitive strategies, along with a menu approach to matching personnel activities to competitive actions, see Randall S. Schuler and Susan E. Jackson, Linking competitive strategies with human resource management practices, in *The Academy of Management Executive* (St Paul, Minn.: West, 1987); Schuler, Human resource management.

11. See, for example, L. Dyer, Studying Human Resource strategy: An approach and an agenda *Industrial Relations* 23(2) (1984); E. C. Smith, Strategic business planning and human resources, *Personnel Journal* 61(8) (1982), 606–610; N. Tichy, C. Fombrun, and M. Devanna, Strategic human resource management.

Sloan Management Review (1982); T. Wils and L. Dyer, Relating business strategy to human resource strategy: Some preliminary evidence. (August 1984) Presented at the Academy of Management meetings in Boston, 1984, provide excellent summary articles.

12. See R. S. Schuler and I. C. MacMillan, Gaining competitive advantage through human resource management practices. *Human Resource Management* 23(3), (1984) 241–56.

13. See Cascio, *Costing Human Resources*.

2

An Overview of Strategic Management

The basis of strategic management is making choices. This chapter introduces strategic management concepts and defines important strategic management activities. Several objectives have guided our inclusion of various issues. First, the content of strategic decisions is distinguished as much as possible from the process of strategic decision making. While distinctions and interactions between strategy formulation and strategy implementation are discussed, this book focuses on the content of strategic choices rather than the process by which such decisions are made. Our focus is on designing a desirable set of strategic options for a firm to consider. A second objective that guided our selection of issues is to clarify the foundations of strategic management activities. Underlying themes and assumptions of strategic management tools and techniques are identified and examined. These themes provide the underpinnings for linking strategy and human resource management. Finally, a summary of strategic management concerns is provided. We believe understanding the scope of strategic activities and the ways in which these issues differ from traditional operating activities in an organization makes a reciprocal relationship between human resource management decisions and strategic choices easier to maintain.

Strategic management entails a series of judgements, under uncertainty, that are directed toward achieving a specific future interaction between a firm and its industry or marketplace environment. Imbedded in this definition is the assumption that a firm has a clear set of strategic goals in mind. It is also presumed that much of the information used to make strategic choices is probabilistic, ambiguous, at times contradictory, and often incomplete. Developing a strategic plan includes the determination of a source of competitive advantage and the means by which the desired interactions between a firm and its market environment are to be attained. This view of strategy contains a number of important assumptions and themes crucial to an understanding of strategic human resource management.

COMPONENTS OF STRATEGY

It often seems that strategy is in the eye of the beholder. Henry Mintzberg has identified five P's of strategy that can be mixed and matched to form a mosaic of strategic descriptions.[1] If strategy is considered a *plan*, it refers to the consciously intended course of action a firm has selected to deal with a situation. Recognizing that not all plans are fully realized, and not all strategic actions are the result of foresight, Mintzberg also suggests that strategy can be considered a *pattern*, defined as a consistent stream of actions that may be, in part, the result of a deliberate plan and in part the result of emergent actions premised on some common underpinnings. At a more tactical level, strategy is sometimes envisioned as a *ploy*, a specific maneuver rather than a long-term series of activities. Adopting a perspective that views organizations relative to other actors rather than an internal decision-making view, strategy can be envisioned as a *position*. Strategy as a position refers to the location of a firm relative to competitors and other important actors in the environment. Finally, Mintzberg contends, strategy can be seen as a *perspective*. From this last vantage point, strategy is the personality, or gestalt, of an organization.

Each of these dimensions of strategy presents an important facet of developing a human resource management strategy. For human resource considerations to be included in strategy formulation activities, human resource issues must be deliberately analyzed and integrated into the decision process. The attitudes and attributes that result from human resource management practices, along with other functional area activities, generate consistent patterns of activity within a firm. Traditional strategic human resource management practices have relied on using human resources to tactically outmaneuver a competitor (e.g., use a more knowledgable sales force) or to secure a better position in the marketplace (e.g., greater responsiveness to customer complaints). Finally, the attitude that accompanies a reciprocal interdependence between strategic management activities and human resource management activities alters the fundamental culture of an organization in important, often subtle, but very pervasive ways.

Regardless of the particular perspective adopted at a particular decision juncture or point in time, descriptions of a firm's strategy should include the following components. First is defining the *product* and *market scope* a firm selects. Product-market considerations include a description of the particular goods and services to be provided, accompanied by distinguishing features that characterize the intended use and attractive attributes of these products. Product-market descriptions include a delineation of those features that differentiate a firm from its competitors. Typical product characteristics include cost, quality dimensions, optional features, durability, reliability, and service alternatives. Market dimensions refer to geographic regions, customer buying characteristics, size and diversity of the target market population, and other distinguishing characteristics. A comprehensive description of product-market scope essentially describes what a firm intends to do, and who should be interested. An externally based and an internally derived view of product-market scope are presented in the section on product and market orientation.

A second basic component of strategy is the determination of a *source of competitive advantage* and the identification of the key *competencies* that are needed to accomplish a sustained competitive position. As mentioned in the first chapter, competitive advantage is what sets a firm apart from other business engaged in similar activities or pursuing similar customers. Two primary ways to achieve competitive advantage will be discussed in more detail later in this chapter.

A third essential component of strategy is *resource deployment*, which depicts how a firm intends to allocate its financial, informational, technical, time (i.e., rules for establishing priority), space or facility, and human resources. The resource deployment choice has perhaps the most direct and obvious link with strategic human resource management issues. A portfolio view of resource allocation is summarized in a later section.

A fourth component of strategy is *synergy*, a muliplier effect that results from making choices that create mutually beneficial interactions among a firm's activities. In highly complex situations, synergy is the reason why groups typically make better decisions than individuals. Synergy explains why mass production operations generally require broad and efficient distribution networks. Synergy is the result of hiring highly creative individuals, guiding them with clear, specific, and challenging goals, and providing sufficient autonomy and resources to generate state-of-the-art software. Mutually beneficial interactions among the diverse actions of a firm permit use of many forms of expertise, talent, and compensatory capability. To the extent a firm generates synergy, it also creates multiple options for achieving any particular goal. Systems engineers refer to this as equifinality. The additional flexibility derived from having many paths to a given objective is often a key element in maintaining a strong competitive position in a highly competitive industry. The search for synergy is a basic incentive for strategic human resource management.

Nucor, one of America's largest and most successful minimill steel operations, illustrates these components. Nucor's product-market scope is the production of high-grade, thin, rolled steel and various light bar products for a variety of industrial uses from oil drums to forging billets. The key competitive advantage is price. Nucor enjoys a number of distinct competencies ranging from innovative and low-cost production techniques, to high human resource productivity, to economies of scale, to modern equipment and highly motivated employees. The human resource selection, training, staffing, and compensation practices lead to production synergies that result in technology advances and high-quality, highly flexible operations. Nucor invests heavily in its employees, in both financial and informational resources.

COMPETITIVE ADVANTAGE AND DISTINCT COMPETENCE

Perhaps the most pervasive concept underlying strategic management is the notion of competition. In order to be an effective competitor, a firm must make two important choices. First, it must decide upon the type of competitive advantage it intends to pursue. Second, it must determine its scope of operations (i.e., the diversity of products it will produce and the range of markets it will serve).

Two basic types of competitive advantage are identified by Michael Porter: competitive advantage based on cost leadership and competitive advantage based on differentiation.[2] A competitive advantage based on *cost leadership* means that a firm attempts to be the low-cost producer of a good or service within the marketplace, while selling the good or service at a price advantage relative to the industry average. This type of competitive advantage requires a firm's outputs to be perceived as roughly comparable to the goods or services offered by competitors. In contrast, competitive advantage based on *differentiation* relies on a firm's ability to offer something both unique and valued to its customers. A firm using a differentiation strategy charges a price premium as a reward for its uniqueness.

Competitive scope refers to the breadth of target market segments a firm intends to serve. This distinguishes a firm that constrains its activities to meet specialized needs of a narrowly defined market niche from a firm that attempts to identify the common product-related characteristics that appeal to the entire marketplace. A firm choosing a broad target market directs its attention toward the industry as a whole. A firm selecting a narrow target identifies specialized industry segments with clearly marked and relatively stable boundaries toward which it directs its efforts. In general, firms that select a narrow scope have more limited growth opportunities yet more freedom in selecting other dimensions of strategy than do firms that choose a broad scope.

Competitive Strategy Options

A cost leadership strategy means that a firm intends to be the preeminent low-cost producer of a product within its industry. A firm electing this strategy serves many industry segments, and, at times, may cross traditional industry boundaries in its effort to secure economies of scale or cost advantages from suppliers or within distribution channels. Effective performance requires that all available sources of cost advantage must be used. A cost leader typically sells a standardized product with few, if any, frills. BIC Incorporated's approach to the writing instrument industry provides an example of the successful use of cost leadership. A cost leadership strategy cannot ignore differentiation, however. The product must be acceptable to customers at a price roughly equivalent to a firm's rivals. If such parity is not achieved, any advantage resulting from lower costs of production will be nullified by a need to severely discount market price.

Often overlooked opportunities for managing costs include exploitation of linkages with external organizations and interactions among support activities in the value chain. A *value chain* is the collection of primary activities (e.g. operations, marketing) and support activities (e.g. procurement, infrastructure development) necessary to design, produce, deliver, market, and support a product. The value chain is a tool to systematically consider disaggregated sets of activities in a way that facilitates the search for cost advantages and sources of uniqueness. Interactions within and between activities in the value chain offer opportunities for valuable competitive contributions from employees. Some firms capitalize on cost-related first-mover advantages, such as obtaining supplier or distribution channel discounts or marketing economies related to brand recognition. Other firms seek gains from being an early follower by allowing a pioneer to work the bugs out of a product. Selecting appropriate discretionary policies can enhance a firm's cost position in a number of ways. Human resource practices can play an important role in each of these competence areas.

A firm pursuing a differentiation strategy attempts to be unique within its industry along attributes that are widely valued by a large proportion of potential customers. Such a strategy involves the identification of one or more factors seen as important to buyers (e.g., innovativeness, special options) and then positioning the product or service to meet those needs precisely. Hewlett-Packard's scientific instrument products rely on this strategy. This quality orientation allows differentiators to charge higher prices for their products. The particular product attributes that are important vary by industry and often by industry segment.

Sources of uniqueness can be enhanced by proliferating differentiation throughout the value chain. The use of high-quality raw materials or nontraditional packaging, for example, can help establish uniqueness. Unique features can be more readily appreciated by potential customers if a firm makes sure that actual product use is consistent with intended product use. This may involve reliance on customer service representatives or the provision of consulting services. A uniqueness-based firm employs various signals to reinforce the need for differentiation. Frequently, these firms bundle information with the product to facilitate both effective use and marketing distinctions. At times a firm can change the rules that govern competition to secure uniqueness.

If a firm relies on cost-related distinct competencies, but concentrates its attention on a more narrow target market, the result is a cost focus strategy. A *cost focus* strategy reflects a firm's choice to be the low-cost producer within a structurally attractive segment of the total marketplace. Structurally attractive means that the target segment is substantially different from other parts of the industry in its preferences or buying habits. Generally this means that the boundaries of the market segment are relatively stable, and that these boundaries can be defended from encroachment by more broadly targeted competitors. Thus, a firm adopting a cost focus strategy is the lowest cost producer that meets the basic needs of a unique market segment. Local distributors of industrial cleaning supplies illustrate this approach.

A *differentiation focus* strategy requires a firm to identify industry segments with special needs, and to meet these needs more precisely than any other competitor. Thus, a successful differentiation focus strategy requires a segment of potential buyers that have quite different needs from the larger industry. Such segments must at present be poorly served by more broadly targeted competitors for the segment to be structurally attractive. Similar to a cost focus strategy, the target market is more narrow than with a pure differentiation approach, but the basic skills needed are quite similar. The Jeep product line illustrates this approach.

The combination of individual choices comprising a competitive approach and breadth of focus yields several successful *strategic configurations:* (1) cost leadership with low differentiation and a broad focus, (2) cost leadership with low differentiation and a narrow focus, (3) high cost with high differentiation and a broad focus, (4) high cost with high differentiation and a narrow focus, (5) low cost with high differentiation and a broad focus, and (6) low cost with high differentiation and a narrow focus. The latter two options are particularly difficult to achieve. Each of the strategies can be successful depending on industry characteristics and a firm's areas of competence. (Note: a high cost with low differentiation combination would not be successful)

The Competency Connection

Sustainable competitive advantage, whether it reflects a low cost or a high differentiation position, is the result of a set of distinct competencies developed by a firm that lead to its favorable position within its industry. *Distinct competencies* are the processes and outcomes in which a firm is able to achieve excellence. Competencies can range from creativity, to financial management, to manufacturing efficiency, to quality control. Every activity a firm undertakes offers a potential for developing a distinct competence. Clearly, we believe an important distinct competence for any firm is the effective management of its human resources. As will be discussed in greater detail in the section on a firm's value chain, the management of human resources cuts across all of a firm's primary and support activities and can, thereby, provide means to lower costs or enhanced differentiation throughout a firm's scope of operations.

A number of specific distinct competencies are associated with a cost leadership strategy. Some of the more common of these are capitalizing on economies of scale or economies of scope, maintaining a highly productive work force, using efficient machinery and facilities, maintaining high-capacity utilization, and other similar manufacturing skills. Cost leadership also relies on efficiency in distribution as well as operations. Moreover, many cost leadership firms develop the means to share technologies across departmental and product lines. Knowledge and understanding of the human resource implications of these types of capabilities plays a major role in effective strategic human resource management.

Competencies associated with differentiation typically reflect operating flexibility, high product and manufacturing reliability, product styling, and product durability. Differentiation firms often emphasize creativity and innovation, market research, and an ability to generate new ideas for improved product use. It is not unusual for numerous options in financing, delivery schedules, technical service, and product or service guarantees to be available to customers. The knowledge, skills, and abilities that lead to high levels of differentiation are quite different than those human resource capabilities that lead to effective cost leadership.

Competitive advantage is important because it permits a firm to achieve above average performance over the long term. Competitive advantage does not refer only to the specific strengths and weaknesses of a firm, but to the purposes toward which these capabilities are directed. Determining an effective source of competitive advantage is perhaps the most fundamental strategy formulation question a firm will answer. We believe that human resource considerations should be a part of that formulation process.

Competitive Advantage and Strategy Themes

The underpinnings of the view of competitive advantage just described rest with an understanding of the structural forces that shape industry competition, and with an understanding of a firm's value chain.[3] Together, these factors describe the important internal and external factors that determine the success or failure of a firm's strategy.

Industry Analysis.   Five forces dominate the characteristics of an industry: (1) degree of rivalry among participants, (2) bargaining power of buyers, (3) bargaining power of suppliers, (4) threat of entry by new competitors, and (5) threats from substitute products.[4] In combination, these forces determine both the potential for industrywide profitability and the segmentation, leverage, and stability of an industry.

Rivalry within an industry is high when there are a number of roughly equal competitors. Intense competition is particularly likely when products are relatively undifferentiated, exit costs are high, and the industry is in a steady state condition. The relative influence of related industries, such as buyer and supplier groups, reflects the extent to which substitutes are available, whether or not their product or service is essential to a strong competitive position within the industry, and the costs of switching from one firm to another. At times, vertical integration offers a means to develop a more level playing field. Substitute products are generally compared to the industry product in terms of cost and utility. The greater the comparability between an industry's product and potential substitutes, the greater the threat. Barriers to entry, such as brand loyalty, high capital requirements, extensive distribution channels, and large-scale investment, can be a two-edged sword. The same barriers that offer some protection from encroachment by new competitors may raise exit costs for industry participants. This means that even if the industry becomes unattractive from a structural or competitive standpoint, exit may be either difficult or expensive for dominant firms. The combined and relative strengths of these five forces reflect the underlying technical and economic features of an industry. An understanding of industry structure is a prerequisite for identifying the range and number of generic choices that can be successfully maintained within a particular industry.

Value Chain.   A value chain depicts the primary activities and support activities a firm must accomplish to successfully engage in any competitive strategy in a disaggregated manner. Primary activities in the value chain include inbound logistics (e.g., raw material management, inventory systems), operations (e.g., manufacturing, testing), outbound logistics (e.g., warehouse management, financing), marketing and sales (e.g., advertising, sales force management), and service (e.g., spare parts, repair options). Support activities in the value chain include development of a firm infrastructure (e.g., planning and control systems), human resource management, technology development (e.g., management information systems, research and development), and procurement (e.g., materials handling, supply activities). A network or matrix of activities results when primary and support activities are combined. This network identifies the variety of specific avenues through which a firm can pursue each of the

An important constraint on competitive advantage is that the full range of options may not be truly available to every firm. Recognizing the requirements of a cost leadership strategy, there can be only one successful cost leader in any industry. There can be several sustainable cost focus, differentiation, or differentiation focus strategies within an industry, provided the focusing firms choose different target segments, and differentiators select different attributes to exploit. Several firms can select low-cost and high-differentiation approaches if there is little overlap in target market.

However, in a commodity-based industry, or in a marketplace with few structurally attractive segments, a firm's choice may be severely constrained. Moreover, as an industry matures, its structural conditions are expected to change, as are the emphasized portions of the value chain. The need for modifying a firm's competencies to maintain a certain type of competitive advantage can be underestimated easily.

One of the clear benefits arising from a competitive advantage based on the management of a firm's human resources is that such an advantage is difficult to copy. A firm's strategic human resource management is a unique blend of procedures, personalities, styles, capabilities, and organization culture. Imitators of human resource strategies generally fall short of the original.

PRODUCT AND MARKET ORIENTATION

There are a number of ways to categorize the product and market orientation of various firms. Two of the most useful are market domain[5] and growth vector.[6] The market domain model describes product-market scope in terms of a firm's overall adaptive relationship to its environment and the subsequent need for internal fit with the external choice. The initial orientation of this approach is externally focused. The growth vector approach depicts product and market choices reflecting an internal bias. Different choices are described relative to a firm's current product and market position. Each of these approaches is an important contribution to human resource management issues for both strategy formulation and implementation.

An Adaptive Perspective on Product-Market Scope

Strategic adaptation is a process by which a firm selects and maintains a viable product-market domain and develops internal mechanisms to effectively compete in this strategic target area.[7] Adaptation includes a process of external and internal alignment. Four different approaches to achieving a two-part alignment are common.

Defender firms identify and protect a portion of the total market in an effort to create a stable product-market domain. Growth is generally achieved through market penetration and some limited product development. The primary implementation concern is how to produce and distribute goods or services to maximize efficiency. This requires strict control of organizational activities and external interactions. Standardizing goods and procedures is a typical solution. Defender organizations, therefore, must demonstrate strong capabilities for managing for efficiency, but have a low requirement for managing complexity. The human resource practices in these firms are directed toward stability and efficiency.

Two requirements for successful maintenance of a defender strategy stand out. First, the industry and the product attributes must be relatively stable. Second, a specific market domain must be identified, and differences between this segment and other portions of the market must be maintained. Note the similarity between these requirements and the requirements for a successful focus strategy as described by Porter. If a firm is successful as a defender, it is difficult for competitors to undercut its position in the absence of serious market or technology shifts. The risks associated with a defender strategy include ineffectiveness resulting from undue concern with efficiency and a reduced ability to identify or exploit new opportunities.

Prospector organizations face demands that are nearly mirror opposites from the conditions facing defender firms. The product-market domain for prospecting firms is in a continual state of development as these firms seek to locate and exploit new product and market opportunities. As a result of constant redefinition in scope and target markets, such firms must manage a great deal of complexity in external relationships and in internal interactions and interdependencies. Prospector firms, therefore, must score high on their ability to manage complexity, but have a relatively low requirement for managing to achieve efficiency. As one would guess, the human resource practices in effective prospector organizations are quite different from effective human resource activities in defender firms.

For a prospector strategy to be effective, success must not depend on efficiency. For example, a prospector strategy would be most difficult to implement in an industry dominated by experience curve management or economies of scale. Product development, market development, and diversification are all viable options for growth. The primary risks of a prospector strategy are low profitability due to an excess of cash-user businesses. Resource allocation errors that result in under-use, overextension, or misuse of resources are also common. Prospector firms are able to respond rapidly to technological and market shifts, and thereby capitalize on environmental turbulence. As a consequence, prospector organizations are often active in shaping the competitive dimensions of their industries.

Analyzer firms play a dual role. They maintain a strong core of stable products and customers while simultaneously attempting to develop new product and market opportunities. Analyzer organizations are required to manage their core businesses and generate sufficient resources to fund modifications in a product-market domain in a highly efficient manner. Yet, these firms must also manage high levels of complexity in their efforts to balance conflicting demands, expectations, and competencies, and to undertake new ventures. High levels of both efficiency and complexity management are needed to maintain organizational equilibrium. Effective strategic human resource management is particularly complex in analyzer organizations.

Analyzer firms attempt to minimize risk while maximizing the opportunities for profits. These firms should operate in industries that do not have rapid or unpredictable market or technology changes. In addition, analyzer firms should support an active applied research group that enables quick adoption of innovations. The pressure placed on balancing efficiency and complexity makes a firm more vulnerable to ineffective operations, and if internal or external balance is lost, analyzer firms may have difficulty re-establishing equilibrium. The information processing demands on analyzer firms are very high.

Firms able to achieve only low levels of efficiency and manage low levels of complexity are generally maladaptive, and are termed *reactors*. Reactor organizations present an unsuccessful prototype. A reactor firm does not establish a clear relationship with its environment, nor does it develop organization structure and processes to fully fit a selected strategy.

Organizations become reactors for three reasons: they lack a clear, articulated strategy, they have not developed sufficient congruence between their strategy and their structure, or they have not made appropriate changes when faced with a shifting environment. These problems identify important pitfalls in strategy formulation and implementation and can serve as important warning signals. Lack of reciprocity and iteration between strategic management decision and human resource management choices is a clear path to becoming a reactor organization.

Underlying Themes and Assumptions of Market Domain Perspectives

Every organization must develop solutions to three fundamental problems: The entrepreneurial problem involves defining a firm's product-market domain. This is not done in terms of specific products to be offered or customers to be served, but in terms of domain characteristics with regard to stability, permanence, and predictability. The engineering problem for a firm is to operationalize the solution to the entrepreneurial problem by developing appropriate planning and control systems, communication networks, decision-making procedures, organizational structures, and so forth. The administrative problem involves stabilizing organizational activities, implementing organizational processes, and designing a firm's culture.[8] An *adaptive cycle* reflects an organization's set of choices regarding these three strategic problems. The four organization types presented in the model depict different patterns of behavior with regard to managing the adaptive cycle, reflecting internally consistent approaches to defining a firm's relationship with its environment.

Several assumptions underlie strategic adaptation. First, the environment is seen as influencing, but not determining, organizational choices and behavior. Thus, the importance of management decisions and actions is reinforced. Second, none of the organizational types is seen as ideal. Each type of solution carries with it an accompanying set of risks. However, a reactor response to entrepreneurial, engineering, and administrative problems is offered as an uncompetitive strategy. Third, the notion of fit, or congruence, is an important component of adaptation. A firm must achieve at least minimal fit with its external environment and simultaneously achieve fit among internal organizational processes. As a corollary, tight fit is offered as a key to competitive success, and early fit is suggested as a means to achieve competitive advantage.

Limitations on a Market Domain Perspective

The primary limitation of this perspective on product and market choice is its operationalization. Little guidance is given in helping firms identify where they are positioned with regard to the organizational prototypes. This problem is intensified in that few organizations are likely to adopt a pure defender, prospector, analyzer, or reactor position. Many firms are likely to exhibit some characteristics of two or more of these prototypes, or to be in a transition phase. A defender firm, for example, that finds its primary market entering decline, should evolve toward an analyzer or prospector mode of operation. This transition might take a number of years, and during the adaptation period the firm would be very difficult to classify.

A secondary limitation of this model is its neglect of competitive issues. The competitive dimensions of a particular product-market setting might significantly affect the competency requirements of a firm. For example, a defender firm attempts to seal off a certain segment of the market. This is generally accomplished through competitive pricing and efficient operations. In today's increasingly global economy, however, it is not unusual to find mature, and therefore potentially standardized and stable, product-market areas to be the targets of aggressive and innovative encroachment by new competitors. This means that defender organizations are often required to maintain a capacity for flexibility as well as stability, innovation as well as efficient standardization, and environmental scanning as well as internal maintenance. Similar problems arise for each successful prototype.

A Strategic Growth Vector Perspective on Product-Market Scope

An important aspect of a firm's strategy is the identification of a common thread that provides direction and a unifying feature to a firm's activities. This common thread guides organizational decision makers and permits outsiders, such as potential investors or competitors, to anticipate where a firm is headed. The growth vector describes the direction a firm is heading with respect to its current product and market posture. Ansoff describes four general options available to a firm.[9]

In a *market penetration* strategy, also referred to as a concentration strategy, a firm focuses its energies and resources on expanding the current business. This can be accomplished by increasing the rate at which current customers purchase the product, attracting customers away from competitors, or encouraging nonusers who are similar to current customers to try the product.

Market penetration is a particularly attractive strategy when the market in the primary business is growing or when a firm has no resources or expertise to pursue other opportunities. Common problems associated with a concentration strategy include retaliation from competitors, particularly in a maturing marketplace, and increased dependence on a single product line, which often increases strategic vulnerability to technological or market shifts. For many product and market arenas, increased penetration is only a short-term option if growth is an important goal. If several firms competing for the same product-market segment choose penetration strategies, then saturation and dysfunctional rivalry are likely.

With a *market development* strategy, a firm relies on its current product offerings but attempts to expand the range of uses to which these products are put. This can include market expansion efforts such as extending the geographic territory, introducing a consumer product to industrial markets (e.g., selling bath oil to nursing homes), or selling an industrial product to individual consumers (e.g., business computers offered to the home market).

A market development strategy is an attractive option if new uses are developed for existing products or if new and untapped geographic markets are identified. This strategy is particularly inviting for firms that have demonstrated prior success at product differentiation. Common problems include cultural barriers among diverse geographic regions, unexpected costs in making a product attractive to diverse customers or for different uses, and unanticipated market segment differences that make distribution, service, or product acceptability more difficult or expensive than expected.

A *product development* strategy involves changing the existing products significantly or adding related items to be marketed to existing customers. This can include such activities as increased product differentiation (e.g., regular, diet, caffeine-free, vitamin C-added soft drinks), or developing families of products (e.g., shaving cream, after-shave lotion, soap, powder, and deodorant with the same scent).

A product development strategy is desirable when opportunities exist to prolong a product life cycle through rejuvenation, or when related products emerge that expand the use of an original product. Product development can also be an appropriate vehicle for capitalizing on a company's image or brand association. Similar to market development, problems associated with this strategy include unexpected costs, unanticipated competition or retaliation, or unnoticed market differences across product lines.

A *diversification* strategy entails entering new markets with new products. *Concentric diversification* is accomplished through acquiring or developing related product lines or targeting consumers with similar market characteristics. When the new product or market areas are unrelated to current activities, *conglomerate diversification* occurs. In either case, a firm extends both its mission and its outputs into new, often innovative, territory.

In general, diversification is appropriate when growth potential is low within existing products and markets, when greater opportunities exist in new areas for which a firm has needed expertise, and when a firm has slack resources. Concentric diversification is desirable if a firm wants to increase its efficiency or capitalize on existing synergy. Conglomerate diversification is attractive when a firm wants to reduce the need to actively manage certain types of uncertainty, or when it wishes to reduce dependency on an existing business area. Common problems associated with concentric diversification include increased risk potential associated with technological change, dependence on certain uncontrollable environmental events, or increased difficulty in executing widespread organizational change. Common problems associated with conglomerate diversification reflect increased organizational complexity and conflict. Concentric diversification can increase a firm's ability to manage uncertainty, while conglomerate diversification can reduce a firm's need to manage uncertainty.

Underlying Themes and Assumptions

Many descriptions of a firm's strategy are available. The strategic growth vector offers an important component of strategy that recognizes the need for a unifying concept while avoiding the pitfalls of overspeci- fication. Considering mission in conjunction with product scope makes several contributions to understanding a firm's strategy.

First, a growth vector approach is more useful at times than describing a firm's strategy in terms of industry boundaries. Many firms compete in a number of different industries; the boundaries of industries are contin- ually being redefined, segmented, and described from varying perspec- tives; and new industries can emerge without changing the products or missions of participant firms. A growth vector provides direction both within an industry as well as across industries.

Second, strategy refers to an organization's sense of direction and in- teraction with its marketplace. A growth vector approach reflects both the product-market scope of a firm's strategy and the magnitude and direction of its growth expectations.

Third, the growth vector approach incorporates the concept of synergy. In market penetration, the potential for synergy is strong due to high levels of interdependence and shared expertise. With the two development strategies, synergy often reflects marketing skills or product technology, and can be key to identifying new product or market opportunities. Under diversification, synergy becomes the basis for an organization's unity of purpose, and understanding the sources of synergy can guide the selection of new product and market arenas.

Limitations

There are three primary limitations to the growth vector perspective. First, it is descriptive rather than prescriptive. From a managerial per- spective, this model does little to guide decision making, but it is a useful tool for articulating the differences among the choices being considered. Second, a growth vector approach describes a limited dimension of strat- egy. While it incorporates ideas related to product-market scope, synergy, and growth, it says nothing about competitive advantage or risk. Third, the perspective adopted by the growth vector is organization-bound rather than focused on external situations and events. This makes the vector less useful as a comparative tool across organizations. One firm's market penetration strategy may be identical to another firm's diversification strategy, simply because each firm took an organizational snapshot at a different point in their strategy development.

While the model is intended as a descriptive tool, managers will find that each quadrant can be enriched to identify when a particular strategy is appropriate for consideration and what common problems emerge from its implementation. In this way, the growth vector can be converted to a planning device as well as a strategic illustration.

PORTFOLIO ANALYSIS

The purpose of any business portfolio approach is to categorize the businesses of a multidivisional firm into groupings that reflect their respective competitive positions and the relative attractiveness of the industries in which they compete. This categorization leads to an assessment of the expected resource requirements and resource-generating capabilities of each business. More importantly, categorization points the way for determining appropriate growth objectives and investment—or divestment—strategies for each business. Human as well as financial resources can be assessed from a portfolio perspective.

One of the most popular portfolio approaches was developed by the Boston Consulting Group (BCG). The BCG growth-share matrix categorizes a firm's businesses based on relative market share and on market growth rates. The market growth dimension indicates the market growth rate for a product or product group. Market growth rates range from low to high, and firms often use a 10 percent growth rate as a line of demarcation. Adjustments can be made to either raise or lower this measure to reflect a particular firm's situation. The market growth dimension is often considered a proxy for industry attractiveness, based on the assumption that a rapidly growing market offers greater competitive opportunities than does a market experiencing slow growth. It is also assumed that if a firm has not secured a desirable position by the time its market growth rate falls below 10 percent, the probability of ever assuming market leadership is very low.

Relative market share is calculated by taking a firm's annual dollar sales for a product and dividing it by the dollar sales of the industry's largest competitor. (If the firm itself is the largest participant, then divide its product sales by the dollar sales of the next largest competitor.) Thus, a ratio of less than 1.0 will result if a firm does not have the largest market share, and a ratio of greater than 1.0 will occur for markets in which a firm is the dominant competitor. Relative market share is generally considered a proxy for competitive position. As described below, dominant market share permits capitalization on experience curve cost reductions, economies of scale, and other size-related advantages.

Four categories of businesses result from applying the BCG approach to portfolio analysis. *Problem children* (also known as question marks) have a low relative market share in an industry classified as having high growth. These businesses are expected to require large cash (and other resource) investments to establish or maintain their competitive position, and even larger investment to gain share and become the stars of the future. Most often, problem children businesses are at the early stages in the product life cycle. (Product life cycles are often characterized as having introduction, growth, maturity, and decline stages.)

Products having high market shares in high-growth industries are class-ified as *stars*. These businesses may be self-sufficient in terms of resources or may require modest additional investment. Additional funding is com-mon in industries noted for high levels of technological change coupled with growth. A primary concern is ensuring that stars maintain their solid market position as the industry life cycle progresses and industry growth slows so that these businesses can become the cash generators of the future.

Products that have high market share in slow growth industries are classified as *cash cows*. A cash cow typically generates large amounts of cash, much more than can be effectively reinvested in the business. Both the product life cycle and industry life cycle are considered mature. The competitive position does not need improvement, only maintenance.

Dogs are businesses that are not expected to generate or require sub-stantial amounts of cash, given their low market share and slow industry growth. At times, modest funding is required to maintain even the low competitive position, and a choice must typically be made regarding an appropriate end game strategy for the business to prevent it from becoming a cash trap, in which the continued investment of funds yields no cor-responding benefits for the business or firm.

The BCG model is premised on an assumed link between high market share and strong competitive position. There are two important aspects to this linkage. First, dominant market share is presumed to be both necessary and sufficient to provide a sustainable competitive advantage, meaning firms using this model will compete, at least in part, on price. The link between this assumption and cost leadership and cost focus strategies should be noted. Second, profit margins and the amount of cash generated by a business are assumed to depend on market share. Both aspects reflect the BCG concept that experience curves link high margins with high market share and low per-unit cost.

Several resource-related concepts are important for applying the BCG portfolio model. An increase in market share is presumed to require fi-nancial investment to make operations more efficient, thus permitting price reductions, or to enhance product quality. Similarly, market growth requires financial investment if a firm wishes to maintain its market share because additional production capacity, more extensive distribution chan-nels, and increased coordination of activities is often necessary.

Both product-related and industry-related life cycles shape a business's classification within the model. Product-related life cycles project a natural movement from problem child, to star, to cash cow, to dog. Industry-related life cycles apply vertical pressure and suggest movement from star to cash cow, and from problem child to dog if market shares are maintained but not improved.

The BCG model is closely related to the concept of experience curves.

Experience curve phenomena, wherein unit costs decline by a predictable amount as accumulated volume of production doubles, is applicable only under a limited set of circumstances and achieved only in firms that are managed with this objective in mind.

Controllability is a final assumption. Market growth is assumed to be the result of uncontrollable, external factors, while market share is presumed to be the consequence of investment decisions made by the firm. Finally, the competitive situation is assumed to be stable, with few major new entrants, unpredictable technology changes, or shifts in industry structure.

Limitations Associated with the BCG Model

There are several characteristics of the BCG model that limit its applicability. First, if market share is unrelated to competitive position, such as with firms competing on the basis of differentiation or innovation, the model leads to erroneous recommendations. Whirlpool, for example, is highly competitive and enjoys high profits, yet has relatively low market share. If experience curves, economies of scale, or some other factor do not guarantee that market share, by itself, leads to sustainable competitive advantage, the cash implications for each quadrant may not hold. For example, Rolex watches have a relatively small market share, yet enjoy high margins. In contrast, Timex, despite its dominant market share, suffered severe financial setbacks when new electronic technology was introduced.

Determining an appropriate definition of product can be problematic. Questions regarding whether the entire marketplace or a relatively narrow segment should comprise the market are left to the judgment of the user. Particularly for a firm considering product development or market expansion, such decisions can be quite difficult. The key to a good decision is identifying competitive segments, which should reflect service or functional end uses of a product, rather than more common product or user characteristics. In this way a number of quite different competitive products (e.g., Velcro, snaps, buttons, zippers) might be defined as part of the same competitive segment.

The requirement for a stable competitive situation limits the generalizability of this model. Firms in industries undergoing substantial regulatory change, developing a new technology, experiencing rapid entry and exit of competitors, or encountering major market shifts due to product differentiation or globalization should use this model with caution.

Alternative Portfolio Approaches

Variations on the portfolio model theme are unlimited. While the BCG model focuses on cash flow implications and requirements, PIMS (Profit

Impact of Market Strategy)-based portfolio models concentrate on investments and returns. In both these models, market share is a principle proxy for strategy effectiveness.

The General Electric (GE) portfolio framework developed in conjunction with McKinsey and Company presents an interesting counterpoint for both the BCG and the PIMS models. Where the BCG and PIMS models are generalizable to industries in which the basic conditions are met, the GE model is personalized and designed to be firm-specific. In the original GE matrix a number of indices for business strength (i.e. technology position, image) and for industry attractiveness (i.e. profitability, market diversity) were developed to reflect the distinct competencies and business interests of GE. Other firms might have a substantially different list of characteristics reflecting their own unique organizational characteristics, capabilities, and strategic preferences.

Like other portfolio models, the GE screen offers specific strategy recommendations for the businesses arrayed across the grid. Variations in terms of investment strategy, time horizons for planning, profit expectations and so forth correspond to placement on the GE screen. The number of strategy options is expanded to nine, recognizing greater reliance on managerial judgment rather than calculated plans.

Implications of Portfolio Perspectives

The purpose of any portfolio model is to aid a firm in competitive analysis and resource allocation decisions. As a first step, product-market business segments must be defined. The charting of businesses on a grid that fits the characteristics of the firm allows for a visual analysis of the firm's businesses. The range of options offered by portfolio models encourages a firm to consider a full range of alternative actions from investment and growth to divestiture and harvesting. In this way, portfolio approaches encourage a firm to adopt a realistic, rather than overly optimistic, perspective on the array of businesses to be managed.

A trend analysis that compares past, current, and projected portfolio charts allows a firm to examine how well its objectives are being met. Managers can be confident of their past analytic and judgment skills if the following conditions have been met. First, past investments should have led to improved competitive position. Second, businesses should have moved in an expected manner from cash users to cash generators. Third, investment should have had the anticipated rate of return. If, however, investments have not led to improved competitive position, or if businesses have unexpectedly slipped from high-to low-performance conditions, this is a signal that managers need to re-evaluate their environmental scanning and internal corporate assessment practices.

Problems with projections can arise from a number of sources. Events once important to organizational performance may no longer be relevant. New events may be neglected. Managers may have developed an accurate model of the environment, but may be making poor strategic choices based on that model. The strategic choices may be fine, but they may have been poorly implemented. In some instances, a firm has a reasonable view of the marketplace, makes appropriate strategic choices, implements those choices well, but still fails to achieve desired objectives because the circumstances changed while the strategic process was underway. Portfolio analysis is often necessary, but clearly is not sufficient, to help diagnose these situations.

Assuming reasonable accuracy, portfolio projections indicate the anticipated cash requirement and cash generating capabilities of a firm. This relates directly to the financial resources available to fund human resource-related activities.

The distribution of products across the various cells in a portfolio model indicates the internal balance of a firm. Ideal portfolios vary with a firm's strategic objectives. Firms with strong growth objectives will typically have the majority of their businesses in emerging or growth stages of industry and product development. Firms more concerned with profits will generally have a disproportionate share of their businesses in the more mature stages of development.

There should be cash-generating businesses (e.g. cash cows, high business strength-low industry attractiveness) sufficient to fund cash users (e.g., problem children, medium business strength-high industry attractiveness). Correspondingly, there should be enough businesses with cash requirements to make effective use of the resources generated by a firm.

A firm may wish to gather sufficient information on its competitors to generate portfolio charts for these firms. Such a competitive analysis allows a firm to better anticipate the resource capabilities and investment choices of its competitors. Further, such comparisons allow a firm to evaluate the potential for competitor response should they undertake an aggressive growth strategy. For example, retaliation for an attack on a highly competitive growth business by a firm with few other cash-using businesses and a number of cash generators is much more likely than is an aggressive response by a firm with many potential cash uses and few cash sources.

Perhaps the greatest contribution of any portfolio model is its ability to distill and integrate a large amount of complex and diverse information into a visually understandable and manageable format. Portfolio models are useful both as planning tools and control mechanisms. While the resource and competitive implications of a portfolio chart are not a substitute for managerial judgment and instinct, they are a useful place to begin. Moreover, the use of a portfolio model can focus managerial attention on the most significant questions and areas of uncertainty. As will be seen, this process is crucial for effective goal-setting decisions.

ACHIEVING EXCELLENCE

Tom Peters presents a number of principles for achieving excellence based on his observations of some high performance firms.[10] If the pursuit of excellence was truly that simple, it is surprising that so few businesses are able to achieve this standard and maintain it over the long haul. We view the world through a more complex set of lenses, and it is from a contingency-based perspective that the strategic human resource management model presented in this book was derived.

The principles that guided the development of the model parallel a number of the underpinnings of strategy that have been outlined in this chapter. First, strategists must continually anticipate the effects that current actions and choices will have on future results. Consequently, strategic management is anticipatory and based upon probable outcomes. Second, strategic management is multidimensional, multifunctional, dynamic, and interactive. This means that strategic issues are complex, and that simple, universal, or one-way solutions should be viewed with skepticism. Third, strategic management is concerned with a variety of aspects of fit. A good strategy should yield a beneficial alignment of an organization within its market environment. A good strategy is equally dependent upon a congruence of internal organizational processes and activities. Moreover, a good strategy provides a match between external expectations and internal capabilities. Fourth, strategic management recognizes multiple stakeholders for any organization. As a result, the evaluation of strategic outcomes should rely on multiple measures of performance. It should be noted that not all of these performance measures will necessarily be complementary. Fifth, good performance must be defined specifically and coupled with equally specific competencies if a firm hopes to achieve a sustainable competitive advantage. A general prescription of striving for excellence is not sufficient. Finally, strategic management is both a process and an outcome. In this book we focus on the content of strategic choices, yet we recognize that the elements of any strategic choice either facilitate or inhibit the means by which future strategy decisions will be made.

NOTES

1. For more information, see H. Mintzberg, Opening up the definition of strategy. *In The Strategy Process*, (Englewood Cliffs, N.J.: Prentice Hall, 1988), pp. 13–20.

2. An expanded discussion is contained in M. Porter *Competitive Strategy* (Boston: Free Press, 1980) and M. Porter, *Competitive Advantage* (Boston: Free Press, 1985).

3. Ibid.

4. Ibid.

5. For a comprehensive discussion of these issues, see R. E. Miles, et al. Organization strategy, structure, and process. *Academy of Management Review* (1984) 546–662.

6. H. Igor Ansoff discusses the growth vector in Chapter 6 of his book *The New Corporate Strategy* New York: Wiley, 1988).

7. R. E. Miles et al. Organization strategy.

8. Ibid.

9. H. Igor Ansoff. op. cit.

10. For anecdotal prescriptions for achieving excellence, see T. J. Peters and R. H. Waterman, Jr. *In Search of Excellence*. (New York: Harper & Row, 1982)

3

An Overview of Human Resource Management

Human resource management as a function in a business organization and field of inquiry has been evolving toward greater prominence. Initially, it was thought of as a minor bureaucratic necessity in organizations, one requiring little attention and having few consequences for the success or failure of an organization. However, as the environment has changed, so has the role of human resource management in business organizations.[1] Today, as international competition becomes more intense, business organizations are looking for every source of competitive advantage they can find. Human resource management is one source of largely untapped potential for helping organizations produce higher quality and lower cost goods and services. Consequently, organizations are changing how they think about human resource management and how they integrate human resource management into business operations.

This chapter is an overview of the human resource management function in the modern organization. It begins with a historical perspective on the evolution of human resource management followed by a description of the human resource management system. A discussion follows on why viewing people as resources rather than personnel is crucial to the strategic management process. Assessing human resources has been done traditionally by both appraising job performance and identifying an individual's knowledge, skills, and abilities in a specific job. However, assessing human resources for strategic considerations requires different approaches. Since knowledge, skills, and abilities have different values depending upon different strategic alternatives, new ways of classifying and measuring these characteristics are necessary for creating useful strategic information. These new approaches are discussed in this chapter. Additionally, a broader perspective on human resource management is proposed, extending the traditional boundaries of the organization to include, for example, suppliers and distributors. This broader perspective is vital for integrating human resource management considerations into both the formulation and implementation of strategic decisions.

Next, two kinds of investments are considered: in individual human resources and in human resource management programs. Because financial resources are limited in all organizations, these decisions must be made carefully and in comparison to alternative opportunities for investments. Today, managers can, and must scrutinize human resource investments in the same way financial investments are examined. Furthermore, a return on investment perspective is essential for warranting the human resource management function a serious role in the strategic management process.

Finally, the chapter proposes how human resource management can influence both strategy formulation and implementation. Many have argued that human resource management has always played a significant role in strategy implementation. However, it was not until recently that authors and practicing managers have begun to make a convincing case for including human resource management considerations in the strategy formulation process. The remainder of the book provides managers with the tools for realizing the benefits of strategic human resource management.

THE EVOLUTION OF A PROFESSION

Human resource management should be a serious consideration in the strategic management process, which, historically, it has not been. In order to appreciate the revolutionary nature of our proposition, it is necessary to first gain a historical perspective on the human resource management function.

Several authors have traced the history of human resource management by defining and describing stages or periods of time defined by events and people.[2] Four major forces have been identified as responsible for the emergence of the modern human resource management function: (1) labor union growth, (2) increasing government legislation and regulation, (3) the changing character and composition of the work force, and (4) increasing demands for productivity improvements brought on by foreign competition. The discussion that follows, primarily based on Cascio, traces the evolution of human resource management through a growth stage model that takes these four forces into account.[3]

Most historians trace the origin of human resource management in the United States to the early 1900s, paralleling the growth of organizations during the Industrial Revolution. Before that time, both the size of organizations and the typical technologies employed did not necessitate a formalized human resource management function. But, as organizations became larger, and new technologies that capitalized on specialized jobs became prevalent, the necessity of human resource management as a formal function in the business operation became apparent. However, the human resource management function was viewed as largely an administrative or maintenance activity.

Thus, the first stage of human resource management has been identified as the *file maintenance stage*. This stage was, from approximately 1900 to 1963, the dominant influence on human resource management. During this stage the emphasis of the human resource management function, usually called the personnel department, was on controlling and reducing labor costs. The top manager of the personnel department was typically called the personnel manager, personnel director, or personnel administrator. Major activities included screening applicants, providing orientation, and maintaining employment records. An effective human resource manager had good organizing and clerical skills. Herbert E. Meyer has captured the stereotype of human resource management during this period:

The personnel department has been represented on many a corporate organization chart as an orphaned box—one that came from nowhere and didn't seem to fit anywhere. To many businessmen, including many chief executives, the people who worked in "personnel" appeared to be a bunch of drones whose apparent missions in life were to create paperwork, recruit secretaries who couldn't type, and send around memos whose impertinence was exceeded only by their irrelevance. As a result of this perception, personnel directors, whatever their individual competence, suffered the *sui generis* image of being good-old-Joe types—harmless chaps who spent their careers worshipping files, arranging company picnics, and generally accomplishing nothing whatsoever of any fundamental importance.[4]

It is not surprising, based upon the common stereotype depicted above, that the strategic potential of human resource management was not realized during this stage.

Nineteen sixty-four marks the beginning of the second major stage in the evolution of human resource management. With the passage of the Civil Rights Act of 1964, human resource management gained new importance as a defensive function in the business organization. While many organizations saw compliance with equal employment opportunity and other legislation as the socially responsible choice, other organizations merely wanted to stay out of trouble and avoid the negative publicity and legal costs associated with failure to comply with laws and regulations.

Thus, the second stage of human resource management growth has been identified as the *government accountability stage*, which extends roughly between 1964 and 1979. This stage is characterized by an emphasis on legal compliance, especially in equal employment opportunity. The top manager of the personnel department was still typically called the personnel manager, personnel director, or personnel administrator. Major activities included such programs as designing and implementing affirmative action programs, and modifying or eliminating previous practices found to be illegal. An effective human resource manager had legal skills in addition to the organizing and clerical skills required to maintain and administer the human aspect of the organization.

Nineteen-eighty marks the beginning of the current stage of human resource management development. The decline of many major industries in the United States, such as the automobile and steel industries, along with the increasing prominence of foreign competition, such as the Japanese, Koreans, and West Germans, signaled a new environment characterized as international competition of the fiercest variety and along all dimensions: price, quantity, and quality. These external pressures have once again influenced the nature and role of the human resource management function in business organizations. Today, the emphasis on human resources is not only one of controlling costs, but also of adding value and creating competitive advantage.

Thus, the third stage of human resource management development has been called the *competitive advantage stage*. Today, the label personnel has been replaced with human resources and the personnel department is now called the human resource management department. The top manager is no longer called the personnel manager, but instead is called the human resource manager, reflecting the changing emphasis. Major activities of the human resource management function include assessing the costs and benefits of human resource activities, designing and implementing productivity improvement programs, and providing input regarding strategy formulation. In addition to the legal, organizational, and clerical skills necessary in the past, the modern day human resource manager must also have solid business skills and be well versed in the fundamentals of accounting, finance, marketing, and strategy.

What does the future hold for the human resource management function? It seems safe to predict that international competition will only continue to expand and place a premium on effective and efficient management of all resources, including human resources. Consequently, the competitive advantage emphasis will likely continue to gain prominence as an emphasis for human resource management.

It is also likely that many social and demographic influences will shape the focus of the human resource management function in organizations. In particular, the growing labor force participation of women and the changing demographics of the work force are likely to place new demands on organizations and how they manage their human resources. Social trends suggest that workers of the future will want to see a greater degree of balance between their work and nonwork lives. Major activities of the future human resource management function will likely include adapting to technologies that redefine work and the workplace (e.g., FAX machines, personal computers, cellular phones) and integrating career and family considerations in new and creative ways. The human resource manager of the future (perhaps to be called the human resource integrator) will need legal, organizational, clerical, and business skills, as well as creativity and an ability to adapt programs to changing environments.

But, let's get back to the present: the competitive advantage stage. Human resource managers and their organizations must change the way human resources are viewed. It requires looking at the people in the organization through a different set of eyeglasses. A later section talks about rethinking our assumptions about human resources, but it is first necessary to define the activities that make up the human resource management system.

THE HUMAN RESOURCE MANAGEMENT SYSTEM: A LONGITUDINAL PERSPECTIVE

Modern human resource management theory is based largely on the systems model. A system is a network of interrelated components. Various human resource management activities make up the components of the human resource management system, which is linked to the other organizational systems, such as finance, accounting, and marketing.

The systems model of human resource management is especially useful as an aid to decision making because it encourages the decision maker to consider the ramifications of taking actions affecting one component of the system (e.g, lowering selection criteria) on the other components of the system (e.g., training and development, compensation, performance appraisal).

The human resource management activities that make up the components of the human resource management system have been described by numerous authors, sometimes using different terms for the same concepts. One of the clearest articulations of the components of the human resource management system is provided by Cascio:

- Attraction comprises the activities of (1) identifying the job requirements within an organization, (2) determining the number of people and the skills mix necessary to do these jobs, and (3) providing equal opportunity for qualified candidates to apply for jobs.

- Selection is the process of choosing the people who are best qualified to perform the jobs.

- Retention comprises the activities of (1) rewarding employees for performing their jobs effectively and (2) maintaining a safe, healthy work environment.

- Development is a function whose activities are aimed at preserving and enhancing employees' competence in their jobs through improving their knowledge, skills, abilities, and other characteristics; personnel specialists use the abbreviation KSAOs to refer to these items.
- Assessment involves the observation and evaluation of behaviors and attitudes relevant to jobs and to job performance.
- Adjustment comprises activities intended to maintain compliance with the organization's personnel policies.[5]

Applying systems theory concepts to human resource management is invaluable, however, it does not capture the interactive nature of human resource management decision making that occurs between employer and employee over the duration of the employment relationship. To see that interrelationship between individual and organization over time, we need to add an additional perspective to the management of human resources.

A longitudinal perspective on the human resource management system considers five phases of the employment relationship: prelabor market, active market, joining, sustained membership, and withdrawal.[6] The time span over which this relationship occurs can be very short (e.g., ended by either the organization through dismissal or the employee through voluntary turnover after only a few weeks) or over a number of years (e.g., when an employee stays with an organization and the organization chooses to retain the employee for many years). Next, the individual and organizational human resource management activities that occur at each phase will be described.

In the *prelabor market phase* individuals are learning about general organization functions, jobs, roles, and rewards. It is during this phase that individuals are learning basic skills (general human capital, described later) and work values (e.g., good attendance, hard work). Individuals also acquire occupational training and begin to narrow their focus for occupational choice. Simultaneously, organizations are assessing both product and labor markets, resulting in the formulation of overall business strategies and human resource management strategies. Additionally, as they narrow their focus, organizations develop human resource plans and forecasts.

In the *active market phase* individuals begin the process of job search. This phase ends for the individual when a job choice is made. During this phase, organizations are concentrating on the attraction component of the human resource management system. This entails activities such as recruitment, selection, and placement. Compensation and reward system activities also occur during this phase, since individuals choose jobs based upon anticipated rewards.

The *joining phase* occurs when the individual actually enters the organization as an employee. As the individual learns more about the organization, he or she finds that some expectations are met while others are unfulfilled. This is a crucial period that, if not managed well, can result in early turnover of new employees. Consequently, organizations develop both formal and informal orientation programs for employees during this phase.

The *sustained membership phase* reflects the period of association during which the employee chooses to stay with the employer and the employer chooses to retain the employee. It is during this period of time that the employee contributes to organizational goals in order to receive desired rewards, and the organization manages the employee in order to receive a return on its human resource investment. The individual becomes fully socialized into the organization, learning goals, tasks, responsibilities, and norms. The organization facilitates the socialization process through training and development, performance appraisal, career development, compensation, and job design.

The *withdrawal phase* represents the individual and organizational activities associated with the disengagement process. Individual employees permanently withdraw from an organization due to a variety of causes: voluntary quitting, retirement, termination, or, in some cases, death. The employer must manage the exit process through human resource management activities tailored to the particular cause of withdrawal. For example, retirement planning may take place for those employees who approach their own chosen retirement date. Termination activities (e.g., documentation, corporate security) are necessary when an employee is discharged. The loss of an employee through either voluntary or involuntary turnover usually necessitates a recycling of the active market phase activities as the organization seeks to replace the job vacancy.

The withdrawal phase can also reflect a temporary condition created by either the individual or the organization. The individual may choose not to attend, creating an absenteeism withdrawal, or participate in a general strike, again temporarily withdrawing from the workplace. The employer, likewise, may choose temporary withdrawal (e.g., temporary layoffs, reduced work weeks, job sharing) in order to match fluctuations in the business cycle.[7]

By combining both the systems approach to human resource management with the longitudinal model of human resource management, we are able to better understand the complexity of the decision-making process in managing a firm's human resources. This perspective allows us to see how value can be added, maintained, or lost over a period of time as a result of either individual or organizational human resource management decisions. The next section continues the development of a perspective on human resource management that is consistent with a strategic viewpoint.

VIEWING PEOPLE AS HUMAN RESOURCES RATHER THAN PERSONNEL

One of the definitions you will find in the dictionary for the term resource is "a source of supply or support: an available means; a source of information or expertise."[8] This seems particularly appropriate for describing the human resource in organizations and suggests the potential strategic importance of this resource. Information or expertise can become a competitive advantage.

Classical economics defines resources as the basic inputs used in producing goods and services, or factors of production.[9] There are three main categories of resources: land, capital, and labor. Labor is defined as the physical and mental talents of human beings as applied to the production of goods and services. In contrast, capital refers to buildings, equipment, and materials used in the production process. The term investment is usually associated with the process of producing and accumulating capital. Choices are made between consuming capital now and consuming it in the future. Investments entail some initial costs that are later recouped or payed back at some future point or over a period of time. Until the 1970s, labor and capital were viewed as two distinctly different entities, with little or nothing in common.

Labor economists changed the way human resources were viewed through their work researching the concept of "human capital."[10] Human capital theory views workers as embodying a set of knowledge and skills that can be "rented out" to organizations. The knowledge and skills a worker has is a result of previous education and training, both on the job and formal. Thus, a worker has a stock of productive capital that can be added to by investments in education and training and is only limited by the amount of inherent ability received at birth. It is important to note that human capital can also deteriorate through obsolescing skills and knowledge caused by either an individual's failure to acquire new knowledge or an organization's failure to provide appropriate investments.

Workers undertake three kinds of investments. In addition to investing in their education and training, they also invest in migration and job search. Like investments in education and training, migration and job search entail an initial cost with an expected future payoff. The value of the human capital an individual has accumulated is derived from how much it is worth to employers in the labor market. Therefore, a worker who does little to develop his or her own human capital as the organization adopts new strategies has two choices for future investments in human capital: either alter his or her knowledge and skills to adapt to the organization's strategic needs, or invest in job search and migration to find another organization that values his or her current human capital base.

The specific investment expenditures a person makes in his or her human capital fall into three categories: out-of-pocket or direct expenses, forgone earnings, and psychic losses.[11] Out-of-pocket expenses include, for example, tuition and books, moving expenses, and transportation costs. Forgone earnings represent the income that cannot be earned while, for example, a person attends school. Psychic losses are the costs associated with doing unpleasant tasks (e.g., taking a boring class, taking a temporary assignment at an undesirable location) or the stress associated with the job search.

To justify the personal investment expenditures, an individual expects a return on the investment in human capital, which can be many and varied. For example, a person may gain higher wages, greater job satisfaction, and experience feelings of competence or simply feel in greater control due to an expanded array of options.

So far we have examined human capital theory from the individual's perspective, but what about the organization's perspective? While it is important to understand individual choices and behavior affecting human capital production and accumulation, it is equally important to understand how organizations produce and accumulate their own base of human capital.

Organization are collectives of individuals, each with a unique set of knowledge, skills, and abilities. Employees are selected according to the anticipated short-term and long-term needs of an organization to accomplish its goals and objectives. If you walk into any organization today, you could take a snapshot of its current human resources. This snapshot would reveal the combined effects of previous individual and organizational investments in human capital to enhance the ability of the organization to produce its goods or services.

Organizations invest in employees through hiring, training, and development. As in the individual investment decision, organizations initially expend funds with the expectation of recouping a return on their investment through improved job performance or greater employee flexibility, which leads to higher revenues, greater profitability, and an improved competitive position. This means that investments in workers cause firms' employment decisions to extend over multiple time periods. Consequently, decisions about investments in human resources, like decisions about products, must be made with an eye on the bottom line.

Hiring investments include all the costs incurred in recruiting and selecting employees for employment, such as advertising, mundane paperwork, and selection tests. These costs are, generally, one-time expenditures necessary for attracting and selecting employees. Firms may make large expenditures to increase the probability of getting the best employees by using such methods as valid selection procedures and company visits. This has been labelled the intensive search strategy.[12] Alternatively, an employer can choose a high-wage strategy, presumably

attracting and hiring the best applicants without incurring additional selection costs. Or, firms may make minimal investments (an intensive training strategy) in hiring, using selection procedures of unknown or low
validity, choosing to accept the quality of work force they receive at a
lower investment cost and training them to meet organizational needs.
As a final option, some firms invest little in either selection or training,
but rely on extensive control systems to weed out employees that fail to
make a positive contribution to the firm's competitive strategy (an intensive control strategy). Research suggests, however, that the intensive
search strategy yields the greatest long-term benefits.[13]

Training investment expenditures are comprised of two categories: explicit monetary costs and implicit or opportunity costs. Explicit monetary
costs include such items as salary or fees for trainers, costs of training materials, and training room overhead costs.[14] There are two types of implicit
or opportunity costs: the cost of the trainee's time (individuals in a training
program are less productive than when they are working full time), and the
opportunity cost associated with using another employee as a trainer (an
employee helping another employee learn the job is not as productive during that time compared to the time spent solely performing assigned tasks.)

According to human capital theory, firms may choose between two
basic kinds of training investments: general training and specific training.
General training increases an employee's productivity to multiple employers. It increases a. employee's productivity and hence value to the
firm making the investment, but it also makes that employee more attractive to other firms as well. For example, firms that offer their employees training in basic skills such as reading, writing, and math are
increasing the value of their employees by making them more productive.
However, the increase in productivity due to basic skill enhancement is
transferrable to other employers as well. There is growing evidence that
many employers are willing to provide remedial training to employees
despite the risk associated with increasing the external marketability of
their employees.[15] Another example of general training that many firms
provide their employees is the M.B.A. (Master's in Business Administration). A petroleum engineer with an M.B.A. becomes more valuable
to his or her firm as well as to other employers. Yet, the employer who
bears the cost of the M.B.A. accepts the risk of creating a more mobile
employee to increase the value of an existing employee.

Specific training increases the employee's productivity and value only
at the firm providing the training where he or she is employed. An example
of pure specific training would be that training necessary to operate a
machine unique to the organization. Other examples would include training in the particular procedures one firm uses in a technology common
to an industry. Specific training investments are lower risk training in-

vestments since they increase the value of an employee to the organization without increasing his or her value to other firms.

The concept of specific training has been further refined by Lee Tom Perry to provide more useful information for strategic human resource management decision making.[16] A firm-specific skill that represents technological or organizational expertise can be further broken down to reflect industry-specific and industry nonspecific skills. For example, RJR Nabisco makes products ranging from cigarettes to graham crackers. A salesperson working in the cookie products division has likely acquired over time a knowledge of company ordering and billing procedures, expense account policies, and so on, and a skill in facilitating intracompany transactions. Transfer to the cigarette division will entail learning some new policies and procedures, but much of what was previously learned will be generalized to the new position. This is an example of firm-specific knowledge and skills (i.e., knowledge of corporate policies unique to RJR Nabisco and skill in using them) and industry non-specific knowledge and skills (i.e., knowledge and skill that is not unique to either the cookie industry or the cigarette industry).

Industry-specific knowledge reflects knowledge and expertise about industry technology that is not transferrable across divisions operating in different industries. Our cookie salesperson may have industry-specific knowledge about the production process for graham crackers that is useless in understanding the production process for menthol cigarettes. Thus, the cookie salesperson would benefit by acquiring industry-specific knowledge of the cigarette manufacturing process, resulting in more cigarette sales and greater commissions. The company would also benefit by providing industry-specific knowledge of the cigarette manufacturing process to the cookie salesperson, resulting in more product sales and greater revenue. Both the individual and the company have an opportunity to earn a return on the investment in human resources.

Industry-specific skills can be further broken down into unit-specific and unit nonspecific skills. A company salesperson who sells only cookies and not other food products will likely have acquired knowledge unique to the product line being sold. For example, typical shelf life, product uses, and other information will apply to cookie products but probably not to other food products sold by the company. That unit-specific knowledge is valuable to the individual and the organization only within the context of cookie sales. The knowledge has no value to either the individual or the organization in the sale of other food products.

It is not surprising that when demand for goods and services falls, employers attempt to maintain an inventory of employees for which investments in specific training have been made.[17] Retention efforts are greatest for these employees, and they are the last to be dismissed when layoffs are necessary. Consequently, when demand picks up, hiring strategies can focus on employees with general training, that can be most easily replaced and most quickly socialized into the organization.

Similarly, when a company alters its strategic focus, even some firm-specific skills may no longer have the same value to either the firm or the employee. Analyzing knowledge and skills using the typology described above allows decision makers to determine the strategic value of current employees as well as the kinds of human resource knowledge and skills necessary for different strategic options.

In summary, human capital theory provides a framework for viewing people as human resources rather than personnel. Human resources have several important characteristics. Investments are made in human resources that entail cost outlays and require payoffs or returns. These payoffs or returns frequently occur over a long-term employment relationship between the employee and the organization. Investments are made in order to attract and select desired employees and to enhance their productivity through training and development over the long-term relationship. The value of a particular human resource at any point depends upon the organization's strategies and objectives and the specific knowledge and skills the employee has acquired. That is, a human resource has value only within the context of a particular chosen strategy. And, finally, maintaining the value of an organization's human capital is a joint responsibility between the employee and the organization.

EXPANDING THE BOUNDARIES OF HUMAN RESOURCE MANAGEMENT

It has been customary when describing and prescribing human resource management practices to focus on a bounded environment that includes only the direct or indirect employees of a specific organization. That is, human resource management practices at General Motors are generally described as those that apply to full-time core employees as well as contingent employees (regular part-time employees and supplemental employees) who are on the payroll of General Motors. Trade-offs among using various mixes of employees are usually discussed with a focus on managing intrafirm human resources. Likewise, human resource management programs are also discussed with a focus on their impact on intrafirm human resources.

Recently, Randall Schuler and Ian MacMillan proposed a new perspective on the boundaries of human resource management.[18] They argue that human resource management practices such as selection, compensation, and training and development can be applied beyond the traditional boundaries of the focal organization to other strategic targets, including customers, distributors, servicers, and suppliers. By broadening the perspective on the boundaries of human resource management, organizations can increase the potential impact of human resource management on the strategic management process.

Strategic targets represent upstream and downstream activities in addition to the focal company itself. As Schuler and MacMillan describe it, "Companies can reach backward or reach forward to help shape the HRM practices of other companies."[19] Training store managers in merchandising techniques can improve both store sales for a distributor as well as product sales for the producer. This is an example of what Pepsico does in applying their training and development expertise to enhance their distributors' skills. Assisting customers with their own performance appraisals makes them more competitive and hence more able to purchase a company's products. This is the approach Unifi takes in applying its skill in appraising employee performance to enhance their customer's competitiveness. Training service repair technicians throughout the region in which a product is sold gives customers high-quality service in a timely fashion. Many automobile manufacturers, like Mercedes, train mechanics in service garages in order to differentiate their products from their competitors. Training can also be focused upstream to improve the quality of the resources purchased from suppliers to create a product. This is what Nissan Motors and Honda Motors do to ensure that their suppliers continue to provide high-quality products. They train their suppliers in quality control techniques and methods. Organizations like McDonald's provide comprehensive training to their franchise owners (distributors-servicers) to both maintain the high-quality standard for their product and to make their franchise owners more successful so they can purchase more products.

In addition to strategic targets, Schuler and MacMillan also define strategic thrusts to complete a matrix for a broadened approach to human resource management decision making. *Strategic thrusts* are defined as ways of beating the competition through human resource management practices. There are two fundamental strategic thrusts. One is the cost-efficiency thrust, which focuses on increasing the efficiency of production and consequently lowering the costs of doing business. The other strategic thrust is a differentiation thrust, which focuses on using human resource management practices in ways to distinguish the product or the company from its competitors.

The expanded boundaries of human resource management described by Schuler and MacMillan increase the probability of human resource considerations playing a larger role in the strategic management process. First, a company must determine what aspects of its human resource management function it does very well. Some firms may have particular strengths in training and development, while other firms may have particular strengths in compensation. Some firms may even be strong across all of the functional areas of human resource management. Once a company has identified its strengths, the next step is to direct its expertise to appropriate targets. By using the Schuler and MacMillan concept of strategic targets, an organization that has strength in training and development can not only gain advantage by enhancing the knowledge and skills of its own employees (i.e., of the focal company), but also enhance the knowledge and skills of employees both upstream and downstream in the organizational chain. This view of human resource management is particularly useful because of its flexibility for use in managerial decision making.

In summary, it is useful to expand the boundaries of human resource management to include other organizations that interact with the focal organization. This makes it possible for an organization to reap an even larger return on its human resource management investments. Additionally, it makes it possible for human resource management to play a significant role in the strategy formulation process. Opening the eyes of top managers and CEOs to the potential impact of human resource management on various strategic targets should provide ample incentive for including human resource management considerations in all phases of the strategic management process.

A MODEL FOR INVESTING IN INDIVIDUAL HUMAN RESOURCES

Because training and development is an expensive undertaking, and since it also represents an organization's investments in its human resources, it is vital that decisions regarding these investments be made with good information and sound decision-making practices. An organization can spread its training investment dollars equally across a wide range of employees (e.g., when a new technology is integrated into the workplace that all employees need to understand), hoping for a return on investment for all affected employees. Or, an organization can target specific employees for greater investments than are made for other employees because of expected higher returns on the investments. This decision-making approach is analogous to a stock investor who has two basic options: (1) invest in a portfolio of stocks, some of which entail higher risk and higher potential yields and some of which entail lower risk and lower yields, and hope that the overall average rate of return is sufficient to meet goals, or (2) invest only in high-risk or low-risk stocks and accept the consequences of the choice.

Human resources, as investments, are often in many ways like stocks traded on Wall Street. They are volatile, unpredictable, and affected by a host of environmental factors. Organizations must consider the nature of individuals when making training and development investment decisions, just as stockbrokers consider the nature of the companies they select for investments. For example, some employees might have the ability to learn new skills and knowledge, yet have no motivation to do so. It would be senseless to invest in training and development for these employees when the likely return would be zero. Likewise, it would be equally senseless to invest training and development dollars in an employee of limited ability who could not acquire the knowledge and skill nor transfer it back to the job. The employee may have the motivation but not the ability to ensure a reasonable rate of return on the investment. Organizations need some means for assessing their human resources that provides information useful to the human resource investment decision.

An investment model for individual human resources would consider both potential risks and potential returns. Potential returns would include enhanced job performance and productivity sustained over enough time periods to recoup the investment. A high return would be characterized as increased job performance and productivity sustained beyond the investment pay back period. For example, assume an employee's increased job performance pays for the cost of the training after one year. If the employee continues to perform at the same high level for nine more years, the organization will experience a high rate of return on its training investment in the individual human resource.

As with financial investments, human resource investments also entail potential risks. There are four kinds of risk associated with human resource investments: (1) training cannot be acquired due to lack of ability, (2) training will not be acquired due to insufficient motivation, (3) training will not be transferred to the job (i.e., training will be acquired, but not used), and (4) the employee will not stay with the organization long enough to recoup the investment (e.g., if the pay back period is one year to recoup the investment, and the employee leaves after six months, the investment cost is lost). These four types of human resource investment risk can result in an organization's failure to receive an acceptable rate of return on its outlay. Therefore, it is vital that organizations consider individual human resource investments systematically and with good information.

One approach to assessing the individual human resource investment decision is based upon a model developed by Larry Cummings and Donald Schwab for performance appraisal and development.[20] They describe three training and development programs, or levels of investments in training and development, as used in this context. A high level of investment is identified as a developmental action program (DAP). A moderate level of investment is identified as a maintenance action program (MAP). A low level of investment is identified as a remedial action program (RAP).

Why is a DAP a higher level of investment than a MAP or a RAP? The answer lies in the human resource management activities associated with each level of investment. In a DAP, more extensive participation in decision making between superior and subordinate takes place, more extensive training to increase promotability is provided, and other programs requiring both direct and indirect costs are used. For example, these employees are frequently promoted for vertical development, or provided with greater flexibility in job design for horizontal development. Furthermore, these employees require higher levels of rewards and compensation in order to retain them. Since a developmental action program entails a variety of costly human resource management activities, it represents a high level of investment.

A MAP on the other hand reflects a modest level of investment in an employee. Less extensive training—training to prevent skill obsolescence rather than increase promotability—is provided to these employees. Additionally, less extensive developmental activities are made available to these employees, such as participation in decision making or flexibility in job design. However, rewards and compensation must be competitive with other employers to retain the services of these employees.

A RAP represents a minimal investment in a human resource. It is similar to a stock option in that for a low cost the employer retains the opportunity to increase its investment in the employee should performance improve, but can also decide to disinvest or decline the option should performance deteriorate. Training and development primarily involves setting specific performance goals and providing continuous performance feedback over a probationary period. If the employee fails to improve during the probationary period, the company loses only a minimal expenditure.

Expected return on investment is a function of assessing the individual's past performance and future potential in the organization. Past performance is indicated by, for example, several recent performance ratings. An average of past performance or a performance pattern provides the decision maker with information about what the employee has done in the past. Future potential is assessed by either supervisor ratings of potential or more elaborate procedures, such as assessment centers. While more difficult to measure, future potential provides the decision maker with information about what the employee can do in the future.

A person with high past performance and high future potential is a good prospect for a DAP investment, a high human resource investment. These are employees for which greater training and development investments are justified. The rate of return is likely to be high for both the individual and the organization given the level of investment. Therefore, a large investment in these human resources has lower risk than a large investment in human resources in the other performance-potential categories.

A person with high past performance but low future potential is a good prospect for a MAP investment (i.e., a moderate human resource investment). This level of investment is likely to yield the highest rate of return for both the individual and the organization. A higher level of investment (a DAP investment) would likely yield a lower rate of return to both the individual and the organization. For example, a person with low future potential would either have difficulty acquiring the additional training and development or have expectations for advancement increased unreasonably as a result of the training and development. In either case, this person and the organization would receive a lower rate of return on the human resource investment.

A person with low past performance but high future potential is a good candidate for a RAP investment, a low human resource investment. This level of investment is likely to yield the highest rate of return for both the individual and the organization. It is unwise to invest greater amounts of training and development dollars in these employees despite their high future potential. If their performance improves over time, they may become a better risk for human resource investment, but until they establish a higher performance record, they are a high risk for any greater level of investment. If their performance continues to deteriorate, the organization should completely divest itself of these employees.

The DAP-MAP-RAP model incorporates assumptions about risk associated with ability, motivation, and transfer of training. More explicit measurement of individuals on these factors is necessary to accurately assess the riskiness of the investment. Furthermore, an assessment of predicted tenure is also necessary in order to determine if the investment cost can be recouped and a return received. While more development of this model is needed, it provides a useful heuristic for improving decision making in the area of individual human resource investment decisions. But what about investments in human resource programs? They will be considered next.

UTILITY ANALYSIS: A METHOD FOR ASSESSING INVESTMENTS IN HUMAN RESOURCE PROGRAMS

What should the best human resource programs use to create a more flexible work force? A knowledge-based pay system? Participative decision making? Should these two human resource programs be implemented simultaneously?

What is the return on investment associated with using a valid selection test rather than a current procedure that relies solely upon a selection interview? Can an assessment center that is expensive to set up and operate yield benefits that justify the costs? Does a computer-based training system produce results that justify the expense? All of these questions reflect a bottom-line emphasis for evaluating human resource programs necessary for strategic human resource management decision making.

Until recently, most human resource managers concluded that, while costs could be estimated fairly precisely in dollar terms for human resource programs, benefits could only be described in qualitative terms. For example, a training program might cost $1,200 per trainee to implement. Benefits would be described as the number of trainees who successfully completed the training program, or the percentage of employees who responded favorably to a reaction questionnaire. No attempt would be made to estimate the increase in job performance in dollar terms resulting from an effective training program. Consequently, when budget cutbacks became necessary, human resource programs were the first to be discontinued, since they were viewed by corporate managers as merely costs that could be, and should be, controlled. Unfortunately, this myopic viewpoint, perpetuated by human resource managers who could not demonstrate the benefits of their programs compared to the costs of their programs, has led to the abandonment of many useful programs and the discounting of human resource management contributions to the bottom line.

Today, the techniques of cost-benefit analysis—called utility analysis in the human resource management literature—are both well developed and available to the practicing human resource manager. A utility analysis involves identifying alternatives, drawing up a list of all the factors to be considered for each alternative, measuring the factors on a common scale (e.g., dollars), and then computing the benefits less the costs to determine the net value of each alternative.[21] The decision maker can then compare alternatives and choose those with net values (or returns on investment) that exceed some predetermined minimum standard. It allows the human resource manager to compare a number of human resource programs, such as a drug testing program, job redesign program, or quality circle program, both in comparison to one another as well as against some minimal expected return. Consequently, the human resource manager can use the same methods that the finance manager uses to aid in decision making. It also means that human resource investments can be compared using the same measurement (i.e., dollars) as for other types of investments, such as investments in new equipment.

Admittedly, some human resource program benefits are difficult to measure, such as the dollar increase in job performance resulting from the use of valid selection procedures.[22] While measurement techniques have been developed to overcome these problems, some managers, especially those outside the human resource management function, may be skeptical. However, by using break-even analysis, different assumptions can be made, providing the decision maker with useful guidance despite the lack of precise measures for some variables. For example, rather than estimating the benefits of a valid selection program with a precise dollar figure associated with improved job performance per person (e.g.,

$20,000), break-even analysis allows the decision maker to determine how much selection effectiveness would have to be improved to merely cover the per person costs of the program (e.g., $150). Then, the decision maker can make a more informed decision about investing in the human resource program. Will it likely provide benefits greater than or equal to $150 per person? If the answer is yes, then it is a good investment decision. If the answer is no, then the investment is risky at best, and unsound at worst.

Two major categories of human resource programs can be assessed using utility analysis. Programs that affect *employee stocks* increase valuable characteristics among existing employees to improve their current job performance.[23] Human resource programs, such as employee participation in decision making, performance feedback, training and development, and compensation, can increase knowledge, skills, and motivation. Decisions affecting employee stocks enhance productivity more when they affect a broad range of employees over a long time period, cause large average increases in the value of employee job behaviors, and achieve both effects at minimum cost.

Employee flows occur when employees move into, through, and out of an organization through selection, promotion, demotion, transfer, and separation. Programs that affect employee flows include improved selection procedures, higher yield recruitment methods, and job posting systems for internal transfers. These programs enhance productivity the most when they affect large numbers of employee flows across a long time period, increase the value of job behaviors through better personnel-job matches, and accomplish these goals at a minimal cost.

Decisions about human resource programs—those affecting both employee stocks and employee flows—provide a vital link between organizational strategies, human resource strategies, and operational decisions made by human resource managers. Human resource strategy implementation, such as creating firm-specific skills through training and development, require decisions about specific human resource programs that will accomplish the desired objectives.

Since a chosen strategy can be implemented in various ways, decision makers need some means for selecting the most appropriate alternatives. Utility analysis provides the analytical framework for making these decisions. For example, suppose a firm wants to change from a traditional manufacturing process to a flexible manufacturing system. What kind of flexibility will be required of its employees? Which programs can create that flexibility? Which programs provide the greatest return on investment? Utility analysis can improve the odds of choosing the appropriate alternatives.

In summary, utility analysis provides human resource managers with the tools to assess alternative human resource investments. Additionally, utility analysis allows a human resource manager to demonstrate the bottom-line impact of human resource programs, both the benefits as well as the costs, making it more likely that human resource considerations will be taken seriously in the strategic management process.

MAKING HUMAN RESOURCE MANAGERS INTO STRATEGIC HUMAN RESOURCE MANAGERS

This chapter began with a discussion of the evolution of human resource management from a minor supportive role in business operations to a crucial position in the strategic management of a firm. Achieving a greater role in the strategic management of a firm will, however, require human resource managers to change their thinking about their field, retool their own human capital to meet new challenges, and become more persuasive advocates of the potential and realized contributions of strategic human resource management.

Rethinking human resource management requires looking at human resources and human resource management activities from a different perspective. This chapter suggests that human resources must be viewed as human capital consisting of knowledge, skills, abilities, and other characteristics with value in relation to strategy options. Human resources can lose value through knowledge and skills obsolescence or through lack of fit with a chosen strategy. Human resources can gain value through increased knowledge and skills enhanced by both individual initiative (e.g., an employee who seeks additional training) and organizational initiative (e.g., tuition reimbursement for job-related college courses) when that knowledge and skill is necessary for a chosen strategy. Sometimes human resource value can change when a new strategy makes more valuable some knowledge and skill that was previously less valuable. That is, without additional investment, some human resources become more valuable simply because the organization's goals have changed.

Human resource management activities are interrelated in their impact on an organization's human resources. Separate human resource management subsystems, such as attraction, selection, retention, development, appraisal, and adjustment, cannot be managed as separate functions. For example, increasing human resource knowledge and skill through training and development has an impact on rewards and compensation. To consider these two functions separately could lead to suboptimal outcomes, such as highly trained employees who leave the firm in greater numbers in order to receive higher compensation from competitors.

Furthermore, human resource management activities can have an impact not only on an organization's own direct employees, but also on the employees of suppliers, distributors, servicers, and customers. When considered in advance, these broader human resource activities can have a significant impact on strategy formulation and implementation.

Human resource managers must also retool their own human capital in order to take advantage of the opportunities afforded by strategic human resource management. This means that human resource managers need to obtain a more thorough knowledge and greater skill in the analytical methods of marketing, finance, accounting, and strategic management. Some of this human capital can be acquired through routinely reading business publications, some can be acquired through formal education, and some can be acquired through more active involvement in the organization's nonhuman resource management decisions.

Finally, human resource managers must become more persuasive advocates of the contribution they can make to an organization.[24] Analytical tools such as utility analysis are available that can facilitate the effective presentation of the bottom-line contributions of human resource management programs. However, no tool, no matter how powerful analytically, will be persuasive if it is not used effectively. Human resource managers must create opportunities to provide human resource input into strategic planning and management.

Organizational players, such as the finance, marketing, and strategy people, have long considered human resource managers second-class citizens in the organization. Overcoming historical biases will require persistence on the part of the human resource manager that rises to the challenge.

NOTES

1. For a good discussion of the causes of the changing role of human resource management in organizations see C. A. O'Reilly and J. C. Anderson, Personnel human resource management in the United States: Some evidence of change. In *Current Issues in Human Resource Management: Commentary and Readings.* Eds. S. L. Rynes and G. T. Milkovich (Plano, Tex.: Business Publications, 1986), pp. 18–26.

2. There are several good treatments of the history of human resource management. See, for example, Chapter 2 of W. F. Cascio, *Managing Human Resources: Productivity, Quality of Worklife, Profits.* (New York: McGraw-Hill, 1989); S. M. Jacoby *Employing Bureaucracy: Managers, Unions, and the Transformation of Work in American Industry*, 1900–1945. (New York: Columbia University Press, 1985); and Chapter 2, J. B. Miner and M. G. Miner, *Personnel and Industrial Relations: A Managerial Approach.* (New York: Macmillan, 1985).

3. See Cascio, *Managing Human Resources.*

4. See H. E. Meyer Personnel directors are the new corporate heroes. In *Policy Issues in Contemporary Personnel and Industrial Relations.* Eds. M. G. Miner and J. B. Miner (1977) (New York: Macmillan 1976), pp. 26–31.

5. See Cascio, *Managing Human Resources.*

6. This discussion is based upon an unpublished model developed by Chris Berger of Purdue University. For a similar approach, see E. H. Schein, *Career Dynamics: Matching Individual and Organizational Needs*. (Reading, Mass.: Addison-Wesley, 1978).

7. Alternative forms of employer temporary withdrawal are discussed in L. T. Perry, Least-cost alternatives to layoffs in declining industries. *Organizational Dynamics* (Spring 1986): pp. 48–61.

8. See *Webster's Ninth New Collegiate Dictionary*. (Springfield, Mass. Merriam-Webster, 1986), p. 1,004.

9. For a typical discussion of the economics concept of resources, see P. Wonnacott and R. Wonnacott, *An Introduction to Macroeconomics*. (New York: McGraw-Hill, 1986), pp. 27–29.

10. A classic work in this area is G. Becker, *Human Capital*. (New York: National Bureau of Economic Research, 1975). Most of this discussion is based on Chapter 9 of R. G. Ehrenberg and R. S. Smith *Modern Labor Economics*. 2d ed. (Glenview, Ill.: Scott, Foresman, 1985). For a comparison and synthesis of human capital theory, human resources accounting, and utility analysis, see B. D. Steffy and S. D. Maurer, Conceptualizing and measuring the economic effectiveness of human resource activities. *Academy of Management Review* 13 (2) (1988) 271–86.

11. Ehrenberg and Smith, *Modern Labor Economics*.

12. See J. Ullman, Interfirm differences in the cost of search for clerical workers. *Journal of Business* 41, (2), (1968): 153–65.

13. See Cascio, *Managing Human Resources*.

14. For a detailed discussion of training expenditures see Chapter 10 of W. F. Cascio, *Costing Human Resources: The Financial Impact of Behavior in Organizations*. 2d ed. (Boston, Mass.: PWS-Kent Publishing, 1987).

15. See the *Wall Street Journal* Feb. 9, 1990 "Back to basics," R14-R15 M. Charlier.

16. L. T. Perry Least-cost alternatives to layoffs in declining industries. *Organizational Dynamics* (Spring 1986): 48–61.

17. Ibid.

18. See R. S. Schuler and I. C. MacMillan, Gaining competitive advantage through human resource management practices. *Human Resource Management*. 23 (3) (1984): 241–55.

19. Ibid.

20. The original model is presented in Chapter 9 of L. L. Cummings and D. P. Schwab, (1973) *Performance in Organizations: Determinants and Appraisal*. (Glenview, Ill.: Scott, Foresman, 1973).

21. See J. Boudreau Utility analysis in W. F. Cascio, ed., *Employment Planning*. (Washington, D.C.: Bureau of National Affairs, 1989), pp. 87–109.

22. See F. L. Schmidt, H. E. Hunter, R. C. McKenzie, and J. W. Muldrow, Impact of valid selection procedures on work force productivity. *Journal of Applied Psychology* 64 (1979): 609–626.

23. See Boudreau, Utility analysis.

24. See Cascio, *Managing Human Resources*.

4

Early Approaches to Strategic Human Resource Management

Preliminary efforts to develop strategic human resource management systems had a number of factors in common. Many approaches were based on similar assumptions about organizations and on accepted ideas about people. As the fields of strategic management and human resource management have evolved over the past decade, a number of these basic premises have been questioned and found wanting. As our knowledge of organizations has grown, we are able to rely on more complex and comprehensive models of how people, groups, and organizational units function. These upgraded models enhance our understanding and thereby improve our ability to predict and influence organizational actions. Situational analyses, rather than static principles, have become the norm for organization design. Our view of employees has also matured. Not only do we see members of an organization as resources, rather than costs or cogs in the organization's wheel, we are better able to take advantage of the potential for flexibility and learning that employees offer. This evolving frame of reference largely distinguishes recent developments in strategic human resource management from earlier efforts.

COMMON ELEMENTS IN EARLY STRATEGIC HUMAN RESOURCE MANAGEMENT APPROACHES

We observe four common characteristics of initial strategic human resource management approaches. These characteristics are depicted in articles written about strategic human resource management and are articulated by managers who adopted early techniques for blending strategy with human resource management. First, early strategic human resource management models emphasize strategy implementation goals over strategy formulation activities and processes. Human resources were considered as means or constraints, or viewed in a supportive role, but human resource activities were virtually ignored as elements in generating or selecting strategic objectives. Rarely were human resources seen as a strategic capacity from which competitive choices should be derived. When human resource issues were infrequently used to suggest or determine strategic direction, the approach was unidirectional from human resource problems to strategic solutions, rather than iterative and interactive. Consequently, the potential contribution that human resources might make to the competitive position of the firm is unnecessarily limited. This perspective practically mandates a one-way dependence between strategic planning and human resource management. As a result, the potential for synergy between these two activities is severely curtailed.

Second, early strategic human resource management models focused on matching people to strategy but not on matching strategy to people. At best, this practice assumes that people are more flexible and adaptable than strategy. This assumption has little empirical support, yet it persists. Such an approach also implies that cause and effect relationships between people and strategic choices are unidirectional. In other words, a strategy was determined to require certain managerial styles, skills, abilities, and human interactions in order for it to be effective. This perspective neglected notions of equifinality, thereby suggesting there is only one set of skills or styles suited to any given strategy. In addition, there is little recognition that people may perform more or less effectively under certain competitive, product-market, growth-oriented, or strategically challenging conditions. The fact that strategies are designed by individuals seems to have been lost as well. Moreover, the knowledge that once in place, strategies influence information and thus shape perceptions, actions, and decisions is ignored.

On the few occasions where firms attempted to match strategy to people, usually because of a low level of substitutability of personnel such as in family businesses, or when a founder maintains entrepreneurial control the causal assumptions were merely reversed. The process did not become multidirectional. Rarely was there an exploration into whether the strategic direction of a firm required an entirely different approach to hiring, training, or any other human resource management activity. The fundamental concepts guiding these functional decisions remained unchanged.

A number of high-tech firms seem to have embraced a similarly myopic solution to a competitive issue. Short product life cycles are a competitive reality for these firms. Some companies have assumed that the need for continuous innovation means a corresponding need for continual turnover in the labor force. New ideas seem to be equated with new people. These firms are in a constant state of hiring and terminating personnel. They do not seem to consider an alternative of nurturing creative ventures or new experiences among a more stable employee population. Early strategic human resource management techniques did not look beyond basic staffing requirements to determine whether the existing organizational culture and expectations facilitated or hindered the selected competitive advantage.

The common goal-related problem of means-ends reversal is a likely consequence of either assuming that strategy dictates managerial skills or that managerial abilities should single-mindedly determine a firm's strategy. For example, a firm, such as Lincoln Electric, that relies on a strong internal culture, promotion from within, and shared experience to provide the incentives and the control systems needed to yield high-quality products at low cost, will have difficulty dealing with the internal organizational conflicts that arise from either internationalization or acquisition as a growth strategy. Without a conceptual reassessment of hiring, compensation, training, and socialization practices, maintaining the existing human resource policies, which once were a means to the strategic objective of low cost products, become an end in themselves. The cultural and human resource management characteristics that provided one source of competitive advantage may preclude consideration of future strategic opportunities.

Third, early models of strategic human resource management rely heavily on organizational or product life cycle phenomena as single and largely uncontrollable catalysts of change. Dependence on this biological metaphor implies that managerial choice is quite limited. More significantly, life cycle models imply determinism and eventual death of the organism. This, in turn, suggests an external dominance of a firm by industry trends, competitor actions, governmental regulations, technological breakthroughs, and other events that accelerate or slow down industry or organizational evolution. The role of managerial choice is downplayed. The consequences of organizational actions are undervalued. The incentive for creative, decisive, integrative strategies is eroded.

While life cycle characteristics are an important part of an organization's climate, strategic choices should be seen as shaping rather than simply derived from organizational life stages. This perspective is not always the case, however. A number of researchers illustrate how organizational structure and managerial processes generally respond to prevailing, or even retrospective, competitive conditions.[1] They further suggest that a shift in structure or methods of organizing generally occur only after adverse economic consequences are experienced as a result of relying on obsolete or ineffective organizational structures and managerial processes. The role of strategic planning is underplayed. Relying on life cycle steps as triggering events rather than as composite responses to organizational and competitive conditions encourages managers to underestimate their potential for choice and influence.

Many of the recent developments in strategic management specifically address this concern. Techniques for conducting an effective industry analysis provide a firm with increasing opportunities to identify and exploit industry leverage points. In fact, the purpose of an industry analysis such as that described in Chapter 2 is to permit a firm to make a deliberate strategic choice. Depending on industry conditions a firm may elect to position itself in such a way that negative industry forces are weakened. A firm anticipating consolidation among important raw material suppliers may elect backward vertical integration to maintain control over important organizational inputs. Alternatively, a firm can aggressively alter the characteristics of its industry. Marketing innovations, for example, can increase brand loyalty and thereby erect a new barrier to entry. A third option is for a firm to actively exploit anticipated changes in industry structure. Such exploitation often requires changes in the knowledge, skills, and abilities of employees. The intent is to capitalize on product shifts, changes in buyer coalitions, entry and exit of current participants, or other similar alterations in the structural forces that shape industry competition. Improvements in forecasting, scenario generation, and utility analysis offer an expanding array of perspectives on strategic conditions to augment life cycle views. These additional perspectives each offer attractive options for framing strategic human resource management issues. Manpower planning and succession planning are only the tip of the iceberg of potential contributions human resource management activities can make to the strategic plans of an organization.

Fourth, most early strategic human resource management models emphasized fit, or congruence, with other management systems while not recognizing the need for a lack of fit during organizational transitions or when organizations have multiple and conflicting goals. Clearly, minimal fit among strategy and human resource practices is essential for effective performance.[2] Researchers have suggested that early fit may provide an important source of competitive advantage. Similarly, some measure of fit between a firm and its market environment is essential. If a firm's products and services are not attractive to a targeted group of potential customers, there is a low probability for economic success. The issue of fit is a matter of degree, however. There is no clear line of demarcation between fit and nonfit. Misfits between task assignments and work group characteristics may be overcome by a tight fit between supervisory behaviors and task requirements. More important to consider, an exceptionally tight fit may cause as many problems for an organization as it resolves. The costs and benefits of tight fit depend on the need for organizational change and flexibility. If organizational change is commonplace, as with highly innovative or prospector organizations, tight fit across all of a firm's managerial processes may be an unacceptable constraint. From a human resource management standpoint, the more tight and pervasive the linkages among all a firm's managerial systems, the more difficult it is to get employees to recognize and accept a need for change, and the more extensive any change effort will need to be.

TARGETED HUMAN RESOURCE MANAGEMENT ACTIVITIES

Most early writers on strategic human resource management focused on a specific functional area or on specialized managerial techniques. The principle focus has been on mainstream human resource management activities such as selection, job analysis, performance appraisal, training and development, or compensation system design. Some looked toward human resource accounting. [3] A human resource accounting approach attempts to assign specific numerical values to a firm's human resources. This is done in an effort to quantify the organization's human capacity and capabilities. Others approach strategic human resource management from a human resource planning perspective.[4] From a planning viewpoint, the intent is to anticipate specific requirements for knowledge, skills, and abilities, and to translate these needs into job classifications. Accurate forecasting enables a manager to project the specific human resource needs in the foreseeable future. Another group of researchers concentrated on developing particular human resource management responses to specific strategic changes in the market environment.[5]

While it is true that many human resource management activities need reorientation if a firm is to develop an effective strategic human resource management plan, a change in techniques is not sufficient. Effective strategic management of a firm's human resources requires a conceptual overhaul of the functional purpose, rather than simply redirection and new methods for achieving traditional objectives. Performance appraisals, for example, must be directly linked with competitive advantage and long-term marketplace effectiveness in a strategic human resource management system. Compensation systems must be evaluated in light of their consequences for a firm's resource base, equity among both internal and external stakeholders, and the competitive position of the firm, as well as in terms of an ability to solicit desired behaviors among organizational members. The ethics, as well as the effectiveness, of training and development programs need to be evaluated. Is it morally correct, for example, to ask an employee to devote many hours of discretionary time to developing skills that are only useful in a single organizational setting, if a firm is not willing to provide a compensating guarantee of long-term employment?

Perhaps the most popular approach to matching a firm's human resources to its strategic interests has been that adopted by scholars and managers who attempt to match the human resource skills, abilities, and activities to particular strategic or organizational conditions dominating a firm's long-term goals or current life cycle phase.[6] In this latter approach, activities such as recruiting, selection and retention, compensation systems, human relations versus traditional versus human resources management styles, and productivity are examined in light of their strategic consequences.[7] Unfortunately, however, few prescriptions for a complete menu of human resource management activities or strategies are offered.

Four different categories of strategic human resource management are discussed in this chapter: human resource valuation (accounting-based approaches), human resources planning (anticipating human resource staffing requirements), consideration of human resource choices as a response to changes in environmental conditions (a match with the external environment), and matching human resources to strategic choices or organizational conditions (developing internal fit). We begin by outlining the assumptions and parameters of each approach. The relevant research and organizational experiences associated with each is then described and critiqued. Primary conclusions and recommendations derived from each of these approaches are examined. Finally, we illustrate the contributions and limitations of early approaches to strategic human resource management by walking through the human and strategic implications these approaches suggest are involved in designing the factory of the future.

HUMAN RESOURCE VALUATION

In many firms, labor costs account for more than 50 percent of the total operating costs of the business, according to a 1982 U.S. Chamber of Commerce report. Human resources are probably the last great cost that remains relatively unmanaged in organizational operations.[8] It has been argued that personnel departments cannot, for several reasons, effectively manage cost improvements through productivity increases. Many personnel operations are limited by inadequate staff. When the number of employees is adequate, human resource management operations are often hampered by training limitations. This often results in personnel trained to use sophisticated human resource management techniques to respond to human resource issues but unable to envision or initiate human resource actions for strategic purposes. As previously discussed, strategic human resource management requires competence in both strategic and human resource management.

Another problem in cost management is that most personnel operations have little power to channel human or other resources into alternate operating line undertakings. In many cases both the scope and the response capabilities of human resource managers are limited by operating managers. This may be because line managers underestimate the potential benefits of a more interactive approach to human resource management. When this is the case, more effective marketing of human resource management contributions can make a difference. Alternatively, managers of other operations may be reluctant to share power with any other functional managers in the firm, even if the organizational benefits of such sharing may be clear.

A final condition limiting a firm's ability to manage human resource costs effectively involves measurement difficulties. Cost improvements are often ineffectively managed due to measurement problems in valuing both human resources and assessing productivity indicators. For example, how should the worth of a particular skill or attitude be assessed? What effect does improved group participation have on unit costs, service capabilities, or product development? Can these effects be measured? Can the contributions that come from improved human resource management be distinguished from the contributions derived from technology improvements? Human resource valuation approaches to strategic human resource management attempt to respond to some of these concerns by considering the economic risk and opportunity losses caused by ineffective personnel management.

TWO VALUATION METHODS

Two human resource accounting methods have gained particular recognition and popularity.[9] One method relies on a cost approach, the other uses a value approach. The difference between these two methods centers on whether an employee is viewed in terms of costs-to-date (the cost approach) or whether an employee is seen in terms of his or her expected contribution to the organization over an extended time horizon (the value approach). Unfortunately, both methods rely on similar proxy measures of employee worth. Cost approaches focus on historical costs incurred to identify, hire, train, and maintain employees within an organization. In essence these methods concentrate on the replacement costs incurred if an employee left and a new employee with similar knowledge, skills, and abilities was put in the same job. Cost methods value an employee based on the investment that a firm has made, or the expenses a firm would need to incur, to duplicate the current contribution of an employee. The current contribution, however, is not explicitly measured. Rather, contribution is assumed to be equal to the sum of the historical costs incurred in the hiring and development process. From a cost-benefit perspective, therefore, cost approaches explicitly look only at the numerator of the equation, grossly underestimating the benefits associated with the investments.

Value approaches consider the present value of an employee's stream of net future contributions to a firm. Rather than looking to historical costs, value approaches attempt to forecast the future. Salary is the most frequently used indicator of expected contribution, based on the assumption that the salary paid to an employee reflects his or her relative contribution to a firm's ongoing activities. A value approach does not consider expenses or time required to enable an employee to make a significant contribution. Rather, value approaches only look at the benefit side of the equation.

Value approaches do not differentiate between an outstanding employee and a mediocre employee with the same salary. More importantly, value approaches do not adjust for strategic or organizational changes. Most organizations have employees who were primary contributors to the firm's competitive position during one phase of operations, but who either through obsolescence or changes in strategy no longer make essential contributions. The salaries of these founding contributors may equal or exceed the salaries of current star performers, yet their expected future contributions would be quite different. Value approaches do not distinguish the first type of employee from the latter.

CONTRIBUTIONS AND LIMITATIONS OF HUMAN RESOURCE ACCOUNTING METHODS

These differences in perspective reflect quite distinct organization cultures. Cost approaches tend to focus on organizational outputs while value approaches concentrate on the employee's output. Unfortunately, neither of these methods provides for a comparison of human resource costs or benefits with the costs of other, perhaps mechanical, resources that would be used to accomplish similar objectives. Nor does either method provide a vehicle for considering a range of different types of contributions a particular employee could make under different strategic scenarios.

Consider a pay-for-skills compensation system, for example. Under these systems, employees are encouraged to develop a wide repertoire of capabilities. If the strategy of the firm continually requires multiskilled workers, as would be the case in a team-based paper mill, the utility of the diversely skilled employee is high. If, however, the skills remain an untapped potential due to industry decline, static competitive options, or a consolidation of product-market scope, the value of diversity may be quite low. Valuation approaches that rely on salary as a proxy for projected contribution do not distinguish between these two situations. Assumptions of static organizational conditions and straight-line projections of employee talents seem to underline value approaches to strategic human resource management.

Beyond measurement problems, there are important contextual difficulties in assessing human costs and contributions. Experts do not agree on who should judge an employee's worth to an organization. In one sense, the judgment issue raises the question of whose bias should prevail. Should an employee estimate his or her potential contribution? Should a boss or peer? Should subordinates? With each of these choices, very different types of organizational contributions are likely to be emphasized.

Moreover, it is unclear how employee valuation information will improve managerial decisions. How should an evaluation of an employee's present value of his or her expected contribution be used to make strategic choices? Can such an assessment be used to compare and contrast various implementation strategies? Should replacement costs for employees be an integral part of strategy selection when a firm is considering changing its target market or product mix? Proponents of human resource valuation approaches to strategic human resource management give little guidance.

As is described in greater detail in Chapter 5, the basic notion of measuring choices managers make in the way their firm selects, trains, and uses its human resources is useful if an appropriate frame of reference is maintained. We suggest that measuring firm and industry specific and nonspecific skills and utility analysis is useful in doing this.

Four problems arise from using human resource accounting-based valuation methods. First, valuation methods that attempt to obtain reliable and valid data are often cumbersome and expensive. The logic used in developing these methods is often obscure. Moreover, some of these techniques make assumptions inconsistent with organizational realities.

Second, it is not clear, since little guidance is provided regarding the use of valuation results, that the benefits of using sound human resource valuation data outweigh the costs involved in obtaining such data. In most instances a valuation approach to strategic human resource management permits either a limited assessment of implementation costs or a narrow comparison of the human input costs associated with a number of strategic options, but does not provide insight into the valuation of human resources relative to other resources given competitive strategy, nor does this approach permit a range of strategies and tactics to be comprehensively considered.

Third, and most importantly, no information is provided on the benefits or costs associated with using human resources in one way versus another. Would it be strategically better, for example, to provide new employees with extensive training that both enhances their effectiveness and increases their potential mobility, or to tie training opportunities to organizational tenure and commitment, thus limiting early benefits but simultaneously limiting early costs?

Merrill Lynch faces this dilemma in its broker training policies. Merrill Lynch arguably provides the best initial training for brokers in the financial services industry. Because of constrained resources, they also provide lower base salaries on the assumption that a better trained broker will be able to more than compensate for lower base pay with higher commissions. For a farsighted employee, this presumption has merit. However, Merrill Lynch has found that a number of more shortsighted and economically oriented new employees take advantage of the extensive training and leave soon after for higher paying positions at other, competing financial services firms. Human resource valuation techniques can provide useful insights into certain dimensions of this dilemma. However, at present, these methods provide little guidance regarding how to define or resolve this strategic human resource management issue.

Fourth, human resource valuation approaches do not provide information on how to improve the value of human resources within a firm in ways that enhance distinct competencies or lead to a wider choice of competitive positions. Moreover, value is not assessed within this framework. Suppose, for example, a firm has a policy of avoiding layoffs. Consider an employee in the airline industry whose primary skills were in working with federal agencies to negotiate and disseminate the fine details of regulation policies. Since it is highly unusual to reduce an employee's salary if his or her abilities become less useful to a firm's strategic objectives, the present value contribution estimate would be inaccurate since, clearly, this employee would need both retraining and redirected attention in a deregulated environment.

Valuation approaches do not provide guidance for measuring such circumstances, nor do they suggest ways to preclude their occurrence. In general, valuation approaches are limited to providing partial answers to strategy implementation questions.

HUMAN RESOURCE PLANNING

Human resource planning is broadly defined as anticipating future business and environmental demands on a firm and then developing a blueprint to meet the personnel requirements dictated by those conditions. A narrow definition of the concept concentrates on meeting personnel needs over some future time horizon. A more progressive approach includes planning for the skills development and contributions, as well as the sufficiency, of human resources. Regardless of specific approach, there is a strong implication that human resource planning could be an important input to strategic decisions. Unfortunately, evidence suggests that the linkage between human resource planning and strategic planning is generally not emphasized in practice.

A partial explanation for this lack of use may be found in the focus of human resource planning literature. Most research focuses on human resource supply and demand forecasting.[10] Many statistical techniques, such as Markov analysis, econometric models, and scenario generation techniques are available for making such forecasts. As with any model-based approach to planning, it is important to ensure that the assumptions of the model fit the conditions of the organization. Given the variety of techniques available, as well as the increasing statistical sophistication of many human resource managers, this is not a primary difficulty.

There are also a number of qualitative human resource planning options offered for consideration. Olian and Rynes rely on the Miles and Snow typology (i.e., defenders, prospectors, analyzers) to develop a number of propositions regarding staffing practices appropriate to implement a given strategy.[11] Their propositions are based on several assumptions. First, they assume that different types of people are required in different organizational settings. Second, they assume that the types of people attracted to a firm reflect the types of recruiting and selection practices used. Third, they assume that selection criteria should reflect organization strategies and goals as well as the outputs from job analysis.

Some of their propositions reflect the type of competitive advantage upon which a firm relies. For example, they postulate that the relative demand for people with functional backgrounds in finance versus marketing will vary with the organization's strategy. Some suggestions reflect assumptions about the ideology of the dominant coalition in a firm. The values and beliefs of the dominant coalition in defender firms is quite different from the values and beliefs of the dominant coalition in prospector organizations. Olian and Rynes propose that secondary selection criteria should reflect the preferences of the dominant coalition. They extend this idea with a series of recommendations designed to insure that the knowledge, skills, abilities, and traits of selected employees meet the work processes, career paths, and structures characteristic of defender, analyzer, and prospector prototypes. Internal versus external recruiting efforts, job preview content and techniques, screening procedures, and decision rules are each examined to hypothesize a good fit with the strategic conditions of different strategy types. Olian and Rynes equate the integration of human resource planning and strategy as devising a series of criteria and tools that enable staffing results to meet strategic choice conditions.

A needs assessment approach is recommended by John DeSanto.[12] He argues that for human resource planning to make a viable contribution to corporate planning, it should begin with an evaluation of the capabilities of the current work force and the anticipated needs for the future labor pool. Human resource planning is seen as the cornerstone of all other human resource management activities. This perspective is justified, in part, by DeSanto's observation that line managers typically neglect to anticipate gaps between current employee abilities and upcoming job demands. The role of strategic human resource management is then seen as predicting and filling in these holes. The primary purpose of human resource planning is to increase predictability, which, it is expected, will lead to an improved probability that human resource needs will be met on a continuing basis. Recruiting activities, training programs, and labor contracts are each seen as valuable tools for implementing human resource plans.

L. James Harvey[13] provides a checklist enabling a firm to evaluate its current human resource planning systems. Included are points related to the time horizon for planning, direct or indirect connections with corporate planning processes, measurability and control issues, and decision processes. Harvey's focus is on the processes that lead to effective human resource planning. Unfortunately, with the exception of budgeting requirements, the content of effective human resource planning is largely ignored. There is no mention of competitive advantage or strategic position.

A SPECIAL CASE: EXECUTIVE SUCCESSION PLANNING

There is one exception to this general rule. Managerial succession planning has been closely linked with strategic business planning. Processes for identifying potential top managers and providing specific developmental career sequences have long been practiced in many firms. As discussed earlier, however, managers are generally chosen to implement selected strategies. Less effort is aimed at adapting strategies to managers and vice versa, and almost no effort is directed toward selecting managers to devise rather than implement strategy.

As a subset of this, succession plans for chief executives have recently received a great deal of attention.[14] Organization size has often been assumed to have a strong influence on the need for succession planning. An underlying assumption is that increased size requires increased bureaucratization. More pervasive bureaucratic systems, in turn, increase the probability that succession will be considered a routine and rational process. Succession then becomes the logical means for introducing sufficient new perspectives and talents into a typically stable organization to maintain adequate adaptability. Through this line of reasoning, it has been argued that large organizations will have a greater frequency of executive succession. However, research that controlled for variations in organization performance and industry differences found the relationship between organization size and frequency of succession to be much less compelling. Succession rates differ widely from industry to industry. The variation in succession rates reflect differences in marketplace volatility and industry maturity.

A more consistent outcome of size is the origin of the successor. As organizations become larger, the likelihood of inside, as opposed to outside, succession increases. It may be that larger firms have a greater number of administrative positions to serve as a fertile training ground for executives. Another possible explanation is that larger organizations are more likely to have candidates with a broader skill and experience repertoire. Diversity in products and markets often accompanies increases in organization size. The challenges of managing a variety of competitive and technological conditions enhance the skill base of many corporate managers. Increased complexity is a common feature of large organizations. Since complexity is often managed through formal rules and informal understandings, this gives an advantage to insiders. Taking these factors into account, it becomes clear that the responsibility of an effective strategic human resource manager for ensuring adequate training opportunities for potential top executives is likely to increase with increases in organization size.

Organization performance also has a strong influence on succession patterns. The underlying rationale is an assumption that CEOs are able to directly affect a firm's performance, in other words, that they have a direct impact on the bottom line. This issue has sparked the interest of scholars and boards of directors alike. Scholars have investigated the issue by assessing the extent to which variation in organizational performance is explained by leadership factors. Boards of directors have examined the question by trial and error. A board of directors explores the performance implications of CEOs every time a dynamic new leader is brought in to turn around a poorly performing business. While a number of highly visible examples such as Lee Iacococca and Frank Lorenzo offer a strong case that a CEO can make a dramatic difference in performance for good or ill, scholars have only been able to consistently attribute a small amount of variance in performance to executive leadership. It is becoming increasingly obvious that while a capable, dynamic, highly skilled CEO can be an important asset, other factors also play a significant role in determining strategic effectiveness. Industry conditions, organization strengths and weaknesses, and environmental threats and opportunities exert a strong influence on organization performance.

Succession plans are particularly evident in multidivisional firms. Often such firms have numerous products at various stages of the product life cycle. Managerial succession planning in these firms seems unduly dependent on having sufficient start-up ventures for the firm's intrapreneurs and sufficient mature business operations for the firm's efficiency experts. Portfolio management seems as related to finding worthwhile outlets for established managerial talents as it is to designing appropriate competitive positions and cash flow sequences.

Achieving a fit appears to be the guiding premise underlying much of the work in managerial succession planning. Fit can be counterproductive from a competitive perspective if a firm operates in a rapidly changing environment, since it may inhibit innovativeness and inappropriately constrain a firm's repertoire of skills. Fit approaches to strategic human resource management can create as many problems as they solve. Hence, managerial succession planning has also been underused as an input in the strategic business plan.

What does this mean to strategic human resource management? Succession planning can be an important and valuable competence for a firm to develop. Under certain conditions, having just the right individual in a key executive role may make the difference between securing a strong competitive advantage and being shaken out of an industry. An ability to recognize these strategically critical turning points may be as valuable a contribution as selecting just the right individual for CEO.

In addition to appropriate situation analysis, a strategic perspective on succession must go beyond traditional concerns with organization size, the need for change, and classic leadership traits. Succession planning should include, at minimum, an evaluation of industry evolution and market conditions. Most significantly, perhaps, effective succession planning should be seen as necessary, but clearly not sufficient, for effective strategic human resource management.

CONTRIBUTIONS AND LIMITATIONS OF HUMAN RESOURCE PLANNING

Human resource planning is relatively underused in most organizations. One reason is that the organization politics involved in fostering the use or neglect of these techniques is generally ignored by their advocates. For example, great care may be taken in designing a statistical model of personnel planning in a particular industry. The model may use readily available data, receive high marks for reliability and validity, and provide comprehensive and useful forecasts. Despite this concern with effective model building, little thought may be given to gaining managerial acceptance of the model's output.

Consider the difficulties encountered if a model predicts that the types of skills a manager has based his or her organizational career upon will be less useful to the firm five years from now due to the introduction of new technology or a shift in raw materials. It is not hard to predict that a personnel administrator will face a real challenge trying to convince the potentially displaced manager that the results of the model are sound.

Other types of problems arise if personnel planning models are used prematurely or given disproportionate weight in the strategic feasibility assessment process. While it is useful to know whether or not sufficient employees having necessary skills will be easy or difficult to find and hire, this knowledge can also contaminate the strategy selection process in inappropriate ways. If one growth strategy calls for an increase in manufacturing personnel, for example, while another approach to growth calls for additional sales personnel, it is not unreasonable to predict that production managers will lobby for the first strategy while marketing managers will prefer the latter option. These preferences may reflect a thorough understanding of labor market projections, but they may just as likely reflect functional biases or self-interest. A large gap exists between available techniques for personnel forecasting and their use. This is in part, because organizational realities are not incorporated in the models.

Both research and practice have shown that planning for the appropriate employee characteristics, reward systems, and training and development programs improve strategy implementation. Many human resource management activities can orient employees toward a particular strategic frame of reference and build commitment to the firm and to the strategic direction. Human resource planning has undergone several evolutionary steps. Initially, the focus was on cost and controllability. Later, it was recognized that effective human resource planning could contribute to a firm's competitive advantage. In particular, efforts were undertaken to ensure that employee values, goals, and behaviors shifted in tune with changes in technology and strategic tactics. It often seems as if human resource planning was directed toward the design of transition roadmaps that enabled firms to change their strategic direction while maintaining a fit among financial, market, human, and information systems.

Dave Ulrich presents an interesting historical perspective on strategic human resource planning.[15] In the first phase, human resource planning frameworks were directed toward the regulatory environment, a primary purpose was to ensure compliance with various policies and regulations. From a strategy perspective, this phase of human resource planning can, at best, be considered as not undermining strategic efforts. As these efforts continued, the role and orientation shifted toward control.   In this phase human resource plans were designed to ensure that employee behavior was consistent with organizational strategies. Selection practices, appraisal techniques, reward systems, and training and development programs were all directed toward a good match between human resource capabilities and strategic objectives. Thinking back on Mintzberg's definitions of strategy, this phase of human resource planning considered strategic human resource management as defining a purpose.[16]

The third and final phase to date, according to Ulrich, requires human resource plans to shape behaviors in order to make a discernable contribution to competitive advantage. This phase is premised on the idea that when an employee's behavior is consistent with a firm's strategy, the strategy is more likely to be accepted due to the congruence between goals and actions. In this phase human resource plans are intended to build strategic commitment as well as influence appropriate behaviors. The issues are strategic, but the focus is still on planning human resource management activities. From Mintzberg's perspective, this phase might entail strategic human resource management as a pattern. At this point, operating professionals and human resource professionals collaborate to develop human resource plans.

We suggest a fourth phase is needed if human resource planning is to fully meet the needs of strategic human resource management. The next step is for human resource managers and strategic managers to collaborate in designing competitive strategies as well as human resource plans. To fully integrate human resource management activities and strategic management activities, human resource managers must be active participants in developing comprehensive strategy plans, ploys, and positions.

STRATEGIC HUMAN RESOURCE MANAGEMENT AS A RESPONSE TO CHANGES IN THE ENVIRONMENT

Strategic management concerns a firm's competitive position within an external market environment. It seems reasonable, therefore, to expect environmental factors such as uncertainty, technological innovation, and demographic changes to affect human resource management strategy. Numerous environmental characteristics have been investigated to determine how they influence human resource management activities or human resource strategy formulation.

Responding to Discrete Environmental Trends

Fombrun, for example, looked at how specific changes in information processing, increased automation in manufacturing, inflation, productivity gains, demographic patterns, philosophies of elitism, and interest group politics affect organizational structures and human resource practices.[17] He considers four dimensions of a firm's environment: technological, economic, social, and political. The argument is offered that changes in the technological environment will include enhanced information networks, increased service activities, and more automation. These shifts are expected to have the greatest effect on service jobs and a general need for retraining employees.

Projected changes in the economic environment include high inflation, lowered productivity, a shift from manufacturing activities to service-related activities, and low attention to innovation and investment. These economic changes are seen as having the most direct effect on compensation alternatives and the initial training of employees.

Changes in the social environment, as noted by Fombrun, center on the aging work force, an increased number of minorities in the labor pool, greater self-concern among employees, and a more highly educated work force. These social changes are related to shifts in organizational development, promotion, and formal appraisal systems.

Finally, the political environment is hypothesized to have the strongest effect on definitions of success, the extent to which organizational commitment and career counseling activities can be effective motivators of behavior. Megatrends identified for the political arena include government by oligarchies, a view that hierarchical management is somewhat illegitimate, reduced power of the United States in world politics, and the increasing influence of special interest groups. Strategic human resource management is envisioned as employee-related responses to these large-scale shifts in the general environment.

Responding to General Environmental Conditions

A more general approach to managing human resources in the face of aggregate environmental change has also been explored. The rising number of discrete environmental challenges, such as raw material price increases, supply shortages, rapid changes in demand, increased international competition, and rising social activism, have been identified as indicators of environmental fluctuation. In most cases a generic solution to environmental turbulence and market changes in general, rather than differential responses to specific problems, is then recommended. For example, Ellis concentrates on identifying an appropriate management style to deal with continuous uncertainty and change.[18] He advocates a management style that is pragmatic, not idealistic, and active rather than passive. Further, Ellis argues that managers should be sensitive and show an emotional or visceral response to events rather than remain stoic. Visible emotional responses are seen as humanizing the workplace. Uncertainty and urgency requires a manager to act quickly under circumstances that are only partially understood. Ellis suggests these characteristics call for a willingness to take limited risks, a certain amount of boldness, and an experimental orientation. As managers are increasingly required to deal with the unexpected, the importance of flexibility increases. Flexibility, in turn, requires an ability to learn from past experiences and a certain level of comfort with changing strategic directions. An ability to respond to change is seen as a more important distinct competence than accurate forecasting capabilities.

Ellis's philosophy is that a flexible, active, practical, and responsive managerial style leads to behaviors that generate numerous alternatives and initiatives. The ability to generate a number of options is seen as an effective strategic response to a continuously changing environment. From his viewpoint, managing human resources strategically creates an organizational climate that fosters the kind of risk taking, learning, and adaptation needed to respond appropriately to turbulent and uncertain environments.

Responding to Specific Situations

A third group of scholars and consultants adopted a one-on-one contingency approach. Contingency views suggest consideration of a specific environmental change and posit a specific, appropriate human resource management response. Lindroth, for example, notes that, according to the Bureau of Labor Statistics, the rate of increase in the work force will be less than the rate of increase in new jobs.[19] This disparity typically comes from technological advances in the 1980s and 1990s. She claims that these countervailing trends will lead to a labor shortage, particularly in lower paying, less desirable service sector jobs. Lindroth suggests creative use of the fringe labor population, like retirees, part-time workers, and temporary help, to mitigate or eliminate this shortage.

Maier investigates innovation cycles and the qualitative and quantitative labor force requirements at each stage of the cycle.[20] His recommendations include a reallocation of educational resources to develop semiskilled workers from unskilled workers, and investment to permit some semiskilled workers to either become more highly skilled or to develop handcraft experience. In addition he promotes increased worker mobility both within firms and from organization to organization. Maier advocates increased industrywide coordination of technological innovation to ensure that the appropriately skilled workers are available to firms at each stage of the innovation process. Industrywide coordination facilitates the movement of workers from one firm to another as the employment needs of each organization change in response to sequential phases of the innovation process.

During developmental stages for new products, Maier contends, highly skilled experts are essential to the decision-making process. A large proportion of skilled workers with craft experience are also needed, along with a moderate number of nonhandicraft skilled and semiskilled employees. As innovation takes hold in the rapid growth stage, the importance of highly skilled workers is maintained at a high level. The demand for skilled and semiskilled workers increases, while the need for craft-experienced workers diminishes. As the product becomes mature, there is a very high need for semiskilled workers and a fairly high demand for skilled workers. The requirement of highly skilled workers is quite low during maturity, however. This cyclical pattern in demand for human resources may contribute to the overlapping S patterns typically observed in product development. It is not uncommon for a substitute product or a new generation improvement to begin emerging at just the time the original product is making strong efficiency gains during the maturity phase.

Felice Schwartz considers an entirely different work force issue.[21] She looks at the increasing need for exceptionally talented managers, coupled with trends in the employment patterns of female workers. Characteristic patterns include the observation that women have traditionally had a greater tendency to interrupt their careers or to plateau at various career stages. Schwartz also claims that the cost of employing women in managerial roles is greater than the cost of employing men in similar roles. It is unclear, however, which events are truly causal and which are consequences. The solution Schwartz offers is a segmentation of the labor market into career-primary and career-and-family primary populations. (The latter notion has been popularized as the "mommy track" since it was presumed that only women would be interested in pursuing a career-and-family option.) In this way employees with certain preferences and characteristics are matched with organizational situations that complement or facilitate their personal choices.

According to Schwartz, career-primary women should be identified early in their careers; given ample opportunities to stretch, develop, and contribute to corporate goals; recognized and included as valuable members of the corporate team; and acknowledged as minority members of a highly stressful environment. Career-and-family primary women, on the other hand, require an organization to plan for and manage maternity leave, offer several avenues of flexibility, such as job sharing, flexible work hours, and at-home work, and provide various family-related support and child care systems.

On the surface, these may seem like attractive solutions. Looking deeper, however, these solutions illustrate how matching human resource considerations with corporate expectations and conditions is easily flawed by an overly narrow focus, or by relying on existing biases and untested assumptions. Consider the irony of a corporation that reinforces division of labor, segmentation of the labor pool, and specialization on the basis on non–job-related factors in terms of the choices it offers to women, yet supports teamwork, collaboration, and work flow concepts in its production and strategic operations. To define parenting as women's work is nearly as archaic as defining motivation as the sole purview of the human resource manager. By adopting a myopic focus, the solution to a single issue can easily lead to problems of an even greater magnitude in other arenas. Unfortunately, this narrowness pervades many of the initial matching approaches to strategic human resource management.

CONTRIBUTIONS AND LIMITATIONS OF A RESPONSIVE APPROACH TO STRATEGIC HUMAN RESOURCE MANAGEMENT

Several problems emerge from past efforts to manage environmental change through human resource management strategies. First, when a comprehensive environmental perspective has been adopted, the research has been limited to correlation studies of environmental conditions with various elements of structure or organizational processes. For example, Dimick and Murray discuss the effects of competitive markets and the lack of special competitive advantages on recruiting and manpower planning.[22] They do not, however, explore how the resulting human resource policies interact with or constrain other organizational processes. Nor do they discuss how human resource practices affect strategic position. A symptomatic problem associated with comprehensive approaches is the lack of theory or model development to guide the search for relationships between strategically important environmental events and human resource management responses. The omission of casual inferences severely handicaps the usefulness of the relationships uncovered. Moreover, the isolation of human resource policies and practices from the activities of other functional units in the organization limits the usefulness of these findings from a strategic perspective.

The more narrowly environmental conditions are defined, the more problematic the recommended solutions become. Lenz, for example, discusses several contingency relationships but offers no conclusions regarding how an improved fit between particular environmental events and organizational processes affect the economic or competitive performance of a firm.[23] In a turbulent environment, the search for fit between environmental conditions and organizational activities involves a constantly moving target.

Moreover, a search for environmentally directed responses may be strategically counterproductive. While intuitively appealing as a goal-directed activity, Miles and Snow argue that if a firm permits the environment to dictate its strategic choices in a reactive manner, the chances of long-term survival are reduced.[24] If, on the other hand, a firm develops a coherent strategy that considers, but is not solely dependent upon, environmental conditions, a more successful strategy is expected. Further, they argue, a firm may be able to influence its environment, and this potential should not be ignored. As discussed earlier, opportunities to exploit an unbalanced industry situation can offer attractive strategic options. In a similar manner, a firm's human resource policies, if viewed strategically, may alter its market position and thereby change the contingencies that should be accommodated.

HUMAN RESOURCE MANAGEMENT AND STRATEGIC CONDITIONS

One popular approach to strategic human resource management has been to see human resource strategies as developing a match between certain strategic or organizational conditions and certain specified aspects of human resource processes or skills.[25] In many ways this approach is the mirror image of efforts to match environmental events discussed in the prior section. While those with an environmental focus concentrated on predicting and reacting to external events, this approach is geared toward anticipating and responding to internal organizational activities and pressures, or at least to internal choices made about external events. While the notion of internal fit or congruence is as appropriate as the need for external alignment, again, an excessively narrow focus limits the usefulness of these approaches.

Matching People to Strategic Conditions

Most studies or recommendations deal exclusively with managers, often looking no deeper in the organization than the CEO or top management team. The implication is that only top managers can have strategic impact. In some ways this is reminiscent of the emphasis on succession planning for CEOs discussed in a previous section. Clearly, high-level executives may have the dominant influence on selecting a mission for a firm, but the means to accomplish these objectives must be developed and implemented throughout the firm. Determining and achieving competitive advantage is the responsibility of all employees, therefore, strategic human resource management must be a pervasive and multidirectional activity.

One approach involves matching managerial skills and interests with the general characteristics of the product-market environment. Such approaches assume that the environment will change very slowly or predictably, if at all. Gerstein and Reisman, for example, recommend a diagnosis of the business situation primarily in terms of the product life cycle. This becomes a precondition for matching executive characteristics to situational requirements. Managerial talents are seen as relatively fixed, apparently downplaying the potential for effective employee development programs. The matching process is seen primarily as a selection rather than a training issue. This may be in part because Gerstein and Reisman focus on managerial behaviors and traits rather than particular knowledge, skills, or abilities.

Gerstein and Reisman's approach includes using role descriptions of executive functions, and technical and managerial responsibilities. Further, this approach involves identifying key relationships and developing a list of skill requirements for each executive position. While the authors provide steps for implementing these tasks, they do little to overcome the problems of identifying and analyzing the appropriate information to either characterize the strategic situation or clarify the manager's role under a specific set of conditions. Further, they do not consider the inevitable need for change as new products and technologies enter the marketplace, or as cost drivers (factors that define the cost structure for a firm) or sources of differentiation factors that contribute to a product's unique value shift.

Other scholars focus on expansion strategy rather than product life cycles.[26] These researchers look at vertical integration (engaging in more activities along the chain from obtaining raw materials to final distribution of the product), related diversification (expanding the product line into new markets or developing new products to serve existing markets), or global expansion (internationalization), for example, rather than considering the emergence, growth, and maturation of product life cycles. However, the managerial characteristics that receive attention do not vary substantially as the types of expansion efforts and strategic conditions vary. Risk propensity, attention to detail, team building versus independent action, communication skills and styles, participative versus autocratic decision methods, and familiarity with financial and marketing functions receive significant attention in nearly every study.

One common claim across these situational matching approaches is the intent to diminish belief in the universal manager myth, which holds that certain leadership or managerial traits will make an individual an outstanding manager regardless of organizational or strategic circumstances. Unfortunately, while the universal manager concept may lose credibility, the universal management team configuration seems to have emerged as a replacement. The composite impression these approaches transmit is the need for a multitalented team of top managers who embrace a standardized mosaic of knowledge, skills, and abilities, rather than a single individual who is able to alter his or her actions to meet situational demands.

Matching Human Resource Management Practices to Strategic Conditions

An alternate approach to creating fit attempts to match, specific strategic choices, with a firm's human resource policies and processes rather than individuals. It is frequently pointed out that while financial, marketing, and technical plans are usually altered to reflect changing strategies, human resource management functions often appear to have been forgotten in the realignment activities. Human resource policies should also be tailored to reflect the needs of the future, rather than mirroring current conditions or past practices. An important problem is identified; it is clear that human resource management practices should not be retrospective. Unfortunately, little is offered toward resolution.

Milkovich and Newman go further with this approach but adopt a more restricted focus.[27] They argue that the compensation mix, comprised of base pay, incentives, and benefits, should be tailored for each phase of a firm's expansion cycle. For example, business units in the start-up phase of the business cycle have a limited, closely related set of products and are just beginning to explore their markets. Cash flow is a problem at this stage, as there are many start-up costs to get the venture running. Earnings and revenue are likely to be low, yet these firms need to be able to attract and retain key personnel as well as encourage innovation in existing personnel.

There are many examples of firms at this stage, especially in the computer software and genetic engineering industries. The mix of pay forms recommended for firms at this stage is a relatively low base pay (to conserve cash), strong emphasis on incentive pay (to conserve cash, emphasize unit and individual performance, and share the results of growth), and low benefits (to control costs).

The same firms at the mature stage will face a different set of conditions. Their product line may now be diversified. Their revenues and earnings are likely to be healthier. The human resource management focus is one of maintaining consistency of programs within the organization, controlling costs, and enhancing efficiency. Consequently, the pay forms reflect greater emphasis on base pay, short-term incentives, and competitive benefits. The compensation strategies noted by Milkovich and Neman offer a specific solution, yet the option is not sufficiently comprehensive to influence the overall human resource management practices of a firm.

CONTRIBUTIONS AND LIMITATIONS OF MATCHING APPROACHES TO STRATEGIC HUMAN RESOURCE MANAGEMENT

The whole issue of fit deserves reassessment. Research has shown that achieving a tight fit among organizational activities is not always desirable. The greater the multidimensional interdependence of various functional activities and organizational processes, the more difficult organizational change becomes. It seems that fit may undermine the flexibility often attributed to self-directed management of human resources. Further, a focus on maximizing fit can be counterproductive if a firm has adopted conflicting competitive goals to correspond to a complex competitive environment.[28] Prospector firms, for example, must be able to continually adapt to a new product-market definition. This entails an ongoing engagement and uncoupling of skills, market orientation, technologies, and many other organizational processes.

Many of the prescriptions offered by those who recommend a matching approach are based on inductive reasoning and observation rather than experimentation. Most of these approaches were developed in response to particular problems that arose when existing managerial talents were unable to generate an effective strategy in a particular organizational setting. Few of these approaches have been linked with organizational performance. In other words, it is not evident that, if these prescriptions were followed, strategic success would be any more likely. It is quite probable that managers would feel more comfortable in an organizational setting that exhibited a good match with their capabilities, but this may or may not enhance the competitive position of the firm.

ONE PRACTICAL EXAMPLE

Combining the best features from prior steps toward strategic human resource management yields a sequential plan that begins with a series of strategic choices followed by a set of human resource management implications or challenges. This is a good beginning, but it does not go far enough. To illustrate this point, consider the evolving discussion surrounding designing the factory of the future.

A host of innovations are evolving a process technology that will form the foundation for world-class manufacturing operations in the next decade. The Office of Technology Assessment anticipates that the magnitude and pervasiveness of change will be sufficient to affect nearly all manufacturing organizations.[29] Computer-aided design (CAD), computer-aided manufacturing (CAM), and computer-integrated manufacturing (CIM) have four common attributes that make this technology substantially different from traditional automation. First, these technologies contain a tremendous capacity for information processing. This will influence production planning, product design, assembly operations, monitoring and evaluation systems, and even the diagnosis of process-related problems. Second, these technologies offer an entirely new concept of flexibility resulting from reprogramming capabilities. Shifting from the manufacture of one product to another may entail little more than exchanging program disks. Routine can be redefined as software programmable rather than repetitive human activities. Third, CAD-CAM and CIM technologies offer the capability of improving quality through increased precision, enhanced reliability, and adaptive control of manufacturing processes. Standards of excellence extend beyond both human capability and human perception in some cases. Finally, the integration potential offered by these technologies redefines the meaning of work flow.

An opportunity frequently cited as offering a potential to reinstate many U.S. firms as world-class manufacturers is the application of computer-integrated manufacturing technology to producing specialized and customized products typically produced in small lot sizes. If a firm's competitive strategy is based primarily on a distinct technical competence, then creating a strong connection between the firm's technical system and its other managerial and organizational systems becomes a prerequisite for effectiveness. As will be shown, strategic human resource management becomes an essential ingredient for success.

To begin with, effective strategic human resource management requires an understanding of the implications associated with particular technology choices. Batch production is appropriate when a product must meet unique requirements for different customers. In such instances innovation, product variety, multiple product options, and experimental attempts to achieve ambiguous goals are priority outcomes. Since demand is unique and highly specialized, the volume requirements for any particular product design are low. This type of competitive position generates three important technical operating contingencies: wide variety, differing degrees of explicitness, and high adaptability.[30] In this context, variety means performing different tasks or manufacturing different products during a given period of time. For example, a skilled mechanic can repair many different kinds of machines in a work day, demonstrating wide variety, whereas an unskilled assembly worker trained to perform a single task exhibits low variety.

Explicitness refers to the extent to which well-defined input parameters, procedures, and output specifications exist for accomplishing a particular objective. If raw materials are well understood, production steps clearly documented and repetitive, and end results easily measured and clearly specified, there is high explicitness. Making a McDonald's hamburger is a highly explicit operation. If raw materials are untested or poorly understood, procedures unknown or unpredictable, and outcomes difficult to measure or specify, the task has low explicitness. Examples of low explicitness include developing leadership, training employees in team building, measuring attitudes, or developing a vaccine for AIDS.

Diversity in products or procedures over time indicates adaptability. A taconite plant exhibits little adaptability, whereas a medical research laboratory demonstrates high adaptability. Batch production takes place when a firm's strategy reflects high variety and high adaptability. The level of explicitness is variable. These three operating characteristics govern the fit between manufacturing operations and human resource management options.

Computer-assisted technology adds additional parameters to the technology. First, there is an increase in the level of sophistication or intricacy of the technical system.[31] This directly affects the knowledge, skills, and abilities required of employees who work within this setting. Second, CIM obviously increases the level of automation and mechanization compared with the more traditional hands-on crafts-person approach to batch production. Third, there is an increase in interdependence among all of the production activities in the system.[32] The magnitude of sequential and reciprocal relationships is greatly increased through the use of a computerized network, which increases expected communication, information processing, and coordination throughout the organization. Fourth, there is a shift in the unit of analysis used for standardization, from product type, to product dimension, or engineering specifications. This increases the level of precision needed throughout the organization's measurement systems, including those directed toward human resource management activities. Finally, there is a redefinition of routineness from known and repetitive to analyzable and programmable. This means that while workers may need to continually augment and upgrade their personal repertoire of knowledge and skills, the firm may consider their jobs to be quite routine.

Human Resource Planning Considerations

There are a number of contributions generated by strategic human resource planning efforts relevant to designing the factory of the future. These approaches acknowledge the need for human resource planning to go beyond personnel projections and assessments and consider the capability, value-based, and competitive implications of staffing issues. In other words, strategic human resource planning means more than just having the right people at the right place at the right time doing the right things. It also means that employees will have the attitudes, values, and strategic orientation enabling them to create a competitive advantage over the long term. Human resource planning perspectives also reinforce the recognition that industry conditions, organization size, and strategy domain interact with staffing choices to yield effective or ineffective human resource management. Human resource planning advocates indicate that strategically oriented succession planning can be a valuable distinct competence. Finally, human resource planning failures reiterate the importance of incorporating political realities and variations in human behaviors into strategic human resource management practices.

Drawing from these strategic human resource planning concepts it becomes clear that the shape of the organization will change dramatically as computer-assisted manufacturing is introduced. Batch production operations are typically characterized by a few individuals at the top of the organization concentrating on strategic issues, and increasingly larger proportions of employees at the middle management and operational levels of the firm. Historically, batch production dependent firms have been constructed to serve the needs and constraints of workers at the operating core. Computer-assisted batch production is designed to serve the needs of the marketplace. Thus, increased environmental scanning and strategic analysis is needed, leading to an increase in the number of personnel engaged in these activities. At the same time, the number of employees directly engaged in production activities is reduced. As a result, an increasing number of employees will be needed at the strategic and technical infrastructure level of a firm, and a shrinking number of individuals will need to be hired for the operating core. This shift introduces substantial power and political shifts as well as significant structural changes.

Changes in the definition of diversification are a likely consequence of changes in manufacturing technique. Concepts of product development, market development, and conglomerate diversification may require re-thinking. For example, are two products that serve entirely different markets, but are manufactured on the same machine with different software instructions, related in ways that are strategically important or only co-incidental? Depending on how this relatedness is viewed, notions of standard costs and appropriate transfer payments, as well as the measurement of production efficiency, will require reassessment. From a human resource planning perspective, the resolution of these issues will provide essential information for job analysis and staffing expectations.

Human Resource Valuation Considerations

Human resource valuation methods make two important contributions to our thinking about the factory of the future. First, these approaches draw our attention to the need for measurement and a comprehensive cost and benefit assessment of human resource practices. Second, valuation approaches support the notion that human resources need to be as actively managed as a firm's financial, informational, and material resources.

Human resource valuation approaches to strategic human resource management suggest that as computer-assisted manufacturing increases, employee worth will be increasingly market based. Moreover, the value of an employee will become more linked with an employee's trainability, adaptability, flexibility, and creativity, and less contingent upon that person's current mastery of specific knowledge, skills, and abilities. Judgmental ability in determining how technology will be used and targeted will take precedence over craft capabilities, which will be replaced largely by machine proficiency, suggesting that strategic human resource accounting methods will need to place a dollar value on potential under shifting criteria rather than on a continuation of past performance.

Matching Human Resources to Strategic Conditions

The various matching approaches discussed throughout this chapter stress the need for strategic human resource management to address selection, training and development, motivation, and other traditional human resource management issues at all hierarchical levels of the firm. Different needs are created by different competitive choices, organization structures, and product-market strategies. These different requirements demand a corresponding variety in human resource management practices and individual characteristics.

In thinking about the factory of the future, several important factors emerge. First, beginning with numerically controlled machines and accelerating with the use of CAD-CAM and CIM, machines have come to contain an increasing proportion of the knowledge, skills, and abilities needed to perform material conversions. In some ways, machines have taken over production activities and workers are now the custodians of machines. Second, while mass production, traditionally associated with highly automated manufacturing systems, reflects division of labor and highly specialized tasks, fully automated manufacturing is based on quite the opposite set of concepts. CIM relies on a synthesis of people, machines, and methods of production, meaning that the costs of suboptimization will increase. Third, these changes in the relationships between people and machines lead to changes in the social structure of the workplace. Social shifts strain traditional line and staff roles, question traditional union and management relationships, and lead to major alterations in the distribution, skills, and orientation of a firm's human resources. Complex strategic choices offer only limited guidance regarding what needs to be matched.

Traditionally, batch-oriented operations are characterized by decentralized decision making and informal management systems. This approach to management requires employees to be largely self-directed, autonomous, and self-controlled. Job satisfaction is closely linked to high-quality workmanship, meaningful jobs, and an ability to see a completed product or project. The increased flexibility and opportunity for innovation offered by CIM can only lead to competitive advantage if choices are guided by some underlying strategy. Decentralization and autonomy means that resources are likely to be used at cross-purposes. Independent activities defeat one of the main advantages of CIM: the potential for lower costs, even with small lot sizes.

This means the managerial system governing product-market decisions, resource allocation and utilization, and competitive positioning must be centralized to coordinate the activities of the entire workflow. To meet these requirements employees will need to be adept at taking directions, developing hierarchical and lateral communication networks, cooperating with other employees and work teams, and subordinating their personal product preferences to strategic and market choices made at top management levels. At all hierarchical levels, the type of employee that meets the expectations of a traditional batch manufacturing operation is quite different from the employee that meets the needs of a batch CIM operation.

Matching Human Resource Practices to Internal Strategic Conditions

The job structure of an organization must undergo a similar modification. Division of labor in an organization generally depends on what an organization believes to be its critical components or contingencies. Divisions can be based on differing activities or functions, volume considerations, environmental geographic differences, professional alliances, or any other distinguishing features of a particular firm. Decisions about division of labor determine how sharp the boundaries will be between line and staff, the firm and its environment, and among different work units.

In traditional batch manufacturing organizations, division of labor was based primarily on task considerations. Human limits on volume, variety, diversity, and stamina largely determined the boundaries within a firm. With batch CIM a strategy-related division of labor is needed. With a strategy-related approach, organizational boundaries are based on competitive concerns rather than technical or human limitations. To the extent that flexibility and innovation underlie a firm's competitive advantage, divisions of activities would be expected to shift in response to prevailing competitive conditions, meaning that human resources must be organizationally oriented rather than job, unit, or product oriented. Moreover, employees must be able to communicate and work effectively with personnel outside their own professional, hierarchical, or product-market areas. Group membership will need to be flexible, and, as a result, steep personal learning curves and accelerated group maturation processes will be important distinct competencies for firms to develop. The implications of these changes for the entire spectrum of human resource management activities are widespread.

Compensation systems in particular will need rethinking. Choices embedded in a firm's reward system reflect decisions regarding which activities are most valued, the relevant time horizon, and whether competition or collaboration should dominate the internal culture. Compensation systems indicate the relative importance of individual, group-level, and organizational-level performance. As a firm increases its reliance on CIM processes to achieve competitive advantage, the compensation system should focus less on individual performance and more on group or organizational-level achievements. This shift acknowledges the increasing interdependence among all parts of the workflow. In addition, the compensation system may have to perform an additional function. Not only must the compensation system reward appropriate behaviors and results, it may need, in a CIM-dominated workplace, to compensate for diminished intrinsic satisfaction. As machines replace humans on the front line of batch production operations, the satisfaction a worker once received from seeing the results of his or her labor are eroded. High levels of motivation and effort are still required and must be developed from other sources. The diminished direct responsibility for production creates an additional challenge for human resource management.

Enabling Human Resource Management Practices to Respond to External Strategic Conditions

The need to actively and continuously scan the environment is reinforced by responsive approaches to strategic human resource management. Human resource management practices should reflect a multitude of environmental characteristics, from technology trends to demographic shifts, to life style preferences, to educational trends. Responsive approaches illustrate the importance of defining problems or opportunities accurately and appropriately. Solutions with too narrow a focus are likely to cause as many new problems as they resolve when integrated into a complex organizational system. Prescriptions with too broad a definition become so general as to be meaningless, or so dogmatic that they ignore important contingencies.

In considering the factory of the future, the fundamental relationship between an organization and its environment needs to be explored. In the past, when efficiency was the goal, organizations generally attempted to make resources and environmental conditions conform to the constraints of mass production. Various buffering systems and rationing processes were used to achieve this aim. High operating costs and a resulting competitive position that cannot accommodate price sensitivity accompanied any deviation from this formula. Since computerized factories are designed to have greater freedom to efficiently respond to multiple and changing marketplace conditions, these restrictions no longer apply. In addition, a wider range of product and market mix options is available, even to cost leader-oriented producers.

Economies of scope, where efficiency is based on diverse products using similar components, often take precedence over economies of scale. As a consequence, employee learning curve phenomena are likely to diminish as production knowledge is increasingly shifted to machines, raising fundamental questions for training and development programs, compensation systems, and staffing practices.

Barriers to industry exit and entry are expected to change in ways that may redefine the concept of industries parallel to the way in which diversification may be redefined. The analysis on any industry's competitive structure will become increasingly complex. Smaller, multimission plants will become economically and managerially practical, drastically altering distribution and control options. Each of these potential changes represents an important choice for managers. Each decision carries with it significant human resource management implications.

SUMMARIZING THE CONTRIBUTIONS OF EARLY EFFORTS TOWARD STRATEGIC HUMAN RESOURCE MANAGEMENT

In summary, then, past approaches to strategic human resource management have suggested ways to match managerial styles or personnel activities with strategic efforts. They have offered methods for forecasting personnel requirements given certain strategic objectives. In addition, they have presented ways to achieve congruence among human resource management practices and processes, a firm's strategy and structure. Each of these approaches has three assumptions in common: that a firm's choice of strategic direction has already been made, that strategy implementation deals solely with means to achieve strategic ends and has no explicit role in strategy formulation, and that the basic issue—whether employee skills, forecasting, processes for career planning, retention, training or a host of other activities—remains constant. These models assume that only the answer or response to the critical issue changes as strategic conditions change.

A number of important contributions were made by initial efforts at strategic human resource management. As illustrated in the previous example, early strategic human resource management models suggest how we might need to change the way we measure and evaluate human resources. Clearly we will need to select, hire, train, and retain different types of employees to effectively staff the factory of the future. Managerial and human resource systems will need to reflect strategic considerations more than human limitations or traditional professional boundaries. The challenge of developing effective compensation systems will become even more complex. Each of these issues is important, and each enhances the contribution that effective human resource management can make to a firm's competitive position.

However, these issues represent a necessary but insufficient interaction between a firm's human resource management and its strategic planning. The implications just discussed reflect a response on the part of human resource management to strategic choices made in an independent forum. Clearly, an effective human resource management response can make an important difference in achieving a desirable competitive position, but this is not the complete answer. A responsive posture does not raise all the necessary questions.

Recent events have called into question the appropriateness of a traditional planning approach. While planning is future oriented and goal directed rather than responsive or historical, planning does rely on linear assumptions and some measure of organizational and environmental stability. Increasingly, strategic managers recognize that some situations are inappropriate for planning. As uncertainty increases and discontinuous events become more frequent, strategic control becomes an important substitute for traditional long-range planning. A similar evolution in thinking is occurring among strategic human resource management experts.[33] Strategic human resource management must also couple short-term, issue-oriented, contingent approaches with long-term, goal-directed processes to be an effective competitive weapon.

NOTES

1. For additional information on the relationship between organizational life stages and strategy, see A. T. Chandler, *Strategy and Structure: Chapters in the History of American Enterprise* (Cambridge, Mass.: MIT Press, 1962); and R. P. Rumelt, *Strategy, Structure and Economic Performance in Large American Industrial Corporations*, (Boston: Harvard University Press, 1974).

2. For more on the role that internal and external fit play in developing an effective organizational strategy, see R. Miles and C. Snow, Fit, failure and the hall of fame. In *Strategy and Organization* Eds. G. Carroll and D. Vogel. Boston: Pitman, 1984) pp. 1–19.

3. For additional information on a human resource accounting perspective, see E. Flamholtz, A model for human resource valuation: A stochastic process with service rewards. *Accounting Review* 46(2) (1971): 253–67; R. B. Frantzreib, L. T. Landau, and D. P. Lundberg, The valuation of human resources. *Business Horizons* 20(3) (1977): 73–80; and C. Fombrun, N. Tichy, and M. A. Devanna *Strategic Human Resource Management* (New York): Wiley, (1984).

4. For an overview of strategic human resource planning, see J. D. Olian and S. L. Rynes, Organizational staffing: Integrating practice with strategy. *Industrial Relations* 23(2) (1984): 170–83; S. A. Stumpf and N. M. Hanrahan, Designing organizational career management practices to fit the strategic management objectives. In *Readings in Personnel and Human Resource Management*. 2d ed. Eds. R. S. Schuler and S. A. Youngblood. (St. Paul: West, 1984), pp. 326–48; and J. F. DeSanto, Work force planning and corporate strategy. *Personnel Administrator* 28(10) 1983 33–42.

5. For additional information on matching specific human resource management activities to particular shifts in the environment, see C. Fombrun, Environmental trends create new pressures on human resources. *Journal of Business Strategy* 3(1) (1982): 61–69; M. Warner, New technology, work organizations, and industrial relations. *Omega* 12(3) (1984): 203–10; and J. Lindroth, How to beat the coming labor shortage. *Personnel Journal* 61(4) (1982): 268–72.

6. See, for example, R. E. Miles, et al., Organization strategy, structure, and process. *Academy of Management Review* 9 (1984): 546–662; M. Gerstein and H. Reisman, Strategic selection: Matching executives to business conditions. *Sloan Management Review* 24(2) (1983): 1–8; and M. Leontiades, Choosing the right manager to fit the strategy. *Journal of Business Strategy* 2(2)(1982): 58–69.

7. For additional information on retention, see J. R. Galosy, Meshing human resources planning with strategic business planning: One company's experience.

Personnel 60(5) (1983): 26–35; on compensation systems, see R. H. Migliore, Linking strategy, performance and pay. *Technological Forecasting and Social Change* 21, (1982): 15–31; on human relations versus traditional versus human resource management styles, see Miles, et al., Organization strategy; and on productivity, see A. Deutsch, How employee retention strategies can aid productivity. *Journal of Business Strategy* 2(4) (1982): 106–09.

8. For an expansion of this argument, see L. M. Cheek, Cost effectiveness from the personnel function. *Harvard Business Review* 51(3) (1973): 96–105; and C. F. Russ, Manpower planning systems: Part II., *Personnel Journal* 61(2) (1982): 119–23.

9. For additional information, see W. Cascio, *Costing Human Resources: The Financial Impact of Behavior in Organizations* (Boston, Mass.: PWS Kent, 1987).

10. For a useful overview of human resource supply and demand forecasting research, see S. Zedeck and W. Cascio, Psychological issues in personnel decisions. *Annual Review of Psychology* 35, (1984): 461–518.

11. For a complete discussion, see Olian and Rynes, Organizational Staffing; and R. E. Miles, et al., Organization strategy.

12. DeSanto, Work force planning.

13. See L. J. Harvey, Effective planning for human resource development. *Personnel Administrator* (1983): 45–112.

14. S. Faux McNamara, CEO succession: A conceptual model. Ph.D. diss. Purdue University, 1988.

15. For a more complete discussion, see D. Ulrich, Strategic human resource planning: Why and how. In Schuler and Youngblood, eds. *Readings*, pp. 57–71.

16. H. Mintzberg, Opening up the definition of strategy. In *The Strategy Process* (Englewood Cliffs, N.J.: Prentice Hall, 1988); pp. 13–20.

17. For additional information on responding to particular environmental trends, see Fombrun, Environmental trends.

18. For additional information on responding to environmental uncertainty, see R. J. Ellis, Improving management response in turbulent times. *Sloan Management Review* 23(2) (1982): 3–12.

19. See J. Lindroth, Labor shortage.

20. See H. Maier, Innovation, efficiency and the quantitative and qualitative demand for human resources. *Technological Forecasting and Social Change* 21 (1982): 15–31.

21. F. N. Schwartz, Management women and the new facts of life. *Harvard Business Review* 67(4) (1989): 65–76.

22. D. E. Dimick and V. V. Murray, (1978) Correlates of substantive policy decisions in organizations: The case of human resource management. *Academy of Management Journal* 21(4) (1978): 611–23.

23. R. T. Lenz, Determinants of organizational performance: An interdisciplinary review. *Strategic Management Journal* 2(2) (1981): 131–54.

24. For a complete discussion, see Miles, et al., Organization strategy. This is also discussed in Chapter 2 of this book.

25. See, for example, Gerstein and Reisman, Strategic selection; L. J. Harvey, Effective planning for human resource development. *Personnel Administrator* 28(10) (1983): 45–52; M. Leontiades, Choosing the right manager to fit the strategy. *Journal of Business Strategy* 2(2) (1982): 58–69; and Migliore, Linking strategy.

26. Perhaps the most noted of these are A. T. Chandler, *Strategy and Structure: Chapters in the History of American Enterprise* (Cambridge, Mass.: MIT Press, 1962); and R. P. Rumelt *Strategy, Structure and Economic Performance in Large American Industrial Corporations* (Boston: Harvard University Press, 1974).

27. G. T. Milkovich and J. M. Newman, *Compensation*. 2d ed. (Dallas: BPI, 1987).

28. C. A. Lengnick-Hall, Fit and misfit: How to achieve efficiency and innovation. *Organization Development Journal* 6(2) (1988): 67–74.

29. See S. W. J. Kozlowski, (1984) Technological innovation and strategic HRM: Facing the challenge of change. In *Readings*, Schuler and Youngblood, eds., pp. 72–81.

30. For a more complete look at the links between technology, structure, and strategy and the use of CIM, see C. A. Lengnick-Hall, Technology advances in batch Production and improved competitive position. *Journal of Management* 12(1) (1986): 75–90.

31. For an expanded understanding of technical sophistication, see H. Mintzberg, *The Structuring of Organizations* (Englewood Cliffs, N.J.: Prentice Hall, 1979); and C. Perrow, A framework for the comparative analysis of organizations. *American Sociological Review* 34(2) (1969): 194–208.

32. For additional information on technological interdependence, see J. D. Thompson, *Organizations in Action* (New York: McGraw-Hall, 1967); and D. S. Pugh, et al., Dimensions of organizational structure. *Administrative Science Quarterly* 13(1) (1968): 65–105.

33. For an expanded discussion, see R. S. Schuler and J. W. Walker, Don't waste time on planning—act: The development of human resource strategy. In *Organizational Dynamics* (in press). Additional information on strategic control is contained in P. Lorange, M. F. Scott Morton, and S. Ghoshal, *Strategic Control* (St. Paul: West, 1986).

5

Critique of Old Assumptions and Articulation of New Assumptions

Managerial analysis usually begins with a problem or opportunity. In general, this means that someone realizes things are not as they should be or that opportunities are being missed for some reason. In order to conduct an effective analysis of the circumstances and arrive at a practical and desirable solution, the situation must be appropriately defined, and accurately diagnosed, and criteria for evaluating resultant plans of action must be established. In each phase of this process, it is essential that the assumptions guiding the analytic processes in use are consistent with the events and relationships being described, diagnosed, and acted upon. This means that if the situation is dynamic, the analytic models used to explore it should also be based on dynamic premises. The same causal relationships that shape the situation should be embedded in the relationships depicted in the analytic tools. While many useful models do not comprehensively capture complex situations, and must therefore be used in tandem with other techniques that reveal different situational variables, the assumptions and relationships of analytic tools should not run counter to those found in the situation being analyzed.

Early efforts toward strategic human resource management have several assumptions in common. This chapter identifies the common elements across many of the initial efforts at strategic human resource management and discusses the problems that arise from these assumptions. Next, an alternate set of assumptions is proposed. Briefly, we propose that the choice of strategy should not be made independently of human resource considerations. We propose that the management of human resources should contribute directly to strategy formulation and implementation. Third, we propose that, as strategic conditions vary, the fundamental questions and issues that should be addressed also vary. The implications of this new set of assumptions are discussed.

TIMING FOR STRATEGIC HUMAN RESOURCE MANAGEMENT

Let's take a closer look at the assumptions underlying early efforts at strategic human resource management. Human resource valuation approaches, human resource planning, and efforts to match or respond to strategic situations assume that the choice of strategic direction has been made prior to considering strategic human resource management. What are the implications of assuming that a firm's choice of strategic direction has been made before attempting the strategic management of human resources? As discussed in the chapter summarizing strategic management, there are at least two basic features encompassed by strategic direction.

First, strategic direction describes the extent to which a firm concentrates on a single business area or expands into new products or markets. This growth vector definition of strategic direction is primarily concerned with variety and interdependence. As a firm enters new product areas and new market segments, the diversity with which the firm must contend increases. Firms that grow in concentric product or market areas assume that a competitive advantage will result from communalities in market characteristics, manufacturing processes, technologies, distribution channels, or any of the other primary and secondary activities in the value chain. Capitalizing on these common elements requires both coordination and collaboration across diverse units and activities. Firms that grow in a conglomerate, or unrelated, manner have a greater concern with maintaining independence. Rather than trying to manage risk by developing a dominant competitive position across a number of closely linked business areas, firms that engage in conglomerate diversification attempt to balance their risk by investing in businesses that do not rely on interdependent actions or events. The benefit is an increased ability to structure self-contained units and a greater likelihood of steady, if not spectacular, performance. The price of this balanced risk position is variety so great that no individual can truly be an expert in all the firm's undertakings.

It is clear that the range of choices, from a single product market concentration, to an expanded group of product and market interests linked by some common elements leading to competitive advantage, to a set of independent business units whose only connection is composite profitability, carry a wide range of human resource implications. The types of skills, knowledge and abilities required in each of these settings is quite different. The anticipated career paths and organizational tenure vary with growth orientation. The need for broad-based communication and information sharing is high when interdependence is high and low when independence is stressed. Communication channels must carry a greater volume and variety of information as diversity increases. The appropriate posture with regard to the environment, and thus the need for and intent of environmental scanning, varies with choice of strategic direction. The importance of responding to or shaping the market environment is much greater with a concentration strategy than with conglomerate diversification. Nearly all the contextual factors that influence effective strategic human resource management will vary in response to the variety and interdependence reflected in growth vector choices.

A second definition of strategic direction concerns product-market domain choices. When a firm decides to be a defender, prospector, or analyzer, that firm is making a choice regarding variability. The product-market and market scope of a defender organization is much more stable than that of a prospector. The goals and outcomes of an organization's strategy are also quite different, depending on the variability of a firm's product-market scope.

When a firm has a stable organizational and strategic context, the focus can be on efficiency. Forecasts can be made with greater accuracy, since trend analysis is a reasonable predictor. Environmental scanning can concentrate on noticing and responding to exceptions and changes rather than assessing the present. The assumption that history will repeat itself is generally accurate, since a defender firm has a vested interest in making sure this is so. Analytic techniques such as intuitive extrapolation, mathematical curve fitting, pattern identification, and analogies are generally appropriate. Problems emerge in a rapidly changing environment when it is difficult to be sure that the causal relationships of the past will hold true for the future. It is also difficult at the early stages of product development, because it is hard to determine an appropriate trend classification when a phenomena is just emerging. Decision making generally focuses on precision, measurability, rationality, and documentation.

When, on the other hand, a firm has a highly variable product-market scope, information is frequently uncertain, ambiguous, novel, and probabilistic. Prospector organizations, therefore, must rely on judgment, compromise, and intuition, rather than computations and precedent. Decisions that work out well may be difficult to replicate. Any choice of expert decision makers entails bias and an implicit definition of the situational parameters. Choices are generally made relying on agreement about goals, but not necessarily about causal relationships. Participation, consensus seeking, and commitment tend to characterize prospectors, whereas delegation, planning, and legitimate power characterize defenders. For most prospector firms, the ability to handle continuous variability comes at the price of low efficiency.

Analyzer firms experience a moderate degree of variability, since one portion of their product and market scope is stable while another is being revised continuously. The balancing act required of analyzers presents perhaps the most complex decision situation. Some of the strategic choices, those in the stable portion of the firm, can be judgments based on a high degree of certainty. Some of the strategic choices—those in the transitory portions of the product-market scope—must reflect uncertainty and opinion. Devising a social and structural system to accommodate these two extremes in information processing presents a complex challenge.

It becomes obvious that the strategic domain choice a firm makes will need to correspond to its job design, selection and promotion, compensation, staffing, and development practices. If a choice of domain posture is made without considering these human resource management elements up front, a firm may choose a strategic direction that is unnecessarily difficult at best and unfeasible at worst.

The implications of determining a strategic direction first and considering strategic human resource management second primarily affect the diagnostic phase of management analysis. Not all relevant information is being considered in the analysis of the situation. Important opportunities may go unrecognized, and important constraints may emerge only after problems are encountered in implementation. Regardless of whether or not human resource issues are considered in the choice of strategic direction, these issues will have a significant influence on the success or failure of the resulting actions. If strategic direction and strategic human resource management issues are considered simultaneously, problems may be avoided and new opportunities are likely to emerge.

CONTENT OF STRATEGIC HUMAN RESOURCE MANAGEMENT

What constraints are encompassed in assuming that strategic human resource management deals solely with means to achieve strategic ends and has no explicit role in strategy formulation? Strategy formulation includes not only the choices associated with strategic direction, but more directly the choice of competitive advantage decisions regarding means to enhance the value chain.

The capabilities and distinct competencies that accompany a low-cost position are dramatically different from the competencies and abilities that lead to a high level of differentiation. Skills needed to effectively maintain a focus strategy are not the same as the knowledge and abilities needed to secure a broad-based competitive dominance. Human resources are a fundamental ingredient in developing sources of competitive advantage. If human resource management issues are not explicitly considered at the strategy formulation stage, these choices must rely on assumptions regarding human resource knowledge, skills, abilities, sufficiency, flexibility, interactions, and a host of other factors. Much of strategy formulation must, by its very nature, rely on assumptions and uncertain information. It seems that nothing is gained and a great deal may be lost by introducing unnecessary uncertainty. It would seem almost unthinkable to devise a strategic plan of action without determining what financial resources would be needed, whether these funds would come from increased equity, increased debt, earnings, divestitures, reallocation of existing funds, or some other source of revenue. It should seem equally absurd to devise a strategy without conducting a similarly extensive analysis of the firm's human capital.

Every point in the value chain is affected by human resource management decisions. Whether human capabilities are essential, ancillary, or incidental to various procurement, inbound and outbound logistics, production, marketing, and sales and service activities can be determined. If a firm competes on low product cost, manufacturing operations can revolve around a highly productive work force or highly automated technical systems. If a firm offers state-of-the-art products, it can reflect highly creative engineers who develop the next generation product ahead of the competition, or it can reflect a highly effective environmental scanning and acquisitions program that purchases state-of-the-art ideas from the environment. Each of these choices either expands or contracts a firm's risk, enhances or inhibits its flexibility, and augments or undermines the sustainability of its competitive position.

The implications of considering strategic human resource management as only concerned with strategy implementation and not strategy formulation hinders the problem definition phase of analysis. Unless human resource management issues are included in strategy formulation, the definition of the issues, and thus management attention, is unnecessarily myopic. Just as a strategic plan, ploy, and position include a description and analysis of its technical, financial, and informational strengths and weaknesses, strategy formulation should be just as explicit and deliberate about considering and including a definition of how it intends to invest in and use its human resources.

FOCUS OF STRATEGIC HUMAN RESOURCE MANAGEMENT

Each of the approaches to strategic human resource management discussed in Chapter 4 assumes a particular issue should dominate the focus of strategic human resource management activities, whether it is the cost of replacing human resources or an emerging environmental trend. This assumption means that the goals of strategic human resource management activities remain the same regardless of organizational or strategic circumstances. Stated differently, assuming a single, consistent focus means that the questions raised for the strategic human resource manager remain the same, only the answers change to reflect different strategic situations.

Does this really seem reasonable? If we look at our personal decision making and planning, the questions we ask as well as the answers we come up with change over time (Is a sixteen-year-old high school student and a forty-five-year-old father of three likely to be concerned with similar events?), over circumstances (Consider the issues that were important on your first job and the issues that emerged after your latest promotion), as a reflection of our resources (The cost-benefit analysis of hamburger versus prime rib is highly correlated with the size of the family income), and in response to our past choices (Is an individual who has just passed the CPA exam and an individual who just retired from the armed forces likely to have similar goals for the next twelve months?). A decision regarding relevant questions affects both the definition phase of analysis and the criteria likely to be used to evaluate the options generated. To keep a single human resource management concern as the keystone for strategic human resource management analysis means that any resulting approaches will offer a good focus for some times, circumstances, resources, and prior decisions, and a poor focus for others.

A NEW SET OF CHOICES

The proposed analytic model relies on a different set of assumptions. We believe these alternate assumptions more accurately reflect both the competitive situation and the complexity and dynamic characteristics that dominate many organizations. In addition, we contend that the proposed assumptions capitalize on the strengths of many of the strategic human resource models currently in effect, but also begin to overcome some of the limitations of these approaches. While the assumptions we offer place an additional analytic burden on strategic human resource managers, the resulting analytic framework offers a significantly wider range of opportunities for gaining a competitive advantage from strategic human resource management.

Simultaneous Consideration of Competitive and Human Resource Management Issues

First, we assume that the strategy has not been chosen. This alters the timing for strategic human resource management in a number of important ways. Perhaps most obviously, strategic human resource management must occur concurrently with competitive analysis. This change alters the analytic process significantly. When strategic planning and human resource planning occur sequentially, the goals, parameters, and many of the constraints governing the diagnosis and definition of the analytic situation have already been determined by the time human resource management issues are considered. This significantly simplifies the diagnostic and decision-making process for strategic human resource managers.

We suggest that the price of this simplification is too high. By allowing external factors and financial or other resource issues to shape the analytic frame of reference, much of the potential for using human resources to achieve a competitive advantage may be missed. In addition, the range of options that remain for human resource managers to consider, even with regard to implementation, is unnecessarily restricted. Perhaps more significantly, using a sequential decision-making process can introduce a ratchet effect to strategic planning. Choices made at one phase of a decision process provide constraints and boundaries for analysis at the next phase. The definition of the situation, criteria for evaluation, and assumptions to be used in diagnosis have already been established by the time the human resource manager enters the picture. In some cases this may leave only mediocre or unattractive options for human resource management consideration. At best, opportunities for enhancing organizational strengths or mitigating organizational weaknesses will not be explored fully. If few attractive options exist, human resource management advocates will at best meet the minimal expectations of the competitive plan, and more likely seek to compromise the previous decision. In either instance, organizational performance expectations are re-established at a new, and necessarily lower, level than envisioned initially. Sequential decision making of this sort is a leading cause of suboptimization.

The price of concurrent competitive and human resource management analysis is not insignificant. Concurrent analysis means that strategic human resource management must become an ongoing process, rather than an analytic task that occurs at discrete intervals. Simultaneous analysis means that just as competitive planners, financial analysts, manufacturing managers, and other corporate leaders must develop increased expertise in human resource management issues, human resource managers must develop business knowledge that encompasses all organization functions as well. Concurrent analysis means that strategic human resource management will be an iterative process. Early choices will need to be tentative and subject to revision. Most situations will require the generation of a number of viable and attractive alternatives, rather than a single feasible response. Cost and benefit assessments across multiple factors will need to replace threshold standards in making strategic human resource management choices.

The advantages of concurrent analysis are also substantial. Human resource management considerations can provide a set of lenses that highlight previously obscured opportunities for product development, market expansion, management of complexity and diversity, and potential sources of synergy across product and market activities. Arthur Andersen's practice of offering regularly scheduled training for worldwide staff in the firm's technology and methodology provides some of the glue that holds this multinational company together. Human resource capabilities may suggest ways to avoid environmental threats or reduce current organizational weaknesses. In some industries, increased price sensitivity may be offset by increased service capabilities, encouraging some buyer segments to pay a premium price in order to obtain consulting benefits, speedy repair, or increased customization. The benefits of concurrent analysis are a more comprehensive definition and diagnosis of strategic circumstances and a wider range of options available to both strategic planners and human resource managers.

Making a Direct Contribution to Strategy Formulation

Second, we assume the management of human resources should contribute directly to strategy formulation as well as to strategy implementation. Equally important, however, we do not assume that human resource considerations should be the sole, or even the primary, factor considered in selecting a firm's strategy. Human resource management concerns should influence strategy formulation to the extent that human resource issues dominate the value chain.

For example, in an employee-owned and -operated organization, human resource management considerations will dominate much of the organizational cultural characteristics and many of the decision parameters. In employee-owned firms equity considerations, an opportunity to influence decision making, and access to information offer both important constraints and significant motivational tools affecting strategy formulation. A competitive choice that relies on tight hierarchical control, secrecy, and numerous rules and procedures will not likely succeed in an employee-owned firm. A strategy that depends on personal initiative, cooperation, and coordination has a much higher probability of success. In an employee-owned and -operated firm, therefore, human resource management concerns may at times drive competitive choices.

In a highly automated metal cutting factory that provides standardized products to large industrial users, human resource management preferences should be much less influential. While human resource management capabilities may still provide crucial sources of competitive advantage in some parts of the value chain, market conditions, product and production process characteristics, cost considerations, and technology factors will more appropriately influence much of the strategy formulation process. Even in this situation, however, including human resource management concerns in strategy formulation allows the firm to exploit all potential sources of efficiency, product quality, and internal synergy. These incremental choices may make the difference between mediocre performance and strategic success, particularly in highly competitive markets.

As with the timing of strategic human resource management, inclusion in the strategy formulation process carries with it identifiable costs. Strategic human resource managers must significantly alter their role within the company. As human resource managers move from outsiders to insiders in the strategy formulation process, their role must change from that of critic and adversary to that of collaborator and problem solver.[1] Strategic human resource managers must be as concerned with the financial, manufacturing, marketing, and competitive implications of their recommendations as they are with the human resource consequences. Strategic human resource managers must be willing and able to demonstrate their contribution to the strategy formulation process in ways that address the interests and concerns of other functional areas. While improved employee satisfaction, for example, may enhance the corporate culture, human resource managers must be able to show how that same culture makes a measurable contribution to competitive advantage.

In addition to changing roles, strategic human resource managers included in competitive strategy formulation will also be held directly accountable for the success or failure of strategic choices. This means that human resource managers must be able to assess and understand industry trends, competitor actions, and other environmental conditions, as well as have expertise regarding the internal workings of the organization. The knowledge, skills, and abilities of human resource managers must grow as their organizational responsibilities expand.

Questions as Well as Answers Change to Fit the Situation

The third assumption of the analytic technique offered in the next chapter presents the most extensive counterpoint with prior approaches to strategic human resource management. Our analysis is based on the assumption that, as strategic conditions vary, the fundamental questions to be addressed also vary. This seems reasonable, since strategic issues should reflect strategic contingencies. Just as, during product development phases, industry infrastructure concerns, research and development, and marketing functional activities are of primary importance, while during maturity stages efficiency issues and manufacturing capabilities are paramount, strategic human resource management issues vary in response to changing strategic opportunities, threats, and expectations.

Moreover, conditions and factors influencing the types of questions to be asked are not necessarily the same contingencies that determine the answers to those questions. The questions asked primarily reflect desired or anticipated organizational outcomes and environmental threats and opportunities. These issues vary with bottom-line expectations and prior organizational choices. Appropriate questions reflect goal-related alternatives and organizational preferences. Issues pertaining to strategic direction and competitive advantage should shape the relevant questions guiding strategic human resource management analyses.

The answers to these goal-oriented questions depend heavily on organizational strengths, weaknesses, and culture. Answers reflect resource capabilities and sufficiency. The answers also depend on a firm's ability to implement changes from prior courses of action and a firm's willingness or reluctance to take risks. Answers are constrained by the inputs and capabilities that can be devoted to addressing an issue. Alternative answers are generated by increased flexibility, understanding of equifinality, learning options, and expanded analytic horizons.

Asking the right questions and developing acceptable answers are both necessary for sustained high performance. For example, consider the situation encountered by a manager who has excessive amounts of information coming into her office. If she defines the problem as one of inefficiency in processing information, she might then ask the question: How can I increase the rate at which I attend to all the information that comes across my desk? Answers, such as developing new procedures for writing responses directly on interoffice memos, automating certain types of information processing, and handling any piece of paper only once before acting on it, filing it, or throwing it away may emerge as a solution. If, on the other hand, the manager defines the problem as difficulty in distinguishing important information from trivial data, the relevant question might be: How should I identify and establish a priority system for dealing with particularly crucial information? As a result, an entirely different set of solutions will be developed. She may develop a more effective scanning and sorting system, identify certain categories of information to receive immediate attention, and delegate certain types of phone calls and requests to subordinates or other units. The way in which an issue is framed has a great deal to do with the types of solutions sought. If the problem is the ignoring of significant information, increased efficiency will not likely yield an effective solution.

OVERCOMING LIMITATIONS OF PRIOR STRATEGIC HUMAN RESOURCE MANAGEMENT APPROACHES

The analytic approach presented in the next chapter suggests ways to address the limitations of prior approaches while integrating their contributions. Specific explanations of how the proposed analytic model, or typology, attempts to overcome the limitations of prior approaches are provided in the following paragraphs.

Human resource valuation approaches are limited by expense. Many require extensive amounts of time, effort, and attention to develop appropriate data banks and methodological techniques. Human resource valuation approaches are limited by the difficulty of putting a dollar value on human contributions or learning. These approaches assume a static environment in which historical trends are a good predictor of future conditions. The proxy measures used to indicate the value of an individual to a corporation are linear and narrowly targeted, and rely on assumptions regarding future productivity and contributions that are not a good reflection of reality. Finally, human resource valuation approaches are limited by problems associated with using the results of human resource valuation calculations. There was little advice provided on how to convert the results of a human resource valuation assessment into data that could be used in making competitive or other strategic choices.

The analytic approach described in this book recognizes that it is important to assess the value of human resource management investment choices and attempt to distinguish the relative contributions of different individuals and work units to the overall corporate strategy. The underlying premise of human resource valuation approaches can make a valuable contribution to strategic human resource management. However, the methodology is seriously flawed by inappropriate assumptions and overly restrictive parameters.

We suggest substituting the concept of firm- and industry-specific skills introduced in Chapter 3, which capitalizes on the potential contribution of human resource valuation by relying on a different analytic methodology.[2] Using firm- and industry-specific skills as a proxy measure for the value of human resource capabilities overcomes many of the obstacles identified with more traditional human resource valuation methods. Technological expertise, political savvy, organizational experience, and other types of knowledge, skills, and abilities useful only within a particular organization are firm-specific skills. Understanding industry structural patterns and methods for technology diffusion, and intuition regarding competitor reactions that reflect only the conditions of a particular industry, are industry-specific skills. Firm- and industry-specific skills have value only within a particular context. When an employee moves out of the specific organizational or industrial arena to which this knowledge, skill, and ability applies, there is a loss of productive value.

For example, knowing a firm's filing system or a color-coded mailroom sorting procedure is firm-specific knowledge. Technical jargon is often industry specific. Terms such as "discounted rate of return" or "leveraged buyout" may be important in the financial services industry but have little meaning in the health care industry. Firm-specific and industry-specific skills are not transferrable in terms of human resource value. Knowing IBM's corporate dress code is not useful to an UNISYS employee. The ability to estimate the minimal passenger load factor needed for a commuter airline to break even has little value to an employee in the food-processing industry. Neither of these skills is useful in a different firm or industry context.

To the extent that an employee's knowledge, skills, and abilities are specific to a certain organization, the employee's mobility and transferability is reduced. However, the employee's value to the firm is enhanced. From the firm's perspective, replacement costs for the employee are increased, since training and development that can only be provided by the firm is required. On the benefit side, the likelihood of requiring a replacement is reduced, since transfer costs for the employee are increased, and the value of the employee to the firm's current operation is enhanced. Relying on firm-specific skills to create competitive advantage makes the resulting competitive edge extremely difficult to copy.

It should be noted, however, that reliance on firm-specific and industry-specific skills can increase resistance to change. Just as it becomes more difficult for an employee to transfer his or her skills to a new organization, it becomes equally difficult for a firm to change its strategic direction or the way in which it attains competitive advantage. This means that the competitive position of the firm is likely to be enhanced as long as conditions remain stable, but the competitive position of the firm becomes more precarious in a turbulent marketplace. Consequently, an assessment of the appropriateness of firm-specific or industry-specific skills must take place in conjunction with an analysis of industry conditions and sustainable competitive position.

A major problem with human resource planning approaches is an overreliance on supply and demand forecasting and response at the expense of other organizational realities. We propose explicit consideration of a firm's values, philosophy, and culture in strategic human resource management decisions to help alleviate this difficulty. This recommendation is linked with the suggested approach for conducting human resource valuation.

If, for example, a firm values long-term employment and does not expect major strategic shifts in either its marketplace environment or own strategic objectives, an investment in creating firm-specific and industry-specific skills is wise. As was pointed out in the preceding discussion, firm-specific skills increase the costs of turnover to the employee as well as to the firm. Agencies such as NASA and private firms such as Hewlett-Packard rely on a combination of organizational concern with employee welfare, employee commitment to the organization, and firm-specific skills to augment the package. The corporate creed known as the HP Way illustrates this kind of interaction. Hewlett Packard's business strategy is based on a several specific elements. First, competitive position is based on excellence in product engineering. In addition, Hewlett-Packard relies on high levels of customer satisfaction, which in turn depends upon thoroughly designed and tested products and outstanding after-sales service. Some of the fundamental ways in which human resources contribute to these competitive advantages are through an emphasis on teamwork, individual responsibility for high levels of performance, meaningful participation in organizational decision making, and learning from other employees. The company has made a commitment to reward top-notch performance with job security, to develop employees and promote from within the firm, and to maintain open, honest communication systems. The result is an extremely effective and symbiotic relationship between competitive strategy and human resource management strategy. Firm-specific skills such as effectively using the company's somewhat unique Management By Objectives program, understanding the informal organization, and work group expertise are key ingredients in promoting commitment, reducing turnover among successful employees, enhancing the competitive position, and, it should be noted, shaping a culture highly resistant to internal culture change.

Human resource planning within Hewlett-Packard has the benefit of drawing upon a large number of employees who expect to upgrade their skills and change their assignments over time. Human resource planning at Hewlett-Packard has the additional restriction of needing to provide appropriate promotion opportunities and job needs for a relatively stable work force.

Other firms may invest in creating industry-specific skills to enhance their current competitive position but are wise to avoid investing in a substantial percentage of firm-specific skills that inhibit mobility or are costly to develop. Fast food firms such as McDonald's choose not to invest in long-term commitment with the majority of their employees. This does not mean that such firms should not or do not have their own unique ways of doing things. It does mean, however, that to be effective and efficient standard operating procedures should be generally simple to explain and learn.

For firms such as McDonald's, firm-specific skills and knowledge should be directly tied to the production process. In addition, there should be few unusual methods or unique organizational features that do not have a direct relationship with the bottom line. By standardizing production processes and designing jobs to minimize mental demands, firms like McDonald's can sustain high turnover in spite of their investment in firm-specific human capital.

Strategic human resource management approaches that focus on responding to environmental change or matching human resources to existing organizational conditions are excessively concerned with developing a tight fit and attempting to generate a one-to-one correspondence between human resource practices and environmental or organizational circumstances. This approach to fit presumes relatively fixed goals and directions. Such a concentration on matching often makes it more difficult for a firm to detect a need for change and to respond appropriately.

Yvan Allaire and Mihaela Firsirotu describe four classifications of organizational and environmental fit or misfit.[3] In the first classification the firm is currently a good fit with its environment, which is expected to change slowly and predictably if at all. This means that the alignment between the firm and its marketplace is expected to continue over the long term. In the second category, the firm is currently out of alignment with its environment, but the environment is expected to change so that the marketplace will align with existing organizational choices. This short-term misfit but long-term fit category can occur either because of temporary business cycles that push an organization out of alignment over the short run, or as a result of a planned preemptive adjustment to anticipated changes in the external environment. In both these first two categories, there is no need for a firm to change the way in which it operates.

The third and fourth categories, in contrast, require radical organizational changes. In the third classification, organizational choices are a good match with the current environmental conditions but are expected to prove a poor fit with the anticipated future. In other words, the marketplace is expected to shift in a way that undermines the firm's competitive position. Since current performance is likely to be quite good, one of the primary problems accompanying this situation is gaining recognition of the need for change. In addition, past experience and specific skills may only be of limited use in securing a desirable competitive position under the anticipated environmental circumstances. These factors heighten resistance to change, hamper recognition of the need for change, and increase problems associated with incremental or evolutionary internal shifts. In order to be successful in the future, a new vision is required.

In the fourth category of fit and misfit, the organization's current strategy is a poor fit with the existing environment, but the environment is in a steady state. Under this set of circumstances, problem recognition is fairly easy since organizational survival is at stake. Problem diagnosis and the design of effective solutions, however, present difficult challenges. There is generally a great deal of uncertainty regarding what should be done. Resources are often limited at this point. Time pressures are usually present. Employee stress is high both because of current poor performance and the likelihood that existing skills may be of limited use in the future. Developing an effective turnaround strategy often requires shifts in power as well as development of new expertise.

To the extent that a tight match between employees and strategic conditions or environmental events has dominated a firm's strategic human resource management practices, problem recognition will be more difficult, diagnosing the situation and developing effective actions will be problematic, and implementing any changes will require negotiation through an obstacle course of power relationships, expectations, skill .deficiencies, and inappropriate world views.

We suggest that the type of fit advocated in strategic human resource approaches advocating matching employees or human resource management practices to organizational or environmental circumstances be considered the opposite of flexibility. The strategic human resource management technique presented in the next chapter encourages a firm to choose a position along the continuum from tight fit to flexibility, to coincide with their assessment of upcoming competitive conditions. This technique contrasts with the earlier recommendation that maximal fit be a driving objective. In this way, maximum congruence is not a primary goal for all firms. Rather, the need for fit should directly reflect the competitive advantage that is expected to result from a high level of congruence among organizational activities as offset by the expected need for transition. This does not negate the potential competitive advantages described earlier regarding organizational fit and competitive position.[4] Minimal compatibility between a firm's product-market strategy and environmental opportunities, and among a firm's managerial processes, remains a prerequisite for long-term success. Early fit may, in some industry settings, provide a source of competitive advantage. Tight fit between a firm and its market environment, and among a firm's structure and managerial processes, is recognized to entail costs as well as benefits, however. Under stable conditions, the costs of tight fit are lower, and the benefits related to competitive advantage are generally quite high. Under this set of conditions, enhancing fit between a firm's human resource management practices and its strategic goals is recommended. Under highly changeable or unpredictable conditions, however, flexibility may offer an improved cost-benefit ratio.

NOTES

1. For an expanded discussion of the responsibility of participation in decision making, see M. L. Lengnick-Hall and C. A. Lengnick-Hall, The neglected role of individual and organizational responsibilities in participative decision making. Proceedings of the council on employee responsibilities and rights annual meeting, Orlando, Fla., 1989.

2. For a complete discussion, see L. T. Perry, Least-cost alternatives to layoffs in declining industries. *Organizational Dynamics* 14(4) (1986): 48–61.

3. Y. Allaire and M. Firsirotu, How to implement radical strategies in large organizations. *Sloan Management Review* 9 (1985): 19–34.

4. For a complete argument in favor of high levels of fit, see R. E. Miles, et al., Organization strategy, structure, and process. *Academy of Management Review* 26(3) (1984): 546–662.

6

The Proposed Approach

A new analytic model for strategic human resource management is proposed. This model combines two fundamental dimensions of strategic human resource management. One captures a firm's strategic direction and goal orientation, segmenting organizations into those with high corporate growth expectations and those with low corporate growth expectations. The second dimension incorporates organizational readiness in terms of human resource knowledge, skills, abilities, and motivation to successfully implement a given strategy. Again, firms can be segmented into those with high levels of organizational readiness and those currently unable to implement a selected strategy.

These two dimensions are then combined to develop a four-celled matrix reflecting four different strategic human resource management situations. These four distinct strategic contingency sets have been labeled development, expansion, productivity, and redirection. In this chapter the basic ingredients of this analytic model are explained, and the characteristics of each of the four strategic conditions is described. Examples of organizations facing representative conditions are provided. The specific issues and problems associated with each of the quadrants are identified. The range of strategic human resource management choices are examined and the advantages and disadvantages associated with various decisions are discussed.

The analytic approach to strategic human resource management presented in this book is illustrated in what we call the growth-readiness matrix, depicted in Figure 1. The model captures the basic features of our proposed approach to strategic human resource management.

Figure 1
Growth/Readiness Matrix

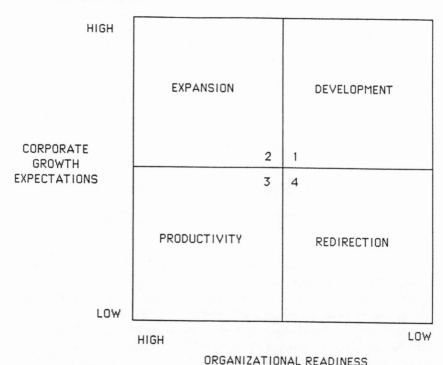

Source: Adapted from C. A. Lengnick-Hall and M. L. Lengnick-Hall 1988. Strategic human
        resources management: A review of the literature and a proposed typology.
        Academy of Management Review 13 (3): 454-470.

CORPORATE GROWTH EXPECTATIONS

Corporate growth expectations are a proxy indicator for the strategic goals of the organizations. The concept of corporate growth encompasses many of the issues relevant to strategy formulation. Consideration of a firm's growth expectations is compatible with the work of scholars such as Ansoff, Porter, Miles, Snow, Meyer and Coleman, and Chandler.[1] A focus on growth is also consistent with the evaluation mechanisms presented by many business publications such as the *Wall Street Journal, Business Week, Fortune, Inc.*, and *Forbes*. In each of these publications, firms are frequently ranked according to market value, sales volume, and change in performance from prior reporting periods.

Much of strategic management centers on goal selection and attainment. As discussed in Chapter 2, specific growth implications are embedded in a firm's choice of competitive advantage, its selection of a domain approach, its identified growth vector, and its reliance on portfolio management techniques. Moreover, the evolution of a firm's industry and the competitive forces that shape that industry also contain important factors governing the ease and attainability of growth expectations.

High growth generally means increased opportunity and expanded competitive challenge. Growth vector aspects of strategic direction can offer one avenue for high growth expectations. Such opportunities might take the form of multiple strategic or competitive options as might occur with a product development strategy or market expansion, for example. A firm's selected domain perspective is also captured in its growth expectations. While a defender organization might expect to expand within a defined product and market area, prospector firms would certainly exhibit high growth expectations. Growth can also include expansion in a firm's source of competitive advantage. In some industries increasing size offers a sustainable competitive advantage. In other industries an extensive and highly diversified product line offers a desirable competitive position.

When considering industry analysis, growth is more easily accomplished if rivalry among industry participants is moderate to low. When competition is aggressive, successful attainment of high growth expectations for one firm frequently carry undesirable implications for its competitors. Increasing power on the part of buyers and suppliers may offer important incentives to expand a firm's horizons and raise its growth expectations. Increasing viability of substitute products may raise the stakes for maintaining the current competitive position if exit costs are high, or may suggest new avenues for product development. High exit costs often accompany high barriers to entry within an industry. The boundaries of an industry often have a strong influence on the realistic growth expectations among industry participants. Industry life cycle phenomena can additionally influence growth expectations. During the early phases of industry evolution, demand frequently exceeds supply, and growth is relatively easy and inexpensive. Growth opportunities are also more readily available during late stages of industry evolution, as some firms choose to exit early. During the more stable periods of development, growth can be quite difficult and expensive to achieve.

Growth relates not only to the traditional notions of the size of a firm, or its dollar value in sales, it also considers the variety in products, market diversity, and the range of activities in which a firm is engaged. When we refer to high growth expectations in this analytic framework, we mean that a firm intends to expand in terms of size, variety, interdependence, variability, portions of the value chain that yield a competitive advantage, or any combination of these factors. High growth means that the firm is focusing on opportunities rather than on threats, and that the firm is expecting to expand upon and challenge its current position and capabilities.

ORGANIZATIONAL READINESS

Organizational readiness measures the current availability or the future obtainability of appropriate human resource knowledge, skills, abilities, and efforts needed for effective strategy implementation. In some ways organizational readiness is a proxy measure for implementation feasibility. In other respects, feasibility is a necessary but insufficient condition for organizational readiness, since both capability and willingness are captured in the measure. Organizational readiness indicates how well the current human resource management outcomes, if managed to achieve their full potential, will meet the needs of the competitive situation and corporate expectations.

Many of the initial approaches to strategic human resource management can be used to provide helpful information in assessing organizational readiness. As noted, human resource planning techniques can help to evaluate whether the appropriate number of individuals are likely to be where and when they are needed, and able to accomplish the necessary tasks. Human resource valuation approaches can offer a limited view of the value of the current stock of human resource capital. Various matching approaches can offer numerous paired comparisons across human resource capabilities or styles and strategic, organizational, or environmental contingencies. In combination, initial approaches to strategic human resource management can provide useful baseline information that enables an assessment of the firm's current, if not its potential, organizational readiness position. When these approaches are augmented by consideration of firm-specific and industry-specific skills, analysis of the firm's desired position of a fit versus flexibility continuum, and assessment of investment options, a comprehensive picture of organizational readiness can be obtained.

OVERVIEW OF THE ANALYTIC MODEL

As noted, there are four cells in the growth-readiness matrix: development, expansion, productivity, and redirection. The four quadrants identified in the analytic model represent four conditions under which organization strategy and our recommended human resource strategy are formulated. For each quadrant, a different strategic human resource issue must be resolved, reflecting our assumption that both the relevant questions and appropriate answers change as strategic conditions change.

If a firm has high growth expectations but low organizational readiness, it is categorized as being in the *development* phase. In the development quadrant, the primary issue is strategy formulation. If a firm has high growth expectations accompanied by high organizational readiness, it is in *expansion*. In the expansion quadrant, resource allocation issues become paramount. A firm with high organizational readiness but low growth expectations is classified as in the *productivity* stage. Strategic trade-off concerns dominate the productivity quadrant. If a firm has both low growth expectations and low organizational readiness it faces *redirection*. In the redirection quadrant, the basic choice is between turnaround and exit.

Analytic Approach

Since the relevant issues vary as strategic conditions change, the specific mix of analytic steps also varies from quadrant to quadrant. As a general analytic approach, a firm should first identify its intended position relative to growth expectations. In a multibusiness organization, the growth expectations of each strategic business unit or division should be determined individually. Next an assessment of organizational readiness to achieve the expected performance given the current competitive conditions should be made. Again, for a single-business organization a single assessment is needed, but for a diversified firm each strategic business unit or division should be evaluated in light of the particular growth expectations, human resource capabilities, and competitive circumstances unique to each unit. Specific guidelines to aid in conducting these two preliminary analyses are provided in the next chapter.

Once the firm or the various businesses have been correctly positioned on the growth-readiness matrix, it is time to begin the second phase of analysis, in which the specific questions and issues unique to each quadrant and the particular conditions influencing successful performance within each quadrant should be considered. Much of the rest of this chapter provides a blueprint for making effective strategic human resource management analyses and decisions under conditions of development, expansion, productivity, and redirection. The specific guidelines, issues, and techniques for undertaking the recommended analyses are provided in Chapter 7.

If an organization has more than one strategic business unit, the next step in the strategic human resource management process is to consider the implications of the separate choices made for each of the business units. This final assessment should consider whether long-term trends are leading in desirable directions. In other words, if all the strategic human resource management decisions are implemented simultaneously, will organizational synergy be enhanced or diminished? Will the repertoire of distinct competencies of the firm be expanded or contracted? Will the firm be appropriately positioned between fit and flexibility? Will the combined strategic human resource management activities promote a desirable and sustainable competitive position?

The final step in any strategic management process is evaluation. Not only should the interactive effects of strategic human resource management decisions and actions be assessed, the accuracy of managerial assumptions, predictions, and expectations should be evaluated. Moreover, the effectiveness of investment, divestment, and human resource allocation decisions must be evaluated. In many instances, this requires a long-time horizon. The longer the period between choice and final observable results, the more important it is to develop incremental checkpoints to assess progress. With the increasing complexity of most organizations, effective strategic human resource control is becoming as important as effective strategic human resource planning.

CONSIDERING EVOLUTIONARY INFLUENCES

Evolutionary forces, such as industry and product maturation, the consequences of increasing organizational size and formality, and familiarity with particular strategic situations, affect the long-term position of a strategic business unit on the growth-readiness matrix. In most cases, evolutionary factors apply pressure to move the strategic situation from the left to the right side of the growth-readiness matrix. This means that as technologies and competitive conditions change, most business units will move from high organizational readiness to obsolescence in knowledge, skills, and abilities.

In part, this reflects changing demands with increasing maturity and familiarity.[2] For example, when a product is first introduced, human resource flexibility is particularly important. Selection, training, and development concerns are high as employees must be hired that have key skills in new and emerging technologies and marketing situations. As product opportunities grow, the ability to identify, add, and integrate new employees on a continuing basis becomes critical. As the product matures further, efficiency concerns are raised, and human resource management options are frequently contrasted with increased automation and mechanization.

In most industries, technological change makes current skills or techniques less competitive over time. While handcraft skills and innovative processes may initially lead to a competitive advantage, standardized production processes, durability and reliability, and service considerations begin to take precedence as markets become more price sensitive. Consequently, there is often a change from a focus on marketing, research, and development activities in emerging industries to a focus on production and manufacturing activities in more mature industries.

It is not unusual for the emphasis on certain portions of the value chain to shift as an industry matures, competition becomes more intense, and markets become more segmented.[3] Most industries undergo evolutionary changes in buyer segments that can be served by a single product offering.

Shifts in related industries, such as raw material suppliers, ancillary product groups, or distribution channels can lead to either increased consolidation or increased segmentation, depending on other factors influencing industry structure.

A reduction of uncertainty generally accompanies industry and product maturation, leading to a change in the information processing requirements for a firm. Lower levels of uncertainty can also lead to shifts in the power that can come from effective environmental scanning. If information and accurate interpretations are readily available, a distinct competence in this regard no longer provides a competitive advantage.

Evolutionary trends also move conditions from the top to the bottom of the growth-readiness matrix for any given strategic business unit. This means that over time, most organizations, or strategic business units in multibusiness firms, shift from higher growth expectations to lower growth goals. As markets become saturated and new competitors enter the marketplace, market penetration or concentration strategy becomes more difficult to achieve. As industries and products mature, growth often becomes less feasible, since there are fewer untapped opportunities. Any gains in market share must come at the expense of competitors rather than from serving unmet buyer needs. In addition, growth becomes more expensive to achieve. Since sales or market share must be taken away from competitors, it is not unusual for price wars or other forms of aggressive retaliation to occur. In some industries, unrealistic growth expectations among large proportions of industry participants have led to extensive overcapacity. This can undermine profitability for the industry as a whole. In other industries, dependence on nonrenewable natural resources provided a cap on aggregate growth expectations. The existence of natural limits frequently provides an incentive for diversification. This, in turn, increases organizational complexity and often leads to an accompanying increase in the costs of doing business. In still other industries, the product life cycle is frequently truncated by substitute products or a newer generation of the original product. Unusually short product life cycles put added pressure on research and development and other avenues of innovation.

While these evolutionary influences are well documented,[4] our concern is that prior approaches to strategic human resource management considered evolutionary events in a deterministic manner, which seems to unnecessarily limit management options. We contend that movement from one quadrant to another results from an interaction between environmental conditions and organizational choices. Prior approaches to strategic human resource management see the manager's responsibility primarily as determining the current stage of development. Once that is accomplished, the appropriate response is seen as relatively fixed. We propose a contingency approach in which organization choices are rec-

ognized as influencing both the rate and the direction of product, organizational, and industrywide life stages.

For example, a firm that invests in research and development or engages
in a joint venture in order to revitalize a mature product may plunge that
product into a second growth stage. Similarly, a firm that neglects product
or technological improvements, or diverts excessive funds from manufacturing operations in stable environments to fund growth opportunities
in emerging areas, can prematurely age the business and accelerate the
maturation process. Marketing and engineering choices regarding style
and fashion options can sustain a growth cycle.

Porter offers an interesting example of this interaction in his discussion
of the roles and responsibilities of good industry leadership.[5] A good
industry leader is concerned with the health of the industry as a whole
as well as with its own competitive position. This often means that the
leader has a strategy and objectives that provide a protective umbrella
under which various followers can profitably compete. A good market
leader must understand the rules of the game in the industry. Furthermore,
a good leader must base its competitive decisions on realistic assumptions
and an appreciation of the forces that govern industry structure. A market
leader that fully exploits experience curve benefits and follows cost reductions with proportional price reductions may destroy the industry's
profitability if there are powerful customers to contend with.

Rockwell International's water meter division offers a useful illustration
of how a firm's choices and actions can have a strong influence on industry
conditions and evolution. In the 1970s, Rockwell charged a price premium
for its superior quality bronze water meter even though it was able to
manufacture the meter at lower costs than most competitors were able
to achieve for less accurate and durable meters. The combination of product differentiation and low cost was achieved through sound engineering,
leading to a design that was easy to manufacture, accompanied by vertical
integration and modern manufacturing plants. A large market share and
shared economies with other operations further enhanced the cost position.

In the early 1980s, competitors introduced plastic water meters. While
the accuracy and durability of these plastic meters was not as high as the
bronze meters manufactured by Rockwell, they were substantially less
expensive. The industry was becoming increasingly price sensitive due
to economic conditions. If Rockwell had chosen to follow industry trends
and redirect their competitive focus away from bronze and toward plastic,
the industry structure would likely have been destroyed. If bronze meters
were phased out, there would be little basis for differentiation left in the
water meter industry. If every firm competes with a similar product, price
sensitivity will likely continue to erode any potential interest in high-
quality, differentiated product lines. This in turn increases the likelihood

of an industry shake-out, followed by the consolidation of remaining competitors at a lower level of profitability once the dust clears. Rockwell maintained its investment in bronze water meters and protected the fundamental competitive options for the water meter industry as a whole. It is clear that Rockwell's actions strongly influences evolutionary trends in product development and the water meter industry. Thus, we contend, the potential for a firm to exert influence on its environment should not be neglected or underestimated.

SUMMARIZING THE ANALYTIC FRAMEWORK

In summary, we see the context for strategic human resource management as derived from two dimensions: organizational goals and the availability and obtainability of appropriate human resource knowledge, skills, abilities, and efforts. Organizational choice has a dominant effect on organizational goals and investment decisions. Goal choices can challenge a firm's capabilities and encourage employees to stretch their talents, or organizational decisions can permit employees to take it easy and invest only minimal effort in organizational activities. Goal choices can recognize and capitalize on industry and marketplace conditions, and thus provide new opportunities for a firm, or these choices can neglect consideration of important environmental realities and be seen as unreachable and, consequently, demotivating.

Investment decisions are equally important and far reaching. A firm can choose to invest in the development of its employees across a broad spectrum of knowledge, skills and abilities, recognizing that some of these capabilities may remain unused for an extended period of time. A broad investment strategy provides a firm with a deep reservoir of talent. Broad investment reflects a preference for positioning a firm away from tight fit and toward some measure of flexibility. In contrast, a firm can elect to only invest in developing those capabilities that have immediate use in achieving the firm's current strategy and goals. Such a limited investment approach may have short-term payoffs in terms of efficiency and financial risk. A limited investment approach generally coincides with a preference for tight fit among a firm's strategy, structure, and managerial processes. However, limited investment and the corresponding benefits often come at the expense of long-term flexibility.

Combined, these goal-oriented and investment choices either expand or limit a firm's horizons regarding growth expectations and organizational readiness. To some extent goal and investment choices set some boundaries on the relevant planning horizon. If the goals are aggressive and the investment expansive, greater uncertainty and potential for change must be accommodated. This means that any strategic human resource management decisions are probabilistic and appropriate for a midrange time horizon. If both goals and investments are conservative and based on relatively certain information and well-tested assumptions, the planning horizon is somewhat extended.

Environmental constraints and opportunities have a dominant effect on the potential for return from investments in a firm's human resources. There are several important implications of this. First, the more closely an organization's vision of its industry and marketplace environment parallels reality, the greater the probability that the firm will recognize opportunities and threats in a timely manner. In addition, such recognition improves the probability that the resulting strategic response will have the desired, or at least the expected, results. Organizations with realistic self-perceptions and external perceptions out-perform firms with overly optimistic or pessimistic frames of reference.

Second, the importance of external influences on the success or failure of a firm's strategy means that a part of strategic human resource management is developing an approach for managing a firm's external contingencies effectively. If human resource policies or practices are only focused internally, important opportunities to shape the environment may be missed. Moreover, if a firm's human resource practices are largely focused internally, shifts in the labor force or in demographic trends are more likely to come as a surprise. This reduces a firm's potential for maintaining organizational readiness. Third, environmental influences on outcomes serve as a reminder that a firm's human resource choices can be no more independent of its environment than its product choices. Both require inputs from the environment, and both expect the marketplace to value the resulting output.

Finally, both organizational choice and environmental factors influence human resource availability and obtainability. Environmental events may reinforce each other to provide an abundance of certain types of human resources and scarcity of others. For example, recent labor statistics suggest that only about 6 percent of all households reflect the two-parent, single wage earner, "Ozzie and Harriet" pattern common in the 1950s. Many of these workers are highly educated and highly motivated, creating numerous opportunities for service organizations, child care providers, and household maintenance firms. This education level creates a potential surplus of middle management talent and at the same time leads to a shortage of people willing to perform entry-level service jobs. Organizations that choose to facilitate dual-career couples through flexible benefits, on-site child care, job sharing or other techniques may have a competitive advantage in securing high-quality human resources. Organizations that expect frequent relocation in exchange for long-term job security may find this choice puts the firm at a competitive disadvantage. Firms that select distinct competencies reflecting the types of skills and abilities resulting from traditional educational programs are likely to have more potentially qualified applicants to choose from in recruiting and hiring employees, yet face greater competition for the best of these workers from firms in a variety of industry settings. Firms that develop distinct competencies around unique or unusual talents—nuclear physics, for example—must select their employees from a smaller sample but are also likely to encounter less varied and more narrow competition for these workers. The approach to strategic human resource management presented here provides a way to systematically explore these complex and multivariate relations.

QUADRANT 1: DEVELOPMENT

The development quadrant is characterized by high growth expectations and a poor level of organizational readiness between strategic contingencies and human resource knowledge, skills, and abilities. This set of conditions can occur in a variety of ways. Perhaps one of the most common reasons an organization can find itself having high expectations but being ill-prepared to achieve them is technological change. At times, lack of investment in research and development or other innovation methods leads to technological obsolescence. When a firm is enjoying the benefits of a highly successful, standardized product, it is often difficult to perceive threats coming from substitutes or new product variations. The steel industry offers unfortunate examples of this type of omission. The lack of effective environmental scanning also leads to technological obsolescence. Failure to identify emerging market segmentation patterns, reluctance to invest in new process technologies, or simple organizational arrogance can lead to a reduced incentive for monitoring the environment effectively. The automobile industry in the early 1970s counted poor market awareness and understanding among its problems.

Perhaps more frequently, technological breakthroughs or entry into an industry by competitors with entirely different skills from traditional competitors leads to an almost instantaneous lack of technological fit and organizational readiness. The introduction of diesel engines, ball point pens, and electric razors offered attractive opportunities for the initiating firms, but created conditions of poor fit and low organizational readiness in a host of other organizations.

When electronic watches were first introduced, for example, electronics technology was largely unfamiliar to traditional watch manufacturers. This new type of watch triggered a growth segment in the marketplace. Suddenly, a firm like Timex, which had caused a restructuring of the watch industry decades earlier, found itself in a situation of poor organizational readiness. The dramatically altered market conditions made Timex's skill in mass-produced mechanical watch manufacturing obsolete. While firms such as Timex still had corporate goals of continual and rapid growth, their mechanical gear-oriented manufacturing technology was abruptly out of date. Their highly formal organization structure, authority-based culture and decision-making systems, and expectations of high rewards for consistent performance presented additional problems in adapting to the altered competitive situation. Knowledge and skills in an entirely different manufacturing technology were immediately required if growth was to be maintained.

Choices for Businesses in the Development Quadrant

Under circumstances of high growth expectations and poor organizational readiness, the first-order choice is strategy formulation. There are three basic options available. One, a firm may choose to invest heavily in its human resources to improve implementation feasibility. Hyatt chose this option when it elected to retrain Braniff employees after acquiring the bankrupt firm. If a firm chooses an investment strategy the assumption is that the organization has a clear vision of what needs to be done. This means that the sources of competitive advantage are identified and the corresponding distinct competencies needed to achieve the desired competitive position are also known. Does the firm need to be able to process a new raw material? Does the firm need to develop increased responsiveness to unique customer preferences? Does the organization need to produce a higher quality product at a lower cost?

Moreover, for an investment strategy to be attractive, a firm must have a fairly clear idea what the target for investment should be. If a firm needs to acquire a new technology, investment needs to include not only the identification, selection, negotiation, and acquisition of an appropriate target firm, but an investment in integrating people from two separate organizations into an effective strategic operation. If a firm needs to be able to make decisions more quickly, investment options may include organizational restructuring, training in delegation, self-management, group decision-making processes, and a shift in the compensation system.

An investment toward improved organizational readiness implies that the firm believes the necessary expertise, capabilities, or motivation can either be developed in-house or purchased from the external environment. This means that not only do managers have a clear idea of what needs to be accomplished and a realistic assessment of how to accomplish these objectives, there is also sufficient time, resources, and availability to prevent an investment strategy from becoming a cash trap. If an appliance repair shop has a poor service reputation, a strategy of investing in training programs, control systems, and compensation changes have a better chance of success if an aggressive competitor is not attempting to take over the target market location. If a small research lab needs top-notch engineers to become competitive, labor market considerations will strongly influence the feasibility of any investment strategy.

As a second alternative response to conditions of high growth expectations and low organizational readiness, a firm may decide to change its corporate goals. A goal change may suggest that the lack of organizational readiness is a permanent or uncorrectable condition. Sambo's restaurants, for example, recognized that rapid growth had taken a severe toll on the firm's infrastructure, management systems, and profits. A number of problems emerged that made further growth increasingly difficult. Rather than alter human resource management practices and corporate investments so that growth could be maintained, corporate management decided to shift its focus from growth to profits after financial difficulties in 1983. A small metal-cutting job shop may discover that its growth opportunities are limited when a number of large customers decide to vertically integrate backwards. Alternatively, a change in goals may reflect the recognition that there are more attractive and feasible opportunities in other business units.

As a third option, a firm may choose to change the corporate operating strategy to capitalize on currently available skills and resources and thus achieve the desired growth objective using a different method or relying on different organizational competencies. This third option reflects the systems concept of equifinality, another way of saying there is generally more than one successful path to any desirable objective. Anheuser-Busch provides an example of this third option with its withdrawal from the soft drink industry and entry into the bakery and snack industries. Anheuser-Busch had very high growth expectations. In addition, the firm had highly efficient operations, wide distribution networks, a strong corporate culture, and a high level of employee commitment. Anheuser-Busch was also noted for effective marketing skills and consistent product quality. Many of these attributes seemed keys to success in the soft drink industry. However, the soft drink industry was mature, dominated by two large and effective competitors, and experiencing slowing growth. Anheuser-Busch's entry into the soft drink industry was unsuccessful and did not help achieve desired corporate growth. The snack food and bakery industries, on the other hand, had significantly lower barriers to entry. However, many of the skills leading to success in the beer industry were also key elements for successful participation in snack foods and bakery goods. By making the switch from soft drinks to snack foods, Anheuser-Busch maintained their growth goals and applied their considerable organizational talents to an industry for which they were better suited. This third alternative retains the growth goals by altering some aspect of the strategy used to achieve them.

Contextual Issues

In order to make an effective competitive and strategic human resource management decision, low levels of organizational readiness must be realistically evaluated. Skill and knowledge obsolescence resulting from the development of a new technology is generally an evolutionary, rather than abrupt, event.[6] The replacement of an existing technology with a new one is rarely immediate. Approximately half of the time, the sale of products using an old technology continues to expand even after a new technology has been established. Sales of an original technology often continue to expand despite a corresponding sales growth in products using the new technology. This is in part because new technologies frequently open new market opportunities not available with the old technology. Even where a new technology is destined to completely replace an existing technology, it generally takes five to fourteen years for the substitution to take place.

What are the strategic human resource implications of this pace and pattern? These characteristics clearly indicate that effective environmental scanning is essential for a firm to develop. Early, accurate, and insightful identification and diagnosis of new technologies can offer an organization the time necessary to explore a full range of competitive and strategic human resource management options.

Effective diagnosis can be a tricky undertaking at times. Most new technologies are crude and expensive when first introduced. Many new products have initial flaws that are often highlighted when the product is first introduced. If a firm is enjoying the benefits of a successful competitive position, it may be seductively easy to underestimate the potential applications of a new technology. If a firm has invested in a high proportion of firm-specific skills and abilities, vested interests may make it hard to appreciate the potential benefits of a new technology. If a firm does not have a high level of readiness to embrace a new technology, the market attractiveness may be downplayed. Jet aircraft, for example, were only believed suitable for military applications when they were first developed. Facsimile machines were thought to only have limited applications when first introduced. Now nearly all business people have FAX numbers on their business cards.

If recognized early, low organizational readiness to compete in future market environments need not require a change in goals or change in strategy. A reasonable lead time can increase the potential payoff from an investment in a firm's human capital. Flawed diagnoses or slow identification of potential threats reduce training and development time, thus eliminating the opportunity for certain types of skill development.

A firm's domain choice also influences how persistent a firm should be in pursuing its growth objectives versus maintaining its current skill base. A defender firm is committed to maintaining its position in an industry. If the dominant skills required to compete effectively change, the firm is obligated to develop and upgrade its current skills repertoire. If organizational readiness cannot be improved, a defender firm must alter its domain posture, redefine its domain to a more specialized market niche, or reduce its growth expectations.

A prospector firm maintains little commitment to industries or product lines. Often maintaining a highly effective base of knowledge, skills and abilities are more crucial issues for these firms than the use to which they are put. Thus, for a prospector, changing goals or the particular strategic environment may be better choices than investing to improve organizational readiness to implement a selected strategy.

Analyzer firms have more freedom and more complicated choices. Analyzer firms are committed to maintaining certain portions of their product and market scope. In addition, analyzer firms generally maintain a base of common capabilities, technologies, and information that helps them maintain their equilibrium. Analyzer firms are also interested in planned growth opportunities and will selectively expand both their product-market scope and human resource capabilities to accomplish this.

Effective strategy formulation is based on assessments of functional and technical capabilities, strengths and weaknesses, and realistic goals. An accurate, timely, and comprehensive understanding of the competitive environment is a prerequisite for making reasonable strategic human resource management choices. If a firm has high growth expectations but is not meeting them due to poor organizational readiness, a number of analytic steps should be taken.

Suggested Analytic Steps

Step 1a: Diagnose the Cause of Poor Readiness. A number of interrelated analytic activities will help a firm make an appropriate strategy formulation choice when a business unit is in the development quadrant. First, the cause of poor organizational readiness should be diagnosed. This step determines whether or not current goals can be achieved with additional investment in human resource capabilities. One way to approach this step is to look for gaps in the value chain. Are skills in operating new automated equipment necessary? Are there too few employees in manufacturing, so that supply is unable to keep up with demand? Is customer service becoming an increasingly important element in the marketplace for a firm that has few skills in customer relations?

In this latter situation, an investment in teaching employees how to handle consumer complaints, upgrading the product knowledge of the sales force, an 800 hot line and knowledgeable employees to staff it, and expanding service and delivery personnel may solve the problem. If the source of poor customer service is a highly transient work force, reflecting insufficient organizational resources to compete effectively in the labor market, investments in training and development are not likely to improve readiness significantly.

Step 1b: Determine Whether or Not the Problem is Correctable. Therefore, a second step in the analytic process is to judge whether or not the omitted capability can be obtained. It is important to determine not only the specific knowledge, skills, or ability that is missing, but to determine whether such talents can be learned or acquired from outside the organization. If the needed skills can be developed through training or education, then a reasonable learning curve should be projected and an estimated time frame determined. If the anticipated time frame for developing a particular human resource competence is too long for effective competitive action, or if a firm does not know how to train someone to accomplish a particular activity, acquiring the human resource skill from outside the firm should be considered. Depending on the organization's culture, a cost-benefit assessment of the make or buy decision is often appropriate.

Often, addressing a lack of organizational readiness requires a complex and extensive set of human resource management and strategic decisions. Apple Computer, for example, recognized that its current human resource management practices and organizational structure were insufficient to generate the needed creativity, flexibility, and speed needed to develop the Macintosh. It recognized the competitive opportunity and growth potential a successful product entry of this kind could offer. Selection, staffing, compensation, training and development, job design, communication and performance expectations, and most other human resource management activities were designed to reflect the specialized expectations and competitive situation faced by the Macintosh group. Consequently, a separate work unit was designed to meet the specialized requirements for this type of start-up venture. In this case, Apple both knew how to generate the necessary knowledge, skills, and abilities among its employees, had the resources needed to invest in these activities, and could accomplish these changes in a relatively short time frame.

In contrast, Anheuser-Busch determined that it could not train employees to become more competitive in the soft drink industry due, at least in part, to the structural forces that influenced industry competition. Anheuser-Busch's lack of competitive success was not dependent primarily on human resource capabilities, and thus could not be corrected by improved human resource management. Sambo's (a restaurant chain) management decided that there was insufficient time to make the major structural and skill-based changes needed and still achieve the original growth goals. It recognized that many of the needed skills and abilities could be learned, but that reaching an appropriate level of competence would not occur in time to turn around the firm's current poor performance before it became financially infeasible to correct the situation.

Step 1c: Determine Whether or Not Improved Readiness is a Cost-Effective Strategic Option. If a firm has both the ability and the time to effect needed changes in human resource management practices or capabilities, then it must determine whether or not this change is cost effective given other organizational resource demands. If increased organizational readiness is not feasible, either in terms of educability or time, then goals or strategic approaches to goal attainment must be changed. This is an example of reciprocal human resource and strategic decision making.

A better understanding of the cause and potential resolution of poor organizational readiness is only the beginning. A diagnosis of the organizational readiness options allows a firm to more adequately assess its internal strengths and weaknesses. The next step is evaluating the reasonableness of corporate growth expectations. To assess whether or not current goals are reasonable, attention must be given to industry structure conditions, product life cycle issues, and the competitive position of the firm.

Step 2a: Conduct an Industry Analysis to Assess Goal Realism. As discussed earlier, growth opportunities are greatest during early and late phases of industry evolution. A firm like Safeway, which attempts to grow rapidly in a mature industry, will require greater resource expenditures and a more significant competitive advantage than a firm like Genentech, a genetic engineering firm that intends to grow during early phases of industry development. This means that the growth expectations a firm develops for a business will almost surely have to change over time. For most firms, the rapid growth expectations that were quite reasonable during early phases of the industry or product life cycle are inappropriate during maturity. The conservative growth expectation accepted during a stable industry period may lead to missed growth opportunities during shake-out periods or when important competitors are exiting the industry.

It is important that firms develop mechanisms for scanning the market environment, which enables them to detect changes in buying behaviors, demand cycles, and long-term shifts in purchasing patterns. Such information provides early warning signals of evolutionary shifts in the industry. Firms also need to keep in mind the potential they may have for influencing industry structure, evolution, and balance. Aggressive marketing may precipitate a shake-out. Benign neglect may extend a stable growth period.

Michael Porter outlines a number of indicators that can be used to anticipate industry evolution.[7] There are a number of signals of increasing demand that accompany high growth in an industry. Market boundaries and buyer groups tend to expand. Customers will often accept uneven quality in goods and services. When demand is increasing, customers are often much more tolerant than they have been during early stages of product development or they will be as the market becomes more saturated. Products often show a variety of technical and performance variations. Despite the variation, overall product quality is generally quite high and performance reliability often becomes a key competitive advantage for complex products and services. High growth is often accompanied by incremental competitive improvements in products and services in order to maintain high visibility and market attention.

Manufacturing operations frequently shift toward mass production during rapid growth. Massive distribution channels and high levels of advertising are also prevalent. Competition usually involves a large number of competitors. In most industries there are a large number of new entrants and mergers and a fair number of casualties among industry participants. Many firms become risk prone during growth periods since easy profitability and attractive opportunities cover many errors in judgment.

There are an equal number of important signals that an industry is entering maturity. With maturity, growth opportunities will likely become more limited. Early indicators that growth opportunities are slowing include signs of market saturation and an increased emphasis on repeat buyers. Trade-ins become a substantial aspect of buying habits. There is often less differentiation among products. Standardization of high quality becomes the norm. Product changes are less rapid and often more cosmetic than functional. Maturity is often accompanied by an increase in market segmentation and occasional efforts among firms with high exit costs to extend the product life cycle. Competition based on advertising and packaging intensifies. Service aspects of the business play an increasingly important role in competitive position. Many firms expand their product line in an effort to secure package sales.

The relative importance of functional areas shifts toward manufacturing. Required labor skills often decline, and more production activities are automated during mature phases of industry development. Distribution channels have an increasing impact on product offerings as they reduce selection to maintain control over their own costs. Cost control is often the key to a desirable competitive position. Private brands often enter the market causing increased price sensitivity. Market share positions and the competitive structure of the industry stabilize, often in such a way that dominant firms protect their advantage. Maturing is a poor time to attempt rapid growth.

Signals that an industry is entering its decline, and thus a firm is wise to develop an appropriate end-game strategy should also be noted. By the time an industry is entering decline, customers have learned a great deal about the product and have generally become quite sophisticated buyers. There is often little product differentiation, and product quality becomes quite variable. Advertising expenditures are usually low. Specialty distribution channels often emerge, in part as a response to overcapacity in manufacturing.

Cost control becomes the key element in securing a competitive advantage. Competitors begin to exit, and the level of competition becomes generally less aggressive. Prices often fall as an industry enters the decline phase, but then rise again once the firms that plan to exit early have done so. Profit margins can be quite variable, depending on the availability of specialty market segments. A firm that is able to capture the replacement or service segments of a declining industry can be quite profitable.

It is important to remember that the evolutionary patterns of industries are not fixed. The actions taken by industry participants can influence both the direction and rate of industry change and evolution. A firm may, for example, develop a new product variation that revitalizes sales and rejuvenates an industry's life cycle. In contrast, firms may limit innovation and concentrate on standardized products in such a way that industry maturation is accelerated. If participants in an industry neglect substitute products, industry growth can be truncated. If participants fail to reinforce barriers to entry, of if they are short of resources and thus unable to resist aggressive moves of new entrants, the industry's evolutionary processes can be drastically altered by new participants.

Step 2b: Evaluate Growth Opportunities Outside Existing Industry Boundaries to Assess Goal Realism. Growth within an industry generally relies primarily on expansion in size and an increased market penetration rate. As has been discussed, high growth expectations can also be achieved by an increase in variety, product or market development, or an expanded number of relatively unrelated activities. When considering whether or not growth goals are realistic, a firm needs to consider these options as well as straight-line extensions of existing activities.

For example, a consumer product may have wide application for industrial use with a minor change in packaging and an extended distribution network. The differences between the consumer and industrial markets may be sufficiently different that the same knowledge, skills, and abilities that yield poor organizational readiness for consumer products may provide a higher state of organizational readiness in industrial goods.

In some cases, the technologies that provided an early competitive advantage in one product-market line could be used to introduce a new line of products in an entirely different market arena. The manufacturing technologies used in making toilet paper and potato chips are remarkably similar. Both products are sold in grocery stores, target similar buyer segments, and rely on similar advertising techniques. While the toilet paper market may be maturing, the potato chip market may be in a more growth-orientated stage of development. This type of related diversification can offer avenues to rapid growth relying on existing capabilities while extending beyond existing industry boundaries.

Variability in product-market offerings provides an additional route to meeting high growth expectations. Prospector firms, for example, are noted for their almost continuous entry and exit in an ever-changing mix of product-market arenas. Human resource management capabilities that no longer provide a source of competitive advantage in one product-market area trigger a search for new opportunities where they can be applied more appropriately. For a prospector organization, the feasibility of meeting corporate growth expectations rests more heavily on effective environmental scanning and an ability to recognize and capitalize on opportunities than on maintaining a high level of organizational readiness to achieve rapid growth in one particular industry or product-market arena.

Step 3a: Assess the Portfolio Implications of a Human Resource Investment Decision. The third analytic step considers the interactive consequences of various strategic human resource choices. If the firm is not in a single business, choices regarding a particular enterprise and the overall growth and diversification pattern of the company need to be reconciled. As discussed in Chapter 2, when portfolio management techniques are used, the strategic and financial objectives of individual businesses or strategic business units are set to meet the needs of the entire corporation. Business-level objectives may not maximize the financial value or competitive position of a particular operation. At times the competitive position of one business will be allowed to slip, permitting human and other resources to be diverted to more attractive long-term opportunities.

Both growth expectations and organizational readiness need to be evaluated during this stage. For example, high growth expectations for a particular unit may be reasonable, and organizational readiness may be sufficiently enhanced so that the goals are feasible, but investing in improved organizational readiness in order to achieve high growth may not be in the firm's best long-term interest. When determining human resource policies, it is important to consider both the goals and organizational readiness within the particular business in question, as well as the growth expectations and general organizational readiness of the firm as a whole.

What are some of the conditions that could lead to this assessment? An organization may have a number of different businesses in the development quadrant and very few strategic business units in other segments of the matrix. When this occurs, a firm must be particularly selective regarding which operations receive human resource management investments. If all of the opportunities were to receive investment simultaneously, the organization is likely to spread itself too thin and end up giving insufficient attention to the unique circumstances facing the individual units. Moreover, if all the ventures were successful simultaneously, the stress of multiple sources of high levels of growth could undermine the firm's infrastructure. This, in turn, can easily lead to a reactive posture, thus undercutting the firm's competitive position.

Step 3b: Assess the Strategic Identity Implications of a Human Re-

source Investment Decision. Another set of circumstances leading to a decision not to invest in improving organizational readiness despite its possible success involves the strategic direction of the firm. Most organizations establish boundaries for the maximum degree of variety, complexity, and variability they are willing to accommodate. For example, this means that while attractive opportunities for diversification might be available, a firm that has reached the limits of variety it intends to accept may turn the opportunity down. To achieve a strong competitive position, a firm needs to have a clear sense of its mission, product-market scope, sources of competitive advantage, and potential for synergy. Not every opportunity will fall within this frame of reference. While such opportunities should not necessarily be disregarded without careful assessment, neither should they be accepted simply because they are available.

Synergy, and a firm's choice to diversify in a related or an unrelated manner, play an important role in assessing the interactive implications of strategic human resource decisions. Valuation concerns suggest that the compatibility of industry-specific and unit-specific skills across businesses should be considered. Investments have a greater potential for a long-term payoff if businesses and, consequently, skills, are related. With increased relatedness, skills and abilities developed in one business unit many have useful applications in other business units over time. Relatedness increases flexibility in application of human resource investment outcomes.

If businesses are unrelated, a firm may have a greater repertoire of skills to draw from. Unrelated diversification offers greater independence and, consequently, a greater range of strategic options. However, when a firm invests in unit-specific skills across unrelated business activities, it may also experience greater difficulty in appropriately recognizing and capitalizing on this potential. When linkages among diverse business units are both uncommon and unexpected, they are less likely to be exploited even when they exist.

In many ways, this difficulty parallels the problems that firms relying on low cost for their competitive advantage experience in recognizing sources of differentiation, or those that differentiator firms experience in attempting to control costs. When an activity is seen as different or foreign, common elements are much harder to recognize. One of the potential benefits of strategic human resource management is that human resource issues cut across all organizational units and activities. Perhaps this commonality will offer a vehicle for recognizing other unlikely sources of synergy.

Step 4: Assess the Extent to Which Investment Specificity is Compatible with the Corporate Culture. A fourth analytic step addresses the time horizon for investment and pay back. As Perry notes, the potential for long-term investment effectiveness needs to be determined.[8] Here the organization's culture as well as its portfolio approach should be considered. If important human resource skills are firm-specific but not unit-specific (specific to a unit within the firm), they provide greater application flexibility, which can be accomplished by having a great deal of shared technology, market similarity, or other forms of relatedness across business units. Alternatively, skill flexibility can be accomplished by focusing on corporate systems rather than developing unique mechanisms and procedures within each unit.

As mentioned previously, achieving firm-specific but not unit-specific skills may inhibit a firm's competitive position if a conglomerate diversification approach has been adopted. Efforts to standardize processes and procedures intended to serve quite different needs and purposes are often counterproductive. If some strategic business units compete on price while others compete on uniqueness, common corporate planning, control, and assessment mechanisms will guarantee a poor competitive showing in at least some operations.

Developing firm-specific and unit-specific skills and abilities is a plus if the firm is committed to employment security and promotion from within. Firm-specific and unit-specific knowledge, skills, and abilities reduce employee mobility outside the organization. If a firm's culture demonstrates a preference for external hiring and promotion, reliance on firm-specific skills should be reduced. When a firm's culture promotes high mobility among employees, firm-specific and unit-specific investments have only short-term benefits. Investment in industry-specific skills and abilities, on the other hand, may offer a competitive advantage. If the investment makes an attractive contribution to human capital at both the individual and the organizational level, such training and development may serve as a recruiting incentive. High-calibre employees may join the firm in order to obtain training; once their productive contribution to the original firm declines, the training enhances their opportunity for exit, offering an attractive solution for both the individual employee and the firm.

A firm's culture also reflects its domain choice. If a firm is a defender-type organization with slowly evolving product and market characteristics, an investment in industry-specific or firm-specific skills is likely to have a pay back over an employee's entire tenure with a firm. Moreover, defender organizations are often prone to fostering organizational commitment among employees and promoting from within. Both these practices are consistent with an investment in firm-specific skills. However, if a firm is a prospector organization with a continually shifting and evolving product-market arena, the return on any investment in firm- or industry-specific skills will be short lived. Analyzer firms may reap long-term benefits from firm- or industry-specific skills that aid in maintaining internal balance or managing complex coordination across business activities. Analyzer firms may also receive a long-term pay-out from investment in firm- or industry-specific skills related to widely shared technologies.

Step 5a: Assess the Compatibility of the Planning and Investment Horizon. A final analytic step involves a firm's strategic choice regarding its desired position on the fit-flexibility continuum. For example, defender firms typically rely on fit. In contrast, prospector organizations depend on flexibility. Analyzer firms are generally positioned somewhere in the middle ranges of the continuum.

As mentioned previously, industry conditions play a significant role in the time horizon for goal planning. If an industry or a product is just entering a particular evolutionary phase, the time period for planning is generally longer than when a transition period is on the horizon. If rivalry is not particularly intense—and most industry participants are content to rely on positioning strategies rather than influencing the balance of factors governing industry structure—the planning horizon is generally longer than if participants are aggressive and active in shaping their industry. If innovation is a key competence among most participants in an industry, change is much more likely. If the majority of dominant firms in an industry compete on a cost-leadership basis, a longer planning horizon can often be anticipated.

If goals represent a long-term commitment and if strategic conditions support a long-term planning horizon, greater investments in achieving organizational readiness are warranted. Under these conditions, investments that move an organization toward greater fit are desirable. On the other hand, if goals are temporary, or if the firm's strategic direction or industry conditions are likely to change, large investments in fit are unwise. For example, it may be shrewd to invest in developing capabilities for dealing with a consolidation in the supplier industry or a major technological shift if the industry structure is fundamentally attractive. This is particularly likely if the firm is in a favorable competitive position. In contrast, investing in skills designed to deal with a temporary shortage of skilled technicians or distribution problems resulting from a labor strike is likely to be wasteful.

As a consequence, it is clear that a firm's map of its task environment is a crucial element in effective strategic human resource management. If an organization does not have an accurate vision of its competitive environment, it is likely to misread or neglect important market signals. If a firm is overly optimistic, it is more likely to assume a longer planning horizon and time period for return on investment than will be available. If a firm is overly pessimistic, worthwhile investments are likely to be shortchanged, and a number of competitive opportunities may be missed.

An organization's speed and effectiveness at implementing proposed changes should also be considered. If a firm has a history of good results, changes resulting from investments are less likely to be resisted. If modified knowledge, skills, abilities, and expectations are considered normal in an organization, employees are more likely to advocate and facilitate investments in improving organizational readiness. If current power co-alitions are likely to lose organizational influence as a result of improved organizational readiness, the speed and effectiveness associated with learning and implementing new skills will be slower than if current power coalitions are expected to benefit from the investment.

Step 5b: Assess the Compatibility of the Demand and Investment Ho-rizons. Resources abundance or scarcity also influences an organization's efficiency and effectiveness in gaining the benefits of investments in hu-man resources. If organizational finances, time, information, or other resources are scarce, if employees are feeling overworked and over-whelmed, new investments are more likely to be viewed with skepticism than enthusiasm. If, on the other hand, there is a surplus of time, financial support, and energy, investment decisions may be seen as attractive, even if expected human capital or competitive returns are low.

These five analytic steps are a template for strategic human resource management under development conditions. Once a firm has determined the cause of poor organizational readiness, assessed the reasonableness of corporate growth expectations, evaluated the interactive implications associated with investing in a particular business, determined the potential for long-term investment effectiveness, and considered appropriate place-ment on a fit-flexibility continuum, it is ready for strategy formulation. At this point, the firm can decide whether it is strategically better to invest in its human resources to improve implementation feasibility, to change corporate goals to reflect the lack of organizational readiness, or to keep the existing goals, while changing the means by which they are to be achieved. In the development quadrant, the primary strategic human re-source issue is strategic direction.

QUADRANT 2: EXPANSION

The expansion quadrant is characterized by high growth expectations and indications of good organizational readiness in strategy and skills. In this sense, expansion conditions suggest a tight fit between strategic aims and current internal structure and human resource practices.

High growth and strong organizational readiness often apply to firms in established competitive positions in the mainstream of a growth in-dustry, for example, Mobile Communication Corporation's position in the telecommunications industry or Target Stores position in the retail in-dustry. Similar conditions could also apply to firms setting new standards of performance in mature industries, for example, Illinois Tool Works' rapidly increasing sales position in general manufacturing.

High growth expectations and high levels of organizational readiness are also present in firms that have established strong competitive positions in attractive market niches. This situation can occur even in mature industry settings and is therefore unlikely to suggest high growth for the majority of industry participants. For example, while zoos are not generally considered part of a growth industry, aquariums are seeing rapid growth opportunities in a number of major metropolitan areas.

High growth expectations can also emerge from a firm's decision to rapidly expand its product-market variety or scope. Firms, such as prospector organizations, may be in a continuous state of high growth and high readiness if they select their acquisitions to capitalize on synergistic organizational competencies. Firms in low-growth industries can also expand their product-market scope to exploit a significant distinct competence. Kaman Corporation offers a particularly creative example of this approach to expansion. Kaman is a market leader in helicopter design and manufacturing. One of the distinct competencies contributing to their strong competitive position is their technology expertise in dampening the "bad vibrations" often associated with helicopter rotors. Kaman capitalized on this expertise in vibration technology and applied it to the music industry. Its ability to dampen destructive vibrations in helicopters enables them to accentuate the "good vibrations" in acoustical guitars, opening doors to new growth opportunities that they were uniquely ready to exploit.

CHOICES FOR BUSINESSES IN THE EXPANSION QUADRANT

Under any of these circumstances, the first-order question for firms in the expansion quadrant involves resource allocation. It is widely recognized that sustained rapid growth offers both benefits and liabilities for an organization. The resource allocation issue confronting strategic human resource managers with businesses in the development quadrant surrounds this cost-benefit issue. What proportion of resources derived from competitive success should be devoted to achieving continued growth? Continued high growth generally requires continued high investment in identifying, hiring, training, socializing, and rewarding employees. What proportion of the resources generated by successful growth should be channeled into managing the effects of growth? Investment relating to managing the effects of growth can include updating planning systems, managing expanded information needs, socializing new employees, and developing linking roles to provide for increasingly complex interactions across related functional activities.

Under conditions of high growth and strong fit the first-order choice is not among a number of competing options, as we found in the development quadrant. Rather, the primary choice for businesses in the expansion quadrant is determining a desirable placement along a continuum ranging from maximizing growth at one extreme to maximizing other organizational objectives at the other. A continuum implies a generally compensatory trade-off between growth and other interests. Increased growth is generally achieved at the expense of increased strain on other organizational objectives. Profit, flexibility, and quality of working life are particularly vulnerable. A decision to devote resources to managing organizational systems or to sharing the benefits of successful growth with a large group of stakeholders may undermine the future competitive position of the business.

Understanding the Choice Situation

Resolving the positioning dilemma depends on a number of related factors. First, the level and relative proportion of human resource investments required to maintain the current position should be assessed, meaning that investments needed to sustain desired growth and maintain continued organizational readiness must be considered. Is it necessary to continue to develop new talents and skills among current and new employees? If so, a large proportion of available resources is likely to be required. Is it only necessary to maintain the current level of proficiency among existing employees? Under this latter situation, the choice between continued growth and a well-managed infrastructure is more concerned with incremental trade-offs than with absolute choices. This question of required investment level and proportion concerns the absolute costs of continued growth.

Second, the relationship between profitability and continued growth needs to be examined. This issue concerns the relative cost of growth. With respect to profitability, the cost of growth may be short term or long term. In some cases, for example, profitability may be quite low initially, while growth is being achieved. However, once a dominant position is established for the business or product line, growth can be maintained without substantial investment, thus allowing profitability to soar. This scenario is particularly common in industries or products dominated by experience curve effects. If a firm has successfully exploited the cost reductions accompanying increased experience, it will likely have a steep cost reduction slope compared to competitors. If the firm has adopted a strategically wise pricing strategy, demand for its product has likely been high. High demand leads to an accelerated accumulated volume of production and to a corresponding rapid descent along the cost reduction curve.

Suppose, for example, exploitation of experience curve phenomena allowed a skateboard manufacturer to achieve substantially lower per-unit costs than the majority of its competitors. If the manufacturer offers the product at a price only a small margin above its initial costs, the initial profitability may be fairly modest. However, as production costs decline on a per-unit basis, a price umbrella can be created if the manufacturer holds the consumer price relatively steady. This price umbrella offers an extremely attractive profit opportunity. The competitive position of the firm is also somewhat protected. If competition becomes intense and other organizations appear likely to erode market share, the low-cost producer can lower market prices to reflect its low-cost position. Such a price reduction generally drives many smaller competitors out of the marketplace, opening the opportunity for a price umbrella to emerge again, albeit at a somewhat lower level.

In other competitive situations, rapid growth requires continuous investment. In high-technology firms, for example, high levels of growth can be sustained only by continuous innovation. Product, process, and managerial innovations each demand accompanying investments in human resources to maintain a strong competitive position. If such investments are not made, a business would soon find itself in the development quadrant situation having high growth expectation but little organizational readiness with which to attain those goals. In this latter instance, a firm must choose between the benefits and costs of continued growth and that of smaller potential size but perhaps larger potential profit margins.

Finally, other performance measures important to a firm should be considered relative to growth. These other interests include performance capabilities that lead to sustained competitive advantage. Examples of this type of objective include promoting market experimentation and maintaining organizational adaptability, high product diversity, and efficient and coordinated linkages among all organizational activities.

Other competing performance measures relate more to quality of work life issues. Examples include fostering employee satisfaction, maintaining opportunities for job rotation, providing flexible time options rather than requiring overtime work, and providing for self-managed teams. Choices regarding organizational structure can also compete with growth objectives. An ability to facilitate collaboration or control among all hierarchical levels or product areas may introduce important size limitations.

The importance of sustaining a strong corporate culture should also be considered. Cultural maintenance usually requires socialization. Socialization, mentoring, and maintenance of organizational myths take resources and human resource management investments. It is not unusual for this latter type of objective to be neglected as a firm concentrates on rapid growth.

Frequently there is not only a trade-off between growth and profits, but between growth and the development of a firm's infrastructure processes and systems. At a minimum, growth erodes organizational and individual slack, and sustained growth over a long period of time virtually eliminates resource cushions. This type of trade-off frequently puts a ceiling on the time horizon for effective growth. Consider the situation faced by a successful restaurant entrepreneur. The business originally had a single location. Food quality was high, service was outstanding, and the relaxing atmosphere encouraged customers to return frequently. The restaurant was also highly profitable. Encouraged by this initial success, the entrepreneur decided to seek additional investment capital and to add six additional locations across the state. Investors were quickly identified and the new operations soon opened.

Unfortunately, growth prospects considerably outweighed infrastructure considerations in the resource allocation process. The entrepreneur now found himself constantly on the road, solving problems in first one location and then in another. Different standard operating procedures emerged in the various locations, reflecting the different preferences and styles of their operating managers. Food quality became less reliable, service was often sloppy, and the atmosphere became hurried and considerably less congenial. The infrastructure was unable to keep pace with growth and the entire chain soon faced bankruptcy. Clearly, choosing between investment in growth versus investment in the essential ingredients needed to maintain the organization not only affects the time horizon for growth but often influences the organization's competitive position.

Contextual Issues

These important resource allocation choices and issues cannot be examined in a vacuum. Again, organization culture and the competitive need for firm- and industry-specific skills play a crucial role in evaluating these issues. Organization culture places both demands and limits on organization processes.[9] Some cultures facilitate growth. To the extent that activities are standardized with common expectations across all organizational units, growth is easier to accomplish. Likewise, if most of the information a firm must contend with is fairly routine, easily understood, and simple to communicate, growth is facilitated. A large proportion of self-contained tasks enable growth to be accomplished more easily. Perhaps most important, cultural uniformity across all of an organization's units and activities is an essential ingredient for achieving growth with little organizational strain. Military organizations, for example, can expand rapidly without substantial changes in organization systems. This is because the culture is relatively uniform and relies heavily on standardization, division of labor, hierarchy, and socialization to coordinate and control activities. This kind of organization can devote a large proportion of its resources to achieving growth, since organizational processes require little innovation or adjustment.

In other firms, the culture may make growth more difficult to achieve.

Firms like Cray Computer, for example, have a culture that presumes individuality and idiosyncratic behavior. As the firm expands, organization processes are expected to change to reflect the unique personalities and skills of new members. In this type of firm, more resources must be allocated to managing the effects of growth. When a culture supports diversity, growth entails an increase in variety, interdependence, and variability, as well as size expansion. Under these circumstances, innovation and increasing diversity are also expected in the organization systems needed to accommodate expansion.

Culture is not the only factor with a facilitative or an inhibitory effect on a firm's expansion capabilities. A high need for firm-specific skills, as for fighter pilots in the armed forces or industry-specific skills, such as skill at negotiating commercial contracts among aircraft manufacturers, affects both the cost and ease of growth. High levels of firm- and industry-specific skill requirements make a given level of growth more expensive to achieve, leaving fewer resources available for managing the effects of growth. Firm- and industry-specific skills also make it more expensive, as well as more difficult, to manage cyclical growth. If an organization staffs its manufacturing operations for peak demand, human resources may go unused during slow periods. If, on the other hand, a firm maintains only the human resources required for production at typical demand rates, additional requirements are placed on human resource management activities. To maintain a viable competitive position, human resource management practices must be developed to accommodate backlogs at certain times and excess capacity at others. While high levels of firm- and industry-specific skills may be costly from some perspectives, the probability of sustained high performance during sustained rapid growth can improve because of greater human resource expertise and reduced training time.

A reliance on more generalizable skills increases mobility among the work force and reduces the need for training time and development expenses, but only for firm nonspecific skills. Training can occur in other organizations or in educational institutions rather than within the organization to the extent that knowledge, skills, and abilities are general. As a result, a wide variation in growth patterns is more easily accommodated if the majority of the human resource capabilities needed for competitive advantage are firm nonspecific and readily available in the labor market. However, lower levels of firm- and industry-specific skills can be a disadvantage if rapid growth is sustained over a long period or if the market environment is extremely competitive.

Sustained growth places heavy demands on a firm's human resources. Reliance on skills that are useful in many firms and industries increases the mobility of an organization's human resource pool. The stress that accompanies continued rapid growth may lead to high levels of turnover if there are inadequate financial or nonmonetary rewards. Providing sufficient incentives to stay with an organization undergoing sustained growth raises the cost of growth.

If the market environment is extremely competitive, problems with human resource raiding may arise. Employees may find that they are highly mobile and that the value they receive for their personal investment in human capital increases if they exploit their mobility. It is not unusual for an organization to provide employees with compensation packages that are internally equitable but that cannot compete with escalating market rates for those same skills. Design engineers, for example, may receive a 10 percent raise if they stay with a particular organization but an 18 percent increase if they are willing to change firms. Some firms overcome this by linking rewards to tenure as well as performance, thereby increasing the costs of turnover to the employee. The more generalizable competitive human resource skills are, the more expensive they may be for an organization to retain. When viewed from this perspective, firm- and industry-specific skills must be assessed in a way that compares development expenses against retention costs.

The issue of fit versus flexibility is also important for making an effective strategic choice regarding desirable placement on a growth versus alternative objective continuum. High growth and strong organizational readiness are conducive to a focus on maximal fit. This fit relationship is supported by human resource planners. A strong match approach is also supported by those who recommend responsiveness to organizational and environmental contingencies. One price of a tight fit is an increased likelihood of means-ends goal reversal.[10] Many firms identify a number of specific behaviors important to achieving high levels of growth. Willingness to work long hours, healthy environmental scanning abilities, and high levels of autonomy are frequently cited examples. These behaviors are then monitored and rewarded from the financial gains resulting from successful growth. Promotion and increased job enrichment opportunities are also readily available incentives under conditions of high growth.

This process is a dual-edged sword, however. While good fit among knowledge, skills, abilities, and growth objectives may make growth easier to achieve, it also makes continued growth the primary means to achieve organizational rewards. However, employee expectations for higher earnings may remain long after the rapid growth period has transpired. Thus, continued growth is likely to become the principal means to achieve financial and status benefits. This reliance upon growth is likely to be maintained even if continued growth is no longer cost effective within the industry setting.

This is one problem with many profit sharing plans. During periods of high growth, employee expectations are raised for higher compensation. As growth declines, profits also may decline, leaving less to share with employees. Sambo's restaurants experienced this problem with their "fraction of the action plan," whereby franchise owners participated in the rewards of expansion. The result was near bankruptcy and corporate takeover.

It is important to keep in mind that, by itself, large organizational size is not always linked with a desirable competitive position. When economies of scale are present, size can be a means to achieve a competitive cost advantage. When brand loyalty has a strong influence on buying behavior, large size can enhance name recognition and lead to related promotional benefits. When broad geographic coverage leads to improved service opportunities, as with airline companies and automobile sales and service operations, size can offer a competitive advantage. If a product purchased because of its exclusivity becomes widely available, size can lead to a competitive disadvantage. If economies in production are related to scope rather than scale, size offers little in the way of a competitive edge. If the increase in sales volume does not compensate for the lower profit margin accepted for a standardized product, size may offer few advantages.

Similarly, expanded diversity and additional variability in product-market scope are not always advantageous. When maximal flexibility is necessary to respond to rapidly changing technologies, a somewhat limited scope may make both market scanning and organizational change easier. When limited diversity is necessary to maintain a strong corporate culture, too extensive a product or market blanket can raise problems. When a highly sophisticated skill base is the key to competitive advantage, continuous revisions in product-market scope can seriously hinder the necessary specialization. Strategic human resource management decisions should reflect the connection between large size or wide diversity among product and market arenas and competitive position. This must be assessed not only for the organization as a whole, but within each strategic business unit's particular industry or business setting.

If increased market share or a wide array of different product and market entrys does not make a substantial and sustainable contribution to desirable competitive outcomes, then high growth goals need to be continually evaluated. Left unchecked across the planning horizon, high growth expectations are unlikely to lead to appropriate human resource or strategic decisions.

Suggested Analytic Steps

Step 1a: Conduct an Industry Analysis to Determine an Appropriate Planning Time Horizon. A number of specific analytic steps contribute to sound resource allocation decisions. First, as was discussed for the development quadrant analysis, relevant trends in product, organization, and industry life cycles need to be identified. An industry's competitive structure reflects the rivalry among existing competitors, the relative bargaining power of buyers and suppliers, the threat from potential substitute products or services, and the threat of new entrants. Each of these factors needs to be evaluated for strategic business units falling into the expansion quadrant. Events expected to accelerate or slow down industry evolution should also be identified and analyzed.

A thorough assessment of industrywide conditions provides information regarding two important issues. One critical question is the relevant planning horizon. Is growth expected to continue for a long period of time? Will growth patterns for the industry be smooth or will they follow a scalloped pattern or an S curve? Will all industry segments grow at a similar rate? Or will there, on the other hand, be uneven pressures that change the competitive playing field and alter the shape of the industry structure?

Step 1b: Conduct an Industry Analysis to Predict the Resource Base Available for Allocation. Expected profitability, at least for the industry as a whole, can also be predicted from an analysis of industry structure. Profit projections are particularly important within the expansion quadrant, since the fundamental question concerns resource allocation. Accurate predictions of the amount and time frame for returns provide a baseline estimate of the resources available for allocation. In many cases the resources allocation choice is governed by certain threshhold considerations. There may be a minimal investment level essential to maintain a viable competitive position. If, for example, new generation products are offered every eight to fifteen months, a firm must have the resources necessary to conduct sufficient research and development to offer new product entrants at this rate. If not, growth prospects are short term at best, and an end-game rather than an investment strategy needs to be considered.

Planning horizons and profitability can be predicted from an assessment of the industry's structure. If suppliers and buyers have relatively low levels of influence over the way in which participants of an industry operate, profitability is likely to be higher than if buyers and suppliers have a great deal of bargaining power. Resources spent on maintaining industry barriers to entry or on rebuffing potential new entrants diminishes profits for industry participants. If substitute products or services offer comparable features, lower prices must be maintained by industry participants than if substitutes are clearly inferior in terms of important performance characteristics.

An understanding of the forces that structure competition in an industry allow a firm to assess whether its current level of profitability is equal to, better than, or lower than competitors. If the current performance of the firm is much higher than comparable businesses, a firm may be better positioned than competitors to both maintain growth and accommodate the effects of growth. Being able to address these dual concerns provides the seeds of a long-term competitive advantage. In this way, industry analysis, along with an evaluation of hiring and training needs, capacity expansion requirements, and so forth, allows a firm to assess the direct costs and benefits of achieving growth.

Step 2a: Identify the Direct Costs of Sustained Growth. A second important analytic step is measuring the costs of sustained growth. Some of the most important direct costs surround an ability to continually recruit, hire, train, and integrate new employees into an active organizational environment. The costs associated with asking current employees to work more hours versus the costs of bringing new employees up to production standards should be evaluated.

Sustained growth is often accompanied by a reassessment of production processes. If the choice is made to automate manufacturing procedures or otherwise change production processes, direct costs of growth may also include the retraining or outplacing of current employees. As would be predicted, previous choices regarding firm and industry-specific skills development play an important role in determining these costs.

Step 2b: Identify the Indirect Costs of Sustained Growth. A firm should also identify the indirect costs of achieving continued growth. Among the most important of the indirect costs is a consideration of fit versus flexibility. As the need for firm or unit-specific skills increases, personal power of successful employees also increases. Since this power is contingent on maintaining existing organization conditions, there is a strong incentive to resist change.[11] To further increase the probability that any change will be resisted, the mobility of these employees is reduced by the extent to which their skills are firm-specific. Resistance to change coupled with organization clout and few alternatives can make a firm uncompetitive as environmental conditions change. Coupling organizational rewards with continued growth further limits a firm's options.

If continued rapid growth can be accomplished only by a substantial investment in firm-specific skills, a firm may incur indirect costs that will surface only when continued growth is no longer feasible. It is important to recognize that not only will growth expectations need to be revised, the ability of the firm to shift its competitive center of gravity may be seriously compromised. Misfit between organizational expectations and environmental conditions may be undetected for an extended period of time because recognition signals severe personal as well as organizational disruption. This presents the classic dilemma where the price of a currently strong competitive position is an inability to meet future competitive conditions.

Step 3a: Identify the Internal Process-related Costs of Managing Growth. The third essential set of analytic activities necessary for effective strategic human resource management in the expansion quadrant surrounds identification of the costs associated with managing growth. Expansion either in size or complexity requires a new look at the value chain. Increased size may increase the need for interaction and integration among some functional activities and provide a rationale for creating self-contained work units for others. Increased volume, for example, may offer opportunities for developing economies of scale in manufacturing, advertising, procurement, distribution, or any other primary activities. Capitalizing on these potential economies often requires changes in job descriptions, communication patterns, performance expectations and compensation systems.

Step 3b: Identify the Externally Derived Costs of Managing Growth. Expansion often leads to more links with external organizational or government agencies. Many regulations, Equal Employment Opportunity legislation or certain reporting requirements, for example, apply only to organizations that exceed a specified size. Some regulations, interstate commerce, environmental protection, and recycling for example, vary with geographic boundaries. Some opportunities, such as small business loans, are only available to firms under a specified revenue base. It is critical to recognize that expansion can generate both threats and opportunities. Growth can lead to new organizational strengths and can also unearth new organizational weaknesses.

Step 3c: Identify the Organizational Structure-related Costs of Managing Growth. At this point, a firm should identify specific organizational structure and process changes that need to accompany growth in size or diversity. Chandler illustrates the difficulty of accepting the need for structural change to accommodate new organizational activities.[12] His research demonstrates that most firms only incorporate the necessary structural changes after the negative economic consequences of neglecting the need for changing organizational configurations and managerial processes in response to strategic shifts are felt.

A particularly important aspect of Chandler's contribution is the recognition that product-market diversity and size have an important structural impact. With increased diversity comes increased complexity and volume. With increased complexity comes a need for decentralization and greater specialization. Consequently, the direct human resource management implications of a change in size and product-market scope include needed changes in job analysis, information processing requirements, decision-making systems, compensation systems, and shifts in the knowledge, skills, and ability requirements at all hierarchical levels.

Galbraith and Kazanjian identify the structural changes often accompanying expansion.[13] An entrepreneurial firm generally relies on a simple structure. According to Mintzberg, simple structures are characterized by informal communication patterns and very little formal planning or coordination.[14] The primary objectives for these organizations are generating ideas and gathering resources. Much of the organization's power rests with being the prime mover. Since financial resources are often scarce, human resources are often expected to compensate for a lack of funding. All resources must be efficiently and effectively used.

As a firm grows in size, perhaps increasing volume or adding elements of vertical integration, a functional structure is generally considered more appropriate. Functional structures offer the advantages of efficiency through specialization, enabling employees to develop some measure of functional expertise. Operating decisions are generally delegated, increasing information-processing requirements at all hierarchical levels. Centralized control is generally maintained in functional structures, facilitated by extensive rules, processes, and standard operating procedures. The disadvantages of a functional structure should also be noted. Narrow specialization can lead to increased organizational conflict and rivalry among different functional units, which can hamper internal mobility of employees as much as their specialized expertise. Line and staff conflicts often emerge in functional organizations, particularly as diversification considerations begin to emerge.

As a firm begins to engage in product development, market development, or any form of concentric diversification, a divisional structure is called for. Diversification means that the firm faces an increased need for structural differentiation to respond to diverse product and market conditions. Interdependence among organizational units often remains high to exploit opportunities for shared economies and other avenues of synergy. The increased volume of activities increases the number of nonroutine decisions to be made. In combination, these factors mean that as a firm diversifies its product line, organizational complexity increases dramatically.

This increase in complexity leads to the need for a divisional structure, which forces decision making and organizational power to appropriately decentralized levels to enable more rapid responses to environmental conditions. The differences in the role responsibilities across hierarchical levels become more distinct. Accountability for performance is sharply increased, raising job analysis, job evaluation, and compensation issues for the strategic human resource manager.

Divisional structures also create some new problems. There is clearly the potential for policy and practice differences across divisional units. In addition, dysfunctional conflict for organizational resources is a common problem. Synergy may suffer from divisional boundaries. The disadvantages of unit-specific skills are augmented, but the advantages associated with firm-specific skills are enhanced.

As a firm further expands its product and market horizons, a strategic business unit (SBU) structural form is often adopted. An SBU approach to organizing relies on elements of both divisional and functional structural forms. It is important to note, however, that these are not the only choices or patterns available. If a firm elects a growth strategy of conglomerate, or unrelated, diversification, a holding company structure is more appropriate than a divisional form. A holding company form maintains independence among profit centers and allows a firm to develop self-contained tasks as a means to manage increased complexity. A diversified firm that increases relatedness across its product lines in order to exploit economies of scale may adopt a centralized functional organizational structure. The important issue for strategic human resource managers is that each structural form carries with it a characteristic set of expectations, advantages, and limitations for a firm's human resources. Structure creates one of the most direct links between a firm's strategic direction choices and its strategic human resource management options.

Often, while firms are growing most successfully, the seeds for future problems are being sowed if organization design does not keep pace with organization accomplishments. PC&D Incorporated had an extremely successful machinery division in the mid–1970s. The board of directors decided that the profitability of this operation was being wasted and so encouraged the acquisition of an electronics firm destined to provide future growth opportunities for the corporation. Unfortunately, the resulting resource investments were so enthusiastically directed toward growth that they undermined the sources of competitive advantages that had made the machinery division a dominant market leader.

This created two sets of strategic human resource management problems. The machinery division was in danger of losing the best of its human resources since it could no longer keep pace with the competition. The electronics division developed a corporate culture that concentrated on growth opportunities to the exclusion of all other performance measures. Both human and financial resources were assumed to be unlimited, and, as a consequence, human and financial resources were wasted. This philosophy undermined the source of competitive advantage in the electronics division. It required a comprehensive reassessment and turnaround strategy to institute an appropriate level of balance once the effects of these growth strategies were recognized.

Step 4a: Identify the Direct Benefits of Sustained Growth. In the fourth step in the analysis process, the value of continued high growth needs to be assessed. In order to make a responsible resource allocation decision, the costs of achieving and maintaining growth should be compared with the expected revenues and competitive advantages. In other words, a formal cost-benefit analysis should be undertaken. Reciprocity between human resource management and competitive strategy is one important consideration in this process. If employees have the necessary skills and abilities, it is not unusual for growth to be competitively feasible yet have little payoff due to the implementation costs of maintaining and nurturing an overworked and overstressed work force. Nor is it unusual for growth expectations that are an outgrowth of prior human resource policies to become competitively undesirable.

Based on the first three analytic steps, a comprehensive cost-benefit analysis can be constructed. As noted the direct and indirect costs of achieving and maintaining growth should be included. Selection, hiring, and training costs are principle examples of direct costs. Indirect costs include individual stress, underdeveloped or undermaintained organizational systems (e.g., management information systems, control systems, personnel policies), increased uncertainty, and increased risk.

Direct and indirect benefits should also be considered. One of the most important potential direct benefits is an improved competitive position. If gains in size lead to improved economies of scale, increased experience curve effects, or increased power relative to buyers and suppliers, an enhanced competitive position may result. Increased diversity may yield a better risk position or opportunities to achieve economies of scope. Diversity and size can also offer avenues to maintain a corporate culture based on reciprocal commitment between employees and the firm. In some industries or competitive situations, growth can promote a reputation as a market leader, which may offer new opportunities to shape the competitive environment. Additional revenues are a common growth-related expectation.

Step 4b: Identify the Indirect Benefits of Sustained Growth. Indirect benefits associated with continued growth may include a more committed and motivated work force, reflecting the enhanced opportunities that may be available for personal development. Growth can also generate a more pervasive sense of the importance or viability of an organization's mission, leading to an increase in shared values among employees and a greater sense of organizational involvement.

Step 4c: Identify the Primary Beneficiaries and Losers Associated with Sustained Growth. Specific stakeholders should also be identified and their relative benefit and cost positions examined. It may be, for example, that organizational shareholders are the dominant beneficiaries of continued expansion, while employees bear the primary cost burden. A firm that chooses to expand its product line by moving its manufacturing operations overseas is often cited as an example of this cost-benefit relationship. In other situations costs and benefits may be more evenly distributed. Short-term reductions in dividends to finance growth may yield long-term value increases for shareholders, for example. At the same time, employees may experience incremental stress or uncertainty but be rewarded with long-term employment security and an increasing resource pie.

However in any strategic human resource management cost-benefit assessment, the equity implications must be assessed. In many firms, corporate culture plays an important role in prioritizing the interests of various stakeholders. This does not mean that employees are always at the head of the line, however. In other firms, reconciling diverse interests is more a political process. In still other firms a concern with equality of effect overrides other considerations. Regardless of the specific stakeholders position, it is important for a firm to identify the expected consequences of various alternatives and, further, to identify the parties to whom those consequences will occur. Finally the advantages and disadvantages of these consequences for particular stakeholders must be reconciled with the corporate culture and value system.

If there is a resulting deficit in the cost benefit equation, a reassessment of goals and the means to achieve growth is in order. This situation is similar to the choices faced in the development quadrant. The difference is that in Quadrant 1 a firm has low organizational readiness in terms of growth, whereas, in the expansion quadrant situation, growth is determined to have lower desirability than initially believed. If costs outweigh expected benefits, or if the cost-benefit pattern is judged inequitable by a firm's management, strategy reformulation is in order.

If a surplus results, an appropriate allocation strategy for these resources is needed. For example, if a growth pattern is expected to be long term and in a relatively stable environment, it may be expected to yield high return on investment and a more secure competitive position. In this situation, resources might be appropriately allocated to managing the personal as well as organizational stress of continued expansion and elevated performance expectation. Continually being asked to do "just a little bit more" takes its toll on the human resources of a firm. It is challenging but also frequently exhausting to be expected to continually exceed past performance. Employees of a firm in stable growth are often less pressured but, some would argue, less motivated than employees in growth-oriented firms.

If long term growth under changing marketplace conditions is expected, resources might be appropriately allocated to research and development or training in an effort to anticipate competitive trends. Marketplace variability must generally be matched by flexibility in the organization. This highlights a firm's desirable position in the fit versus flexibility continuum. In addition, as expectations of continued variability and unpredictability increase, control systems are often given greater weight than planning systems.

What happens when managers attempt to implement a detailed, well-formulated plan of action in a business unit in which events do not follow a smooth, predictable, and well-established pattern?[15] Results are generally not desirable. The root of the problem is not necessarily poor planning or management. Rather, there is a mismatch between the conditions necessary for accurate model building, which is the first step in the planning process, and the circumstances inherent in the strategic situation. The uncertain nature of the tasks to be accomplished and uncertainty surrounding the processes used to accomplish objectives and the precise outcomes that are desirable severely restrict planning effectiveness. Therefore, even with a long planning horizon, the strategic situation may not be amenable to planning approaches.

If growth is expected to be short term, resources might most appropriately be allocated to preparing for organizational transition. With a short-term, one-time need for growth and change, massive shifts are often preferable to incremental changes in strategy and human resource practices. The comprehensive overhaul approach causes greater organizational trauma during the transition, but it allows a firm to maintain a high level of fit between strategy and human resource management both before and after the change.

These four steps provide guidelines for strategic human resource management under expansion conditions. The choice for Quadrant 2 firms is to determine an acceptable position along a resource allocation continuum, which ranges from a situation in which all resources are channeled into achieving growth to one in which all resources are devoted to managing the effects of prior growth. A position somewhere in the middle range is desirable for most firms.

However, it is particularly important to make the choice explicit. Not only does a deliberate choice enable a firm's management to anticipate the types of problems and challenges they are likely to confront in the future, intentional selection of a resource allocation strategy forces explicit consideration of both human resource concerns and strategic interests prior to resource disbursement. It is less likely that the consequences of either neglecting to invest resources toward maintaining organizational stability and slack or reducing the emphasis on continued expansion will come as a surprise to organizational members.

QUADRANT 3: PRODUCTIVITY

The productivity quadrant is characterized by low growth expectations and strong organizational readiness for strategy implementation. These circumstances typically occur when a firm has established a dominant and highly profitable position in a maturing industry or stable industry segment. It is important to recognize that large size is not a requirement for competitive strength. For example, the position established by Mercedes Benz in the automobile industry reflects a very low market share. In contrast, Safeway occupies an equally dominant position in the grocery industry, and is among the largest competitors.

Choices for Businesses in the Productivity Quadrant

If a firm has an established competitive advantage and is not trying to expand rapidly, operations are usually highly effective and efficient. There is less concern with establishing a position, as in the development stages, or with extending the market, as in the expansion stage. Rather, the key question is how to effectively channel the results of productive activities so that they continue to enhance the organization's competitive position. Firms and strategic business units in the development quadrant are highly profitable, and neither financial nor human resources should be wasted. Stated differently, the basic choice is where to channel resources and efforts that are no longer required simply to maintain growth objectives.

There are often several attractive alternatives for channeling productivity returns. One option reflects forecasts of significant changes in the competitive environment. With this option, investment activities can be focused on preparing for anticipated changes in the industry or competitive situation. Under this first alternative, the business unit makes a strategic human resource reinvestment in itself to sustain the competitive position over a longer term future than would otherwise be available.

There are a number of circumstances that would make this first option particularly attractive. If an industry appears to be at the cusp of a transition from one evolutionary stage to another, a need for change is likely. If the firm is in the process of shifting its domain orientation or its product-market scope, change is likely. If a firm has adopted a portfolio approach to managing diversified businesses, it is not unusual for the role of a particular business to change once it has established a secure competitive position and growth is no longer required. As outlined in Chapter 2, these conditions typically signal a shift from cash user to cash generator in a portfolio-managed firm. If a firm has adopted a prospector domain stance, a firm in a low growth but high organizational readiness position might offer an attractive divestment option.

As a second alternative, resources can be invested in related or unrelated businesses in the portfolio. This option is particularly common in firms that have undertaken concentric diversification approaches. With related diversification, firms are more likely to manage businesses as parts of an interdependent portfolio rather than as independent operations. While traditional portfolio views concentrate on the financial resource sharing among a portfolio of businesses, we believe that the sharing of human resource skills and abilities from one business to another offers equally significant strategic benefits.

This option is particularly attractive if start-up operations or businesses in rapid growth situations rely on similar knowledge, skills, and abilities as the strategic business in the productivity quadrant. Such similarity can arise because of common technological skill requirements, parallel marketing channels, related information-processing or decision-making situations, or any of a number of other sources of intradivisional relatedness. Important similarities can also arise if a firm has invested heavily in developing firm-specific skills. In either case, human resource capabilities viewed as slack for a business unit in the productivity quadrant may hold the key to developing or maintaining a competitive advantage for business units in the development or expansion quadrants.

As a third alternative, a business unit can elect to direct its resources toward improving its current competitive position. At times, business units that are strong competitively but offer few growth opportunities for the future are neglected and allowed to slide into a less desirable market position. If the current competitive position is threatened by new entrants into the industry or increasingly attractive substitute products, an investment in rebuilding a strong competitive advantage may be appropriate. Reinvestment directed toward revitalization is particularly attractive if the long-term outlook for the business unit and the marketplace are strong. Major television networks, such as ABC, NBC, and CBS, exhibit this human resource management strategy. Each of these networks continues an escalating investment in its human resource capital despite low growth prospects. To forgo such investments virtually guarantees competitive decline. Maintaining and upgrading the human resource capabilities available to the business unit increases the probability of a long and profitable future. This reinvestment focus includes using resources for improving socialization, mentoring, and developing succession plans in order to compensate for or correct perceived organizational weaknesses.

As a fourth alternative, a firm can begin plans to exit from the business. This may be the most beneficial option for the firm as a whole if substitute products are more likely to replace than compete with existing products. As noted in an earlier discussion, product substitution is generally an evolutionary process. End-game strategies need not be a plan for immediate exit.

Thinking in terms of early exit from a particular industry setting is an attractive option if there are other, substantially more attractive uses for the highly productive human capital that would be released as a consequence of exit. Exit during the productivity phase is generally considered only by organizations diversified into a number of different product-market areas. If a firm operates in a single product-market arena, premature exit is a major risk.

Under conditions of low growth and high productivity, a strategic planning focus predominates in that choices concern trade-offs between current actions and future options. Planning, as opposed to strategic control, is reasonable since low growth opportunities generally indicate increased information certainty and a slower rate of environmental change. High levels of expertise and experience also increase planning capabilities.

Strategic human resource choices made in the productivity quadrant often reflect a higher level of economic rationality than those made in any other quadrant. This heightened rationality in part reflects a perception that the stakes may be somewhat lower than in other quadrant situations. However, increased rationality may in part result because the information available is more complete, less ambiguous, and more likely to be familiar to organization decision makers.

Contextual Issues

As might be expected, concerns with fit versus flexibility become crucial. Undoubtedly, for business units in the productivity quadrant, some degree of fit has been already established. The decision issue becomes whether continued fit should be rewarded to increase profits and efficiency or whether the first steps toward organization change should be encouraged. A clear understanding of the strategic direction decisions of the organization are essential to evaluating the desired degree of fit.

The role a particular business plays in the overall corporate plan inevitably changes as the unit shifts from being a cash user to a cash generator. Clearly enhanced self-confidence and demonstrated competence accompany this kind of role shift. If diverse businesses are managed interdependently, the change in cash flow conditions will also affect other business units in the organization. Businesses accustomed to receiving human resource and other types of investments to aid their own competitive position may, over time, be expected to provide a return on this investment by making contributions to the growth and competitiveness of other units. If fit, rather than flexibility, has been emphasized, this shift in perspective presents a monumental challenge for the strategic human resource manager.

Unit-, firm and industry-specific skills also contribute to or inhibit organization transition. If businesses are related and firm-specific and industry-specific skills have been emphasized, an employee's future prospects may be uncertain, but the options are likely to appear more attractive and secure. If, on the other hand, other strategic business units are unrelated and unit-specific skills have been emphasized, transition is more threatening. Employees have a vested interest in maintaining a strong strategic posture for their business unit. This self-interest may persist even if it is suboptimal for the firm as a whole. Investment in firm-specific skills make other organizational units appear more comfortable and welcoming. Previous investments in industry-specific skills may lead to exit from the organization as prospects for the productivity unit become less challenging.

The organization's reward structure and compensation system play a major role in determining the ability and willingness of employees to change the nature of their strategic contributions. In some firms, high levels of growth, gains in market share, and development of new products receive the lion's share of organizational benefits. Is it surprising that for these organizations, employees in business units in the productivity quadrant are reluctant to forgo even meager growth opportunities to enable investment in other strategic business units?

Suggested Analytic Steps

Step 1a: Conduct an Industry Analysis to Assess the Sustainability of Competitive Advantage. Several analytic steps are useful for firms in the productivity quadrant. First, as with each of the other strategic human resource management situations, evaluating competitive trends helps determine a reasonable time horizon for planning. Sustainability of the current competitive advantage as the product and industry matures should be assessed. At this stage in the analytic process, the assessment of sustained competitive position should be based on the assumption that the business unit will only rely on existing distinct competencies. A comprehensive analysis should include an evaluation of the structural forces influencing industry attractiveness and the environmental trends likely to precipitate any transitions.

Step 1b: Conduct an Internal Analysis to Assess the Sustainability of Competitive Advantage. Any aspects of the value chain that have been neglected or underinvested should be examined. Do any of these neglected areas present a competitive time bomb waiting to explode and undermine the business unit's currently attractive position? It is particularly important to determine whether the current competitive position is viable with a flat level of investment. Coke's position in the soft drink industry can be maintained without major increases in advertising, research and development, or human capital investment. It should be recognized that it is not unusual to find that, even if a firm dominates a particular industry at one point in time, competitive position is dependent on escalating investments. Research and development investments are required to maintain a strong position in the computer industry. Human capital investments are generally required to accompany innovations in products, processes, or managerial systems.

Caterpillar provides an important example of a firm that lost its dominant position by failing to recognize market shifts and new competitive threats. Caterpillar's problems resulted in part from a failure to correctly position itself along the fit versus flexibility continuum. Caterpillar has a strong and internally maintained organization culture. Promotion is generally from within. While this strong culture provided a competitive advantage enabling Caterpillar to develop and manufacture high-quality products, it also promoted an excessively internal orientation among employees. Because their products were the best, Caterpillar managers began to assume they would always be in a dominant position. Because the primary sources of competitive advantage came from human resource management practices, Caterpillar managers neglected to explore their market environment. As a result, Caterpillar was manufacturing some of the best large-scale earth-moving equipment at a time when all market growth was directed toward small equipment sales. This was due to an extremely costly separation of strategic analysis and human resource management practice.

Step 1c: Assess the Extent to which the Sources of Competitive Advantage Can be Protected. An equally important question is whether or not the current competitive advantage is one that can be protected as well as sustained. Often, as industries or products mature, competitors become adept at copying product and marketing competencies of a successful participant. Threats can also come from powerful customers or suppliers of raw materials or component parts, as well as from industry participants. If a large-volume customer believes it is either financially or organizationally desirable to produce a firm's products itself, vertical integration is a real threat. Its potential reinforces the need for thorough analysis and understanding of the forces governing industry structure. An ability to predict the moves, not only of competitors but of businesses in related industries, may be an essential ingredient in successful strategic human resource management.

It should be noted that strategic human resource management practices are more difficult to imitate than product or distribution characteristics. This is because human resource management reflects a unique blend of corporate culture as well as corporate decisions. Even if another computer firm adopted exactly the same policies and practices as IBM, would their employees likely behave and think like IBM employees? Since competition often increases during low growth periods, mimicry and aggression also frequently increase. A wise investment in developing a source of competitive advantage that relies heavily on a firm's human resource competencies can offer some measure of protection. This is particularly true if the investment has been made in firm-specific and industry non-specific skills rather than industry-specific skills and abilities. Remember, however, that the cost of this tighter fit and reduced mobility may be an increased resistance to internal change.

Step 2: Conduct an Industry Analysis to Determine the Desirability of Maintaining the Current Competitive Position. Second, industry structure should be assessed to determine an appropriate planning horizon. As growth slows, supplier firms and buyer segments often undergo significant reconfiguration. It is important to monitor the direction as well as the rate of change. As noted earlier, vertical integration by buyers and suppliers is a possibility. Depending on the competitive conditions in their own industries, suppliers and buyers may consolidate or further increase their segmentation. This alters the external contingencies a firm must manage and can change the knowledge, skills, and abilities required of the human resources engaging in boundary-scanning activities.

Often, trends in contiguous industries can be accelerated or postponed by astute human resource management practices among dominant firms in an industry. Such influences can have a profound effect on potential profitability. If, for example, component parts suppliers consider mergers to increase their economies of scale as well as their relative influence, a firm purchasing a large proportion of these parts may wish to develop contracts that slow this consolidation process. If a high level of competition is retained in the supplier industry, the price of parts is more likely to remain low. This can provide an important ingredient in maintaining profitability among end-user manufacturers.

Substitute products often gain popularity while a firm focuses on efficiency. The comparability of potential substitutes may be underestimated, particularly by highly successful firms. In some situations the marketplace may become unattractive over time, regardless of competitive position. Increasing pressure from both buyers and suppliers, relatively low barriers to entry, and a continual barrage of potential substitutes can for many firms erode industry profits to unacceptable levels. The natural tendency is for management to be internally focused to increase profits, yet low-growth industries require extensive environmental analysis.

Step 3: Determine the Relevant Planning Horizon. Third, a time horizon for planning should be determined. Understanding the current strategy's viability and the industry's long-term attractiveness provides important parameters for allocating human and other resources. The information gathered in the first two steps of this analytic process provides the raw materials for this phase of analysis. The question, however, involves timing, not attractiveness or sustainabilty.

If the planning horizon is short, fit should be de-emphasized. With a short planning horizon, investment resources should be channeled to other units rather than reinvested in the productivity business. More importantly from a strategic perspective, the skills necessary for transition should be rewarded. This may contrast sharply with the existing reward and compensation system. With a short planning horizon, the business unit will want to position itself closer to flexibility on the the fit versus flexibility continuum.

If the planning horizon is long, fit should be balanced with flexibility. With a long planning horizon, sufficient resources should be reinvested in the unit to maintain competitiveness. This allows the benefits of productivity to be harvested for a much longer period. Extended availability of investment potential benefits the entire corporation. With a long planning horizon, unit-specific, firm-specific, and industry-specific skills should continue to receive rewards, as long as they make a substantial contribution to competitive advantage.

Step 4: Conduct an Organizational Needs Analysis. Finally, a needs analysis of the entire organization should be conducted. Both strategic needs and human resource needs should be identified, examined, and evaluated in terms of feasibility, costs, and benefits. Interdependencies among various needs should be recognized. At this point choices regarding strategic direction, domain preferences, and sources of competitive advantage are particularly important.

The needs assessment process provides a shopping list for resource allocation decision making. Since the productivity quadrant represents a time of potential transition, it is important to ensure that alternatives are developed through a creative process. Otherwise, it is not unusual for established precedents leading to successful performance to limit the generation of options. It is equally important that the process be collaborative. Since many options are likely to require major shifts in the knowledge, skills, abilities, and expectations of the business unit's employees, their involvement in the analysis and decision making process is critical to successful implementation.

Productivity is the time to take stock of a firm's current position and where the firm wants to go in the future. The responsibilities of strategic human resource management involve both managing the process of analysis and decision making and contributing to the eventual decision outcomes.

QUADRANT 4: REDIRECTION

The fourth quadrant, redirection, is characterized by low growth expectations and poor organizational readiness. It is typically assumed that firms facing these conditions are in declining industries, but that is not always the case. Firms that have been unable to achieve a strong competitive position may also face low growth prospects even if the industry continues to expand. Other firms face these circumstances because they have maintained obsolete products or continue to rely on manufacturing processes that are no longer competitive. Examples include small textile mills and many family farms. Low growth expectations coupled with low organizational readiness often arises in firms that focus on excessive fit among human resource skills, organizational culture, managerial procedures, and competitive strategy.

Several firms in the steel industry provide interesting examples of this phenomena. Despite changes in technology and an increasingly competitive international market arena, many large integrated steel mills stubbornly maintained their open-hearth furnaces, extensive and integrated product lines, and cumbersome size. It was not until domestic minimills and foreign competitors eroded substantial portions of their market share that these large, integrated steel mills recognized a problem. Only after severe negative economic consequences was it accepted that their outdated production processes, highly formal organization structures, and control-oriented management styles were leading to organizational demise. Managers acknowledged quite late in the game that the the problems were not just the results of a cyclical downturn in demand. With this recognition came the opportunity for change. It is this type of opportunity that characterizes the redirection quadrant.

Choices for Businesses in the Redirection Quadrant

The choice facing businesses in circumstances of low growth expectations and low organizational readiness is between turnaround and exit from the industry. Stated differently, a firm must decide whether to redirect employee activities or alter the objectives for the business unit. It is important to recognize that an opportunity for turnaround does not guarantee that an investment in internal revitalization and change is in the best interest of the organization. The types of changes necessary to compete effectively in a shifted marketplace will at times undermine a firm's source of competitive advantage in other product lines. As noted earlier, increasing price sensitivity is a common feature of industry and product maturation. For example, a firm that relies on differentiation across a broad but related product line might find it difficult to shift one product toward a cost leadership approach without undercutting the necessary flexibility, creativity, and uniqueness that serves as a competitive advantage with the remaining products.

Contextual Issues

Both human resource and competitive considerations are essential to consider when making a choice between turnaround and exit. From a human resource management perspective, if turnaround is chosen, retraining, restructuring, and realignment are needed. Allaire and Firsirotu identify a number of important pitfalls that firms should keep in mind as they consider a revitalization or turnaround strategy.[16] One of the most critical, from a human resource management standpoint, when management does not realize it is embarking on new territory. Knowledge, skills, and abilities that may have been essential for achieving a competitive edge in the past may no longer offer a strategic advantage. Recognizing the limitations of existing skills and capabilities may be hindered by the emphasis placed on identifying similarities between the existing operation and the new direction.

General Foods encountered this problem when it first entered the fast-food business with Burger Chef. Initially, General Foods tried to manage the new business in the same way and with the same people that had led to their success in food processing. When attempting revitalization or turnaround, firms should be attuned to the need for a change in organizational culture, requirements for interdependence, collaboration with successful existing operations, and the possibility of needing entirely different human resource management practices.

A second potential problem area concerns the health of a firm's human resources. Even if strategic revitalization or turnaround activities are desirable and widely accepted, they still require massive amounts of learning and adapting to be effective, which places enormous stress on the employees involved in the process. Existing internal and external alliances are often shattered. Existing competencies are no longer valued to the same extent. While the vision or strategic direction may be clear, the outcome is certainly not guaranteed. Each of these factors raises the emotional and, quite possibly, the physical costs associated with revitalization and turnaround.

From a competitive standpoint, a firm must determine whether or not the cost-benefit ratio associated with radical change exceeds the cost-benefit ratio resulting from a planned exit from a particular business arena. If the probability of turnaround success is not high, revitalization investments may become a cash trap. This can waste both financial and human resources available to an organization.

There are four alternative exit strategies to consider. If the industry's structure is appropriate, and if the firm can achieve the appropriate types of distinct competencies, assuming a leadership role presents one possibility. A successful leader, even in a low growth situation, can be highly profitable. According to Michael Porter, achieving leadership generally requires the purchase of market share, and possibly operations, from competitors who intend to leave the industry early.[17] Acquisitions of this type can provide the necessary human resource and technological talent needed to assume a dominant industry position. Information-processing activities are also extremely important. In order to maintain high levels of motivation among employees, the development and disclosure of credible information about industry conditions and the organization's intended strategy are essential. For some firms this may present a new human resource management challenge. Firms that wish to become leaders during industry decline should also work to reduce or eliminate exit barriers for competitors. To the extent that rivalry can be reduced, profitability can be enhanced.

A second type of planned exit strategy is concentrating on securing a dominant position in an attractive niche. This option also relies on a clear understanding of industry conditions and organizational strengths and weaknesses. A niche strategy can allow a business unit to retain and capitalize on existing knowledge, skills, and abilities relevant to only a small segment of the marketplace. If a firm has selected a concentric diversification strategy, if the outputs of the business unit in the redirection quadrant facilitate achieving competitive advantage in other organizational units, or if exit costs are high, this can be a particularly attractive option.

A harvest strategy presents a third alternative for planned exit. The purpose of a harvest strategy is to maximize the resource flow from the unit. New investments are severely restricted or eliminated entirely. The residual strengths of the business are relied upon to generate profits. A harvest strategy is an option only for firms in fairly strong competitive positions. The earlier redirection circumstances are recognized by strategic human resource managers, the more likely a harvest strategy will be a viable option.

The final exit strategy option is quick divestment. This strategy assumes that the business or its assets will be attractive to another firm. From a strategic human resource management perspective, early divestment relies on employee mobility. If a quick exit is selected, turnover, both voluntary and involuntary, and relocation within the firm are often required.

Organization culture and employment philosophy provide important constraints or opportunities associated with each of the various alternatives. For example, a firm with a strong commitment to employment security will likely have higher human resource exit costs than a firm that fosters hiring from outside the organization and frequent turnover. Often, when a firm reaches this stage of development, organization culture is firmly established. Equally often, values that have dominated during times of growth and implementation ease are maladaptive when faced with end-game choices such as harvesting, developing a niche, or preparing for quick divestment in a particular business. Thus, a firm's choice of location along the fit versus flexibility continuum strongly influences the feasibility of certain alternatives.

Prospector firms become particularly adept at choosing wisely between turnaround and exit, in part because the organization's culture is geared toward a fluid structure and a continually evolving product line and market focus. Most other organization cultures do not help a firm avoid premature divestiture, nor do they reduce the likelihood of creating a cash trap. Many organization cultures encourage these types of mistakes. Defender firms, for example, are often extremely reluctant to let go of operations that at one time were pivotal to their success. This reflects in part the integration of many activities in these firms. Although a particular product line may no longer be competitive or particularly profitable, the name association may be a cornerstone to a firm's corporate image and self-concept. If turnaround is unfeasible and exit is unacceptable, a cash trap is the likely outcome.

An additional cultural issue concerns diversification strategy. With related diversification, severe organizational conflict may arise from attempts to remain competitive in a product area that has undergone major technical changes. It is not uncommon for technical changes in a product or its production process to cause functional conflict rather than functional synergy in firms having technological relatedness among product groups.

A strategy of vertical integration creates similar problems. While cost advantages may result, the increased internal and external linkages generated by a vertical integration strategy erect mobility barriers. In addition, vertical integration increases and the operating leverage of the organization. Increased leverage increases the probability of systemwide repercussions from a change in vertical integration patterns. A heavy reliance on vertical integration extends the boundaries of the human resource management issues that must be considered.

Competing demand for human resources raises another set of important issues. The need for human resources in other, growing areas of the firm should be considered. If new employment options exist elsewhere in the firm, previous reliance on either unit-specific or industry-specific skills will affect a firm's ability to capitalize on these opportunities. Both the direct and indirect costs of transfer and the anticipated effectiveness of employee performance in new business areas must be carefully considered.

Suggested Analytic Steps

Step 1: Determine Whether Low Growth Prospects are Industrywide or Firm-specific. A number of analytic steps are necessary order to make strategic human resource management choices within the redirection quadrant effective. First, it is important to determine whether the industry is experiencing widespread decline or whether the firm is poorly positioned. In other words, do declining growth expectations and poor organizational readiness result from internal organizational choices or external trends and events? When a substitute product replaces the existing need for a product and ensures that future demand will only be for replacement parts, the phenomena is industrywide. This situation occurred when receiving tubes were replaced by integrated circuits. Under these conditions, turnaround is related to a firm's ability to adopt and succeed with the replacement technology. If the industry is declining, any turnaround strategy directed toward the current product would, at best, have a short-term pay back.

If the downturn is firm-specific—for example, the circumstances encountered by small textile mills facing industry consolidation—then a change in strategy or tactics might lead to renewed competitiveness. If the industry is concentrating on standardized, low-cost production, are there opportunities for differentiation? Are new market segments becoming available? In other words, are there opportunities for a firm to redeploy its talents to more productive uses within the same product and market arena, thereby raising growth expectations? If so, this could put the business unit in the development quadrant.

Step 2: Diagnose the Cause and Extent of Poor Organizational Readiness. Second, the cause of poor organizational readiness needs to be examined. If lack of organizational readiness reflects a poor organizational strategy, analysis to determine a new source of competitive advantage is needed. It may be that employees are better suited to implement a new strategy than they are to perform under existing conditions. Different responses are appropriate if poor organizational readiness signals a lack of any distinct competencies or the omission of basic requirements for a particular business, than if poor organizational readiness reflects a lack of fit between a particular set of skills and abilities and a specified strategic focus. Woolworth's competencies are effective in the variety store industry and could potentially offer a source of competitive advantage in a similar retail situation. These same competencies, however, were ill-suited for discount store competitive conditions, as Woolco's failure illustrated. When skills are obsolete or do not meet basic business requirements, a firm has a slim human resource base to work from. When a strong skill base exists but has been misdirected, the potential for strong performance exists given the right circumstances and appropriate application.

Step 3a: Identify the Proportion of Skills that Are Firm-specific and the Proportion that Are Industry-specific. Third, an evaluation of turnaround feasibility and exit feasibility depends, in part, on the extent to which firm- and industry-specific skills are present and the extent to which these skills meet the needs of the current competitive environment. As discussed previously, firm-specific and industry-specific skills have a more narrow range of use than general skills. This more limited scope can be either an advantage or a disadvantage, depending on the competitive situation.

Step 3b: Determine the Extent to which Firm-specific and Industry-specific Skills Can Contribute to Competitive Advantage in the Future. If firm- and industry-specific skills comprise a high proportion of the human resource skill base, and such skills are compatible with the competitive environment, turnaround feasibility depends on whether additional skills can be learned in a timely manner. Under these conditions, basic business requirements have been achieved, but a source of competitive advantage may be eroding. Examples of firms identifying this diagnostic situation include hotels and restaurants that have improved service and made a comeback. Exit, under these circumstances, is less desirable because it wastes opportunities.

If firm- and industry-specific skills comprise a high proportion of the human resource skill base, and if these capabilities do not meet competitive needs, turnaround will create significant amounts of organizational conflict. Not only will employees have to learn new skills, they will have to abandon those capabilities rewarded in the past. In addition, exit will be quite difficult, since the mobility of these employees is impaired. This is perhaps the most painful choice situation facing a firm. The issues surrounding what to do with family farms illustrates this dilemma.

If firm- and industry-specific skills comprise a low proportion of the skill base, but if those skills fit well with the competitive conditions, as in software development firms, turnaround is feasible if appropriate new skills can be acquired in a timely fashion. If turnaround is either unfeasible or undesirable, exit is less complicated by organization values and personal limitations. Since employees may be quite mobile, a firm may be able to acquire some of the needed skills and develop others. This can affect the time horizon for improved organizational readiness significantly.

If firm- and industry specific-skills are low but incompatible with competitive conditions, both competitive restructuring and a shift in a firm's values are needed to effect a turnaround. This was the situation faced by AMC prior to its acquisition by Chrysler. Exit may be a desirable choice in a multibusiness firm. In single-business organizations, merger or acquisition by a firm that possesses the needed expertise is often seen as a desirable alternative. Generally, a merger or acquisition shifts a firm's values and personality as fully as it alters its strategy and capabilities.

Step 4: Determine the Exit Costs for the Business Unit. A final analytic step involves an assessment of exit costs. Exit costs are in part a function of the mobility associated with firm-specific skills development. More generally speaking, exit costs are increased if knowledge, skills, and abilities are specialized and thereby difficult to convert to alternate uses. In this way, while an ability to type accurately and rapidly on a manual typewriter may, at one time, have been considered a very general skill, this capability is not easily converted to alternate uses when a firm acquires a word processing unit. Similarly, knowing how to diagnose problems with vacuum tubes loses considerable value with the introduction of integrated circuits. Noncompetitive but specialized human resource assets, just like other specialized assets, must be redirected toward other uses paralleling the original competitive situation or their value is greatly diminished. The number of midlevel managers structured out of large organizations as they introduce new technologies painfully illustrates this situation.

If a firm has an organizational culture that relies on long-term employment and concern for individuals, as with the HP Way mentioned earlier, exit costs may be extremely high if a firm's human capital is not well suited to current business conditions. Often, firms facing this set of circumstances search extensively for new opportunities that can rely on existing skills. When Cummins Engine decided to invest in CIM technology in its main engine plant, it simultaneously developed a related diversification strategy to open employment opportunities for displaced workers. From a competitive perspective, a firm with a tenure-oriented culture is wise to continually insure that the human capital it maintains is both flexible and a source of competitive advantage.

Exit costs can also include labor settlements and the costs of breaking contracts with customers and suppliers. While initial payments can be calculated as direct costs, indirect costs should also be projected. What is the cost of the loss of credibility associated with premature exit from an industry? What are the costs in employee commitment and corporate culture arising from layoffs or early retirements? What are the competitive costs of giving up on a business? Will other organization units be as willing to take risks in the future?

These four analytic steps provide the information needed to make an effective redirection decision. An evaluation of the industry condition provides a better understanding of the competitive situation and an indication of the planning time horizon. An assessment of the firm's current competitive position permits an assessment of both turnaround and exit options. Evaluating the feasibility of accomplishing needed changes further refines these alternatives. Understanding exit costs and alternate uses for human resource capital helps to establish decision priorities. Often, no choice is truly desirable, and most options contain significant risks. If consideration of the future is incorporated during productivity phases, these problems can frequently be reduced.

NOTES

1. Additional information regarding growth expectation can be found in H. I. Ansoff, *The New Corporate Strategy* (New York: Wiley, 1988); M. Porter *Competitive Advantage*, (New York: Free Press, 1985); R. E. Miles, et al., Organization strategy, structure, and process. *Academy of Management Review* 3 (1978) 546–662; A. T. Chandler, *Strategy and Structure: Chapters in the History of the American Enterprise* (Cambridge, Mass.: MIT Press, 1962).

2. For additional information regarding the ways in which sources of distinct competence are likely to change at different evolutionary stages, see C. W. Hofer, (1977) Conceptual constructs for formulating corporate and business strategy. Boston: Intercollegiate Case Clearing House; P. Kotler *Marketing Management* (Englewood Cliffs, N. J.: Prentice-Hall, 1988).

3. M. Porter discusses industry evolution in *Competitive Strategy* (New York: Free Press, 1980).

4. See, for example C. A. De Kluyver, Innovation and industrial product life cycles. *California Management Review* 20 (1) (1977): 21–33; G. S. Day, *Analysis for Strategic Market Decisions*. (St. Paul: West 1986); R. H. Hayes and S. C. Wheelwright. The dynamics of process-product life cycles. *Harvard Business Review* 57, (2) (March-April 1979): 127–36; Porter, *Competitive Strategy*.

5. Porter, *Competitive Advantage*.

6. For an expanded discussion, see A. C. Cooper and D. Schendel, Strategic responses to technological threats. *Business Horizons* 19(1) (1976): 1–9.

7. Porter, *Competitive Strategy*.

8. L. T. Perry, Least-cost alternatives to layoffs in declining industries. *Organizational Dynamics* 14(4) (1986): 48–61.

9. Galbraith and Kazanjian, *Strategy Implementation*.

10. I. C MacMillan and P. E. Jones, *Strategy Formulation: Power and Politics*. (2d ed) (St. Paul: West, 1986).

11. Ibid.

12. Chandler, *Strategy and Structure*.

13. Galbraith and Kazanjian, *Strategy Implementation*.

14. H. Mintzberg, *The Structuring of Organizations*. (Englewood Cliffs, N.J.: Prentice Hall, 1979).

15. For additional discussion, see C. A. Lengnick-Hall and D. H. Futterman, Getting a handle on complex units. *Personnel* 62(3) (1985): 57–63.

16. Y. Allaire and M. Firsirotu, How to implement radical change strategies in large organizations. *Sloan Management Review* 26(3) (1985): 19–34.

17. Porter, *Competitive Strategy*.

7

Application of the Strategic Human Resource Management Model

This chapter presents a decision flow outline of a step-by-step process for strategic human resource management. This decision process summarizes the various choice points described in the proposed model for strategic human resource management and highlights the interactive nature of competitive strategy and human resource management activities. We propose that this approach be used to bridge the gap between theoretical descriptions and the practice of strategic human resource management.

Reciprocal interdependence between a firm's business strategy and its human resources strategy underlies the proposed approach to the strategic management of human resources. This perspective is depicted in Figure 2. Both human resource and business strategies are seen as composite outcomes. In each system many functions, events, and relationships influence organizational results. The crucial interaction is between multidimensional demand and multifaceted readiness. Each is an input to and a constraint on the other.

The following decision pattern can be used to guide managers through a systematic use of the proposed model Checklists are provided to encourage a comprehensive approach to each analytic step.

IDENTIFYING THE RELEVANT STRATEGIC HUMAN RESOURCE MANAGEMENT DECISION QUADRANT

The first step in the strategic human resource management process is to identify the organization's or the business unit's position on the growth-readiness matrix. The position of a business unit depends on corporate

Figure 2
A Perspective of Competitvie Strategy and Human Resource Management Strategy Interdependence

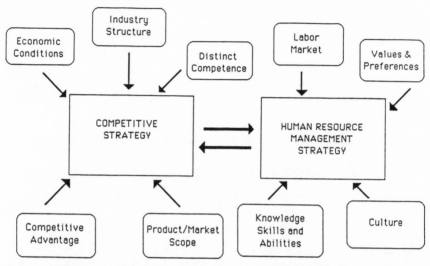

Source: Adapted from C. A. Lengnick-Hall and M. L. Lengnick-Hall. 1988. Strategic human resources management: A review of the literature and a proposed typology. *Academy of Management Review* 13(3): 454-470.

growth expectations and the level of organizational readiness to achieve those objectives. If a business unit has high growth expectations and low levels of organizational readiness, it is placed in the development quadrant. If a business unit has high growth expectations and high levels of organizational readiness, it is positioned in the expansion quadrant. If a business unit has low growth expectations and high levels of organizational readiness, it is categorized in the productivity quadrant. Finally, if a business unit has low growth expectations coupled with low levels of organizational readiness, it should be classified in the redirection quadrant.

Let's first consider corporate growth expectations. As indicated in the model description growth expectations include intended expansion in sales volume or organizational size, increases in product-market scope, and increases in the variability of a business unit's activities. The following checklist can be used to assess the growth expectations of the business unit.

Checklist 1
Assessment of Corporate Growth Expectations

1. How rapidly is sales volume expected to grow during the plan-
   ning period?   slow   1 2 3 4 5   rapid

7. To what extent is the competitive
   strategy well understood by all
   employees?   low   1 2 3 4 5   high

The first three questions on this checklist focus on extrinsic factors likely to enhance motivation. The last four questions address issues of intrinsic motivation and likely goal conflict. An individual is more likely to internalize goals and desired behavior if expectations are clear and if organizational purposes are widely known and accepted.

Strong or exceptional ratings of knowledge, skills, and abilities in Checklist 2, coupled with high levels of motivation in Checklist 3, indicate high levels of organizational readiness. Low scores on either ability level or motivation suggest low levels of readiness. Understanding the source of low readiness is an important part of diagnosing the situation.

It is important to recognize that ability and motivation are not compensatory. Regardless of how much effort individuals put into tasks, if they do not have the knowledge, skills, or ability needed to do their jobs, their performance will be in adequate. Likewise, if an individual has all the necessary capabilities but does not apply them to the task at hand, low levels of performance will result.

Based on the previous assessments, a business unit can be categorized as in the development quadrant, the expansion quadrant, the productivity quadrant, or the redirection quadrant. The next phase of the analysis considers the relevant strategic human resource management issues and analytic steps on a quadrant-by-quadrant basis.

STRATEGY FORMULATION IN THE DEVELOPMENT QUADRANT

The fundamental decision to be made by business units in the development quadrant involves strategy formulation. A choice must be made to either invest in the firm's human capital in order to improve organizational readiness, to alter the business unit's goals to conform to the existing level of organizational readiness, or to alter the way in which current knowledge, skills, and abilities are used to achieve competitive advantage.

The first step in the process is to diagnose the cause of poor organizational readiness. Much of the analysis needed for this step will have been done in order to properly position the business unit on the growth-readiness matrix. Using Checklist 2 to evaluate the adequacy of existing knowledge, skills, and abilities and Checklist 3 to determine the motivational aspects of readiness allows a strategic human resource manager to diagnose the underlying cause of poor organizational readiness.

If the source of poor organizational readiness is motivational, then any improvements in organizational readiness will likely require revisions in the firm's reward system. Knowledge, clarity, and acceptance of goals should also be examined. Unless employees know what they are supposed to accomplish and accept responsibility for the contributions they are expected to make toward a firm's competitive position, individual motivation to perform is not likely to be high.

Organizational culture will need to be examined to determine whether or not performance expectations and skill acquisition practices are facilitated or hindered by the existing organizational climate. Consider, for example, a firm in which creativity is needed to achieve competitive advantage. Even if employees with outstanding innovative skills and abilities have been hired, if the organizational culture concentrates on punishing failure rather than rewarding successes, the potential for a distinct competence in innovation is unlikely to be realized.

If the source of low organizational readiness is inadequate knowledge, skills, and abilities, the firm faces an entirely different set of issues. While Checklist 2 provides a menu of the specific competencies required, an assessment needs to be made as to whether or not the problem is correctable. Checklist 4 provides some guidance regarding issues to consider in assessing the correctability of knowledge, skills, and ability deficiencies.

Checklist 4
Assessing The Correctability of Low Organizational Readiness

1. Can the necessary knowledge, skills, and abilities be learned by current employees?
2. Is the firm able to provide the appropriate training and development to teach these knowledge, skills, and abilities?
3. What is the expected time frame for achieving adequate performance levels in the new knowledge, skills, and abilities?
4. Does the competitive situation permit an adequate time for learning to take place?
5. Can the necessary knowledge, skills, and abilities be acquired from outside the organization?
6. Does the firm have the resources necessary to fund the acquisition?
7. Can employees having the necessary knowledge, skills, and abilities be integrated effectively within the existing organization?

Answers to Checklist 4 indicate whether or not capability deficiencies can be corrected in sufficient time to secure a desirable competitive position. It is equally important to determine whether or not improving organizational readiness is a cost-effective choice. An analysis of cost effectiveness assumes that the primary objective can be achieved with a given level of investment. To address issues related to cost effectiveness, direct and indirect benefits as well as direct and indirect costs need to be evaluated. Checklist 5 outlines the issues that should be considered in assessing cost effectiveness.

Checklist 5
Evaluating Cost Effectiveness of Investments to Improve Organizational Readiness

1. What are the financial costs of developing the necessary knowledge, skills, and abilities in-house?
2. What are the financial costs of acquiring the necessary knowledge, skills, and abilities from the external market?
3. What are the opportunity costs of a financial investment in developing or acquiring needed knowledge, skills, and abilities?
4. What are the human costs (i.e., displacement, stress, organizational conflict) of developing or acquiring the needed knowledge, skills, and abilities?
5. How rapidly will the new knowledge, skills and abilities become obsolete?
6. Are any indirect financial benefits to be derived from investing in the needed knowledge, skills and abilities? (i.e., potential for shared economies, new skills could be transferred to other units at lower cost)
7. Are any secondary competitive benefits expected from developing or acquiring the necessary knowledge, skills and abilities? (i.e., increased organizational flexibility, enhanced corporate image, more sustainable competitive edge in related product lines)
8. Are any secondary human resource benefits expected from developing or acquiring the needed knowledge, skills, and abilities? (i.e., increased self-efficacy, enhanced organizational commitment, greater motivation potential inherent in the job)

An assessment of these costs and benefits will not be the same for every organization, even if the quantifiable aspects of the cost-benefit assessment are similar. Organizational culture, the values and beliefs that guide human resource management activities, and strategic orientation will all influence how these costs are interpreted. For example, in a research and development laboratory enhanced self-efficacy may be an extremely important secondary benefit of any investment in human capital if it increases the rate of innovation. For a defender firm competing on cost leadership, increasing organizational conflict may present an excessive cost. A situational analysis of a firm's unique blend of human resource management practices, competitive strategy, and organization culture needs to accompany any effective cost-benefit assessment.

If the needed knowledge, skills, and abilities cannot be either developed or acquired from outside the organization, or if the cost-benefit analysis shows a negative return, an investment in improved organizational readiness is unlikely to pay off in terms of competitive advantage. In addition, if the cost effectiveness of an investment in human capital is low, the resources and energies of the firm might be better put to alternate uses.

The next stage in the process is to assess goal realism. Two sets of issues need to be considered. First, realistic growth expectations within the current industry setting need to be evaluated. To do this, a diagnosis of the current industry structure should be undertaken along with an assessment of trigger events likely to foster a transition in the current competitive situation. Checklist 6 provides some guidance in conducting an appropriate industry assessment.

Checklist 6
Analysis of Industry Structure and Transition Potential

1. Is the current level of competition in the industry high, moderate or low? Many roughly equal competitors, slow growth, few product differences, high exit costs, and high fixed costs of operation signal high levels of rivalry.)

2. Are events on the horizon likely to trigger a change in the level of competition? Acquisitions can introduce a new personality to the playing field, and technological innovation can alter the equality among competitors and introduce important product differences.)

3 Do customer groups or customer industries have a great deal of influence on the operations of the firm? For example, do they purchase in large volume? Is there a threat of backward integration?

4. Are significant changes in buyer habits or preferences anticipated?

5. Do supplier groups or industries significantly influence the way in which business is conducted in the industry? For example, are substitute products available? Are switching costs high or low? Is the supplier industry dominated by only a few companies?

6. Are any changes such as consolidation, new technology, or increased regulation anticipated in either buyer or supplier industry structures that will alter their relationship with the firm?

7. Are there effective industry-wide barriers to entry such as economies of scale, brand loyalty, proprietary technology, and specialized human resource capabilities?

8. If new firms should enter the industry, what is the likelihood of effective retaliation? (The potential for retaliation increases if the industry has a history of aggressive competition, if resources are available, and if the growth rate for existing products is slow.)

9. Are there attractive substitute products available? (It is important to consider both products being developed within the industry and products that might serve a similar purpose developed outside the industry.)

10. Are the rates of product, process, and managerial innovation high, moderate, or low? Can innovations lead to a sustainable competitive advantage?[1]

As competition within an industry increases, and as industry participants lose ground to customer groups, suppliers, or substitute products, industry attractiveness and, consequently, industry profitability are expected to decline. Transition periods can offer opportunities for growth or serious competitive threats, depending on a firm's competitive position and existing store of distinct competencies. A thorough understanding of the industry condition for the forseeable future is the first aspect of assessing whether or not growth expectations are realistic.

Analyzing the industry permits an evaluation of the potential for increased market penetration. Additional opportunities for rapid growth come from outside the current industry boundaries. At this point, the potential for product development, market development, and conglomerate diversification needs to be evaluated. Checklist 7 provides some guidance for this activity.

Checklist 7
Assessing Growth Opportunities Outside the Current Industry

1. Have new, untapped geographic markets been identified?
2. Have new uses been developed for the existing product?
3. Has the firm demonstrated previous success with product diversification?
4. Can the product life cycle be prolonged if new product features are added?
5. Does the company's image facilitate brand loyalty and product line identification?
6. Will the introduction of related products expand the use of the original product line?
7. Does the organization have slack human, physical, and financial resources?
8. Does the firm have a set of distinct competencies that create synergy in different product and market arenas?
9. Does the firm want to increase its ability to manage risk?
10. Does the firm want to decrease its need to manage risk?
11. Would the firm benefit from a reduced dependency on current industries?
12. Does this organization continuously undergo revision in product-market scope?

If the answers to the first three questions are yes, significant opportunities for market development may exist. To determine whether or not these opportunities present reasonable risks for the firm, it is important to consider any cultural barriers that may exist, to predict any unusual costs that may arise, and to explore any differences in market segment structure, buying behavior, or competitive advantages.

If the answers to questions four, five, and six are yes, the firm may want to seriously consider product development opportunities. Risks include unexpected cost differences across product lines and unnoticed market differences, even among related products. In addition, expanding the product line may trigger competition from unexpected sources or retaliation from existing competitors.

If the answers to questions seven through eleven are yes, diversification may offer attractive opportunities. While diversification may offer attractive product, market, and profit opportunities, it is also likely to generate a preference for growth for growth's sake. In addition, diversification generally requires a change in organizational structure and culture. Increased organizational complexity and an enhanced potential for dysfunctional conflict often accompany diversification. These two factors mean that secondary costs must be evaluated very carefully.

If the answers to questions eight and twelve are yes, the firm is likely a prospector. As noted, prospector organizations often thrive on growth in new products and markets, which is, however, generally accomplished by divesting more mature operations. Identification as a prospector suggests that strategic human resource management must be conducted at a corporate, rather than at a business unit, level.

At this stage in the decision-making process, a judgement needs to be made as to whether the high growth expectations are realistic. If an increased market penetration strategy seems unlikely, and if industry growth rates are low, successful expansion in the current product-market arena is doubtful. If few opportunities exist outside industry boundaries, or if other organizational concerns make expansion of the product-market scope undesirable, then the growth expectations of the business unit should be reassessed.

Next, the interactive consequences of investing in improved organizational readiness to enable exploitation of growth opportunities need to be addressed. At this point, the strategic human resource manager needs to consider the effect of decisions regarding the particular business unit in question on the organization as a whole. At this stage each business unit can be considered part of the firm's portfolio.

As was discussed in Chapter 2, one of the fundamental issues in portfolio management is balance. Business units using more of a firm's human capital and financial resources than it can generate must be balanced by business units generating greater human capital and financial resources than are needed to maintain the desired competitive position. If a firm wants to increase predictability in organizational performance, it is generally preferable to have business units distributed rather evenly across industries and products at different life cycle stages. If a firm's overriding objective is profitability, it makes sense to have a greater proportion of the organization's business units in fairly mature products and industry settings. If the firm wishes to emphasize growth, a greater proportion of the business units should be in early stages of product and industry development.

There is no single optimal blend of business unit characteristics. A desirable mix reflects a firm's distinct competencies and source of competitive advantage, its culture and values, and its strategic objectives. To the extent that a firm competes on differentiation across related product and market segments, an investment in human capital is expected to have a synergistic payoff. To the extent a firm has a clear strategic focus and corporate identity, it is better able to tolerate the risks of investment in unique or previously untried human resource capabilities.

The fourth stage in strategy formulation for business units in the development quadrant considers issues related to tight fit among the firm's strategy, structure, and management processes, as well as human resource knowledge, skills, and abilities versus a loose coupling among these factors in order to enhance organizational flexibility. The first issue is determining the business unit's current position in terms of fit versus flexibility. Checklist 8 can be used to identify the business unit's current position with regard to a tight fit.

Checklist 8
Determining The Business Unit's Current Fit Versus Flexibility Position

1. To what extent has an investment been made in unit-specific skills?   low   1 2 3 4 5   high

2. To what extent has an investment been made in firm-specific skills?   low   1 2 3 4 5   high

3. To what extent has an investment been made in industry-specific skills?   low   1 2 3 4 5   high

4. To what extent has an investment been made in general skill development?   low   1 2 3 4 5   high

5. To what extent are organizational policies tightly linked and coordinated?   low   1 2 3 4 5   high

6. To what extent do human resource management activities depend on other organization activities?   low   1 2 3 4 5   high

7. What degree of emphasis is placed on division of labor?   low   1 2 3 4 5   high

8. What degree of emphasis is placed on specialization?	low	1 2 3 4 5	high
9. What degree of emphasis is placed on efficiency?	low	1 2 3 4 5	high

If a business unit has circled primarily fours and fives, then a tight fit has been emphasized in human resource management decisions. The more ones and twos that have been circled, the farther toward flexibility the business unit is positioned on a fit versus flexibility continuum. This analysis provides a baseline measure of the business unit's current position. Let's now consider whether or not that position is appropriate.

Checklist 9 is intended to guide a strategic human resource manager through consideration of the most desirable position on a fit versus flexibility continuum.

Checklist 9
Strategic Desirability of Fit Versus Flexibility

1. To what degree has minimal fit been achieved within this business unti?	low	1 2 3 4 5	high
2. To what degree does early fit provide a source of competitive advantage?	low	1 2 3 4 5	high
3. To what degree does a tight fit provide a sustainable source of competitive advantage?	low	1 2 3 4 5	high
4. Does this business unit require an ability to change rapidly to meet customer preferences?	yes	1 2 3 4 5	no
5. Does this business unit require an ability to change rapidly to meet customer performances?	yes	1 2 3 4 5	no
6. Are the triggers of change in the industry predictable?	yes	5 4 3 2 1	no
7. Are the directions of change in the industry predictable?	yes	5 4 3 2 1	no
8. Are the human resource management activities across different business units in this firm complementary?	yes	5 4 3 2 1	no

To the extent that a business unit has circled primarily fours or fives on Checklist 9, a tight fit provides an important and enduring source of competitive advantage. If a business unit has circled mostly ones and twos, flexibility in human resource management activities is expected to be an important distinct competence for the business unit.

At this point the results of Checklist 8 and Checklist 9 should be compared. If the current position of the business unit and the strategically desirable position on the fit versus flexibility continuum are compatible, this match should be maintained. If, however, there are incongruencies between the current position and the desirable position, low organizational readiness may offer an attractive opportunity for reconciliation.

The final stage in the analysis requires the strategic human resource manager to consider time horizons. Can organizational readiness be achieved in time to improve the competitive position of the business unit? If not, such an investment in human capital will be difficult to justify, unless secondary benefits are extensive. Will the improved competitive position be maintained for a sufficient period of time to receive an adequate return on investment? If not, an investment in improved organizational readiness while feasible and competitively attractive, is not likely to be a cost-effective use of the business unit's resources.

Armed with the results of these analyses, a strategic human resource manager is now prepared to make a choice in terms of strategic formulation. Should the business unit invest heavily in its human resources in order to improve organizational readiness? Should it change its corporate goals to better reflect internal organizational considerations or environmental contingencies? Should a change in the competitive operating strategy be implemented to better capitalize on existing knowledge, skills, and abilities? At this point, a choice should be made regarding strategic direction.

RESOURCE ALLOCATION IN THE EXPANSION QUADRANT

Business units in the expansion quadrant have achieved high levels of organizational readiness and embraced high expectations with regard to growth. The basic strategic human resource management issue is effective resource allocation. What proportion of resources should be devoted to achieving continued growth, and what proportion should be channeled into managing its effects?

Deciding on a relevant planning horizon is a fundamental requirement for any effective resource allocation decision. In the expansion quadrant, the relevant time frame is primarily dependent upon how long existing competitive conditions are expected to continue. If a business unit is positioned at an extreme flexibility position, external competitive trends can possibly be counteracted, but in most instances an appropriate planning horizon reflects industry conditions and evolution.

A second fundamental prerequisite for an effective resource allocation decision is an identification of the amount and nature of the resources to be deployed. If the resource base is small, the expected value of accurate information increases, since errors in allocation are magnified by resource scarcity. If the resource base is quite large, it may be more cost effective to rely on approximately correct information so that resources can enter the productive cycle more quickly. With a large resource base the costs of minor misallocations are less severe.

Checklist 6, introduced in the discussion of business units in the development quadrant, can be used to gather relevant information for both of these decisions. Knowing the industry structure that provides the environmental context for business unit competition can indicate time-related limits and profit projections. Increased stability in industry conditions extends the planning horizon. A favorable industry structure increases the attractiveness of continued participation and provides a greater store of resources to fund continued growth.

Next, the costs of sustaining rapid growth need to be identified. We begin with consideration of the direct costs.

Checklist 10
Identifying the Direct Costs of Sustained Growth

1. What are the costs associated with hiring sufficient personnel to sustain rapid growth?
2. What are the costs associated with developing necessary unit-specific skills among new employees?
3. What are the costs associated with developing necessary firm-specific skills for employees new to the organization?
4. What are the costs associated with developing necessary industry-specific skills among employees new to the industry?
5. What costs are involved in socializing new employees into the existing work force?
6. What costs are involved in compensating employees for working longer hours, adding new jobs responsibilities, or relocating to new areas?

A number of the techniques developed in early strategic human resource management efforts are helpful in identifying the direct costs of growth. The contributions these methods make to effective strategic human resource management particularly in the expansion quadrant should not be underestimated. Human resource planning tools and valuation techniques are especially useful.

To adequately assess the total costs of sustained growth, indirect costs, must also be identified. Indirect costs relate primarily to the toll that sustained rapid growth is likely to take on human resources and strategic perspectives. Growth expectations are often seductive. The rewards of growth can increase organizational dependence on expansion beyond the point where a competitive advantage results. Checklist 11 is designed to aid in identifying the indirect costs of sustaining rapid growth.

Checklist 11
Identifying Indirect Costs of Sustained Growth

1. Is the potential for means-ends reversal exceeding desirable limits due to sustained growth?
2. Is organizational dependence on continued rapid growth exceeding desirable limits?
3. What are the physical, psychological, and emotional costs of sustained growth?
4. Are the business unit's human, financial, or other resources being stretched too thin?

When the direct and indirect costs required to sustain rapid growth are combined, the resource demands associated with a targeted allocation toward growth can be calculated.

Continuing with the focus on the cost side of the equation, the costs of managing growth must also be identified. This enables an assessment of the demand for resources associated with the alternative investment approach. Checklist 12 focuses attention on the costs associated with managing growth.

Checklist 12
Identifying the Costs of Managing Growth

1. What costs will be incurred by making changes in inbound logistics systems as a result of sustained growth?
2. What costs will be incurred by making changes in operations as a result of sustained growth?
3. What costs will be incurred by making changes in outbound logistic systems as a result of sustained growth?
4. What costs will be incurred by making changes in marketing and sales systems as a result of sustained growth?
5. What costs will be incurred by making changes in service systems as a result of sustained growth?
6. What costs will be incurred by making changes in procurement systems as a result of sustained growth?
7. What costs will be incurred by making changes in the firm's infrastructure as a result of sustained growth?
8. What costs will be incurred by making changes in technology development systems as a result of sustained growth?

9. What costs will be incurred by making changes in human resource management systems as a result of sustained growth?

10. What costs will be incurred by making changes in the firm's external linkages as a result of sustained growth?

11. What costs will be incurred by changes in the regulatory environment as a result of sustained growth?

12. What costs will be incurred by making changes in the firm's information processing requirements as a result of sustained growth?

13. What costs will be incurred by making changes in the firm's organization structure as a result of sustained growth?

It is now time to switch our focus from considering the relative demand for resources associated with either sustained high levels of growth or more effective management of the effects of growth, to consideration of the benefits associated with growth. Checklist 13 provides a tool for evaluating the potential benefits of growth.

Checklist 13
Identifying the Strategic Benefits of Growth

1. To what extent are there economies of scale in manufacturing, advertising, distribution, information processing, or other business activities?   low   1 2 3 4 5   high

2. To what extent are experience curve benefits present in this industry?   low   1 2 3 4 5   high

3. To what extent does this business unit rely on cost leadership as a source of competitive advantage?   low   1 2 3 4 5   high

4. To what extent will increased size provide additional leverage given the industry structure?   low   1 2 3 4 5   high

5. To what extent do economies of scope yield a source of competitive advantage?   low   1 2 3 4 5   high

6. To what extent does increased product-market diversity improve the risk position of the business unit?   low   1 2 3 4 5   high

7. To what extent does growth improve the company image so as to enhance competitive advantage?   low   1 2 3 4 5   high

8. To what extent does growth yield improved profit margins?   low   1 2 3 4 5   high

9. To what extent does growth in this business unit offer important human resource opportunities for business units in other quadrants?   low   1 2 3 4 5   high

10. To what extent does growth in this business unit provide a source of competitive advantage to other business units?   low   1 2 3 4 5   high

If the benefits of growth are extensive, a firm may wish to forgo some level of organizational profitability in order to achieve a given level of size or diversity. If, on the other hand, the expected benefits of growth beyond a certain level are modest, a firm may want to devote more of its resources and attention to ensuring that organizational systems keep pace with expansion.

It is important for a strategic human resource manager to recognize that the benefits of growth are not fixed. In fact, it is most reasonable to expect the level of benefits to change over time. In many industry settings, benefits are derived in a step function. There may be minimum and maximum economic plant sizes. Brand loyalty may be difficult to establish below a certain volume of sales, but sales levels beyond a certain threshold may provide few economies or other competitive advantages. For business units in the expansion quadrant, evaluation of the costs and benefits of growth is an ongoing process.

A final step in the analytic process is identifying relevant stakeholders and assessing what they stand to gain or lose by the resource allocation choice. A list of relevant stakeholders might include employees and potential employees, customers, suppliers, firms, and individuals in related industries, special interest groups, and shareholders. For each of these stakeholders it is important to determine exactly what and how much they can expect to gain from allocating resources toward continued growth or from deploying resources to manage the effects of growth. It is equally important to determine as precisely as possible where the resources will come from. Different stakeholder groups may have to make different levels of contribution.

A firm's position with regard to social responsibility has a great deal to do with how a stakeholder analysis is applied. For some organizations, the primary stakeholder is the shareholder. In this situation, strategic human resource management decisions should be made to maximize the long-term net worth of the firm. In other organizations, employee interests dominate. Here the firm may want to make strategic human resource choices that improve the probability for long-term employment or high wages. Clearly, there is no one right answer. However, ethical issues such as these should be made deliberately and with as full an understanding of complex consequences as possible. The resource allocation choices to be made in the expansion quadrant carry with them important value and social responsibility implications.

Decisions made in the expansion quadrant are, in many ways, complex cost-benefit analyses. The costs and benefits of continued rapid growth must be weighed against the costs and benefits of effective management of growth. The trade-offs are often obscure and generally have far-reaching consequences for all stakeholders.

CHANNELING THE RESULTS OF PRODUCTIVE ACTIVITY IN THE PRODUCTIVITY QUADRANT

The strategic human resource management situation in the productivity quadrant is often characterized by choosing among a number of attractive alternatives. While this may be a very desirable situation, it is often not easy to sort through the competing alternatives.

As in the other quadrants, a first step is to gain increased knowledge and understanding of the competitive situation. Checklist 6 again provides the raw data needed for analysis. Several issues are important to resolve. First, it is important to determine to what extent the existing source of competitive advantage is sustainable without additional investment. The answer to this first question suggests what proportion of the resources generated by high levels of productivity are discretionary in terms of their resource allocation options. Second, it is essential to determine whether or not the existing sources of competitive advantage can be protected from aggressive competitors. It may, for example, be possible to maintain existing distinct competencies without additional investment, but these same competencies may provide only a short-term competitive edge. Third, an industry analysis can suggest the length of time the current external competitive environment will remain stable. Stability is a key element in determining the planning time horizon. Fourth, industry analysis is a principle element in assessing industry attractiveness both currently and throughout the planning horizon. This final issue suggests the extent to which continued participation in an industry is beneficial and desirable.

A second phase of analysis in the productivity quadrant focuses inside the organization. Here the question is twofold. First, will existing distinct competencies be both necessary and sufficient to sustain competitive advantage? While the current source of competitive advantage may be both necessary and sufficient to maintain a desirable competitive position, existing distinct competencies may be insufficient to maintain a particular source of competitive advantage as industry conditions evolve. The first question, then, is can high levels of organizational readiness be sustained? If not, there will be a corresponding demand to reinvest productive resources back into the business unit to maintain a strong competitive position.

A second focus of internal analysis surrounds the desirability of the current value chain, distinct competencies, organizational culture, and strategic human resource management practices. This second concern evaluates the current set of distinct competencies through the lenses of fit versus flexibility. A tight fit often accompanies a business unit's position in the productivity quadrant. When considering the use of productive resources, it is essential to evaluate whether or not the previous fit preference and position presents a good set of options for the future.

Checklists nine and ten are particularly useful in making this assessment. However, an evaluation of the preference and requirement of fit versus flexibility (Checklist 10) should be applied toward anticipated future competitive conditions as well as the current situation. To the extent that flexibility is required to meet upcoming competitive conditions, there will be a demand for reinvestment of productive resources into the business unit in the productivity quadrant.

Once reinvestment needs have been determined it is time to consider investment opportunities in other parts of the organization. A needs analysis of this type should rely on high levels of participation and a decision model that fosters creativity. It may be useful to begin with a wish list. In some cases what begins as an outrageous idea serves as a stepping stone to a strong competitive position. A creative process for generating alternatives can also help to uncover as yet undetected problem areas lurking in the firm. There is nothing like the potential for gaining resources to bring previously unmentioned symptoms and unmet needs to light.

The decision situation in the productivity quadrant is attractive. Productive resources can be reinvested back into the business unit that produced them to achieve a number of outcomes. Resources can be reinvested to maintain the current competitive position as industry conditions change or as current distinct competencies lose effectiveness. Resources can be reinvested to secure a desirable position from which to exit an industry as it evolves. Resources can be reinvested to revitalize the business unit and change its center of gravity, potentially moving it from the productivity quadrant to the expansion quadrant.

Alternatively, productive resources can be allocated to other business units in the firm's portfolio. Human capital that is no longer needed in productivity-situated business units or that is more cost effective to use elsewhere can also be deployed in a variety of ways. Business units in productivity can provide the human resources to maintain the organization's culture, provide training in firm-specific skills, or cement the firm's strategic orientation. The competitive success of business units in the productivity quadrant enhances the credibility of the units' human resources as mentors. Resources generated by business units in the productivity quadrant often provide the necessary fuel to create organizational readiness for business units in the development quadrant and to manage the effects of growth for business units in the expansion quadrant.

TURNAROUND VERSUS EXIT IN REDIRECTION

Business units positioned in the redirection quadrant face perhaps the most challenging and potentially painful set of choices for a strategic human resource manager. The elements essential to making a competitive and astute, if not always popular, decision are good information, a clear understanding of the costs and benefits of various choices, and a logical rationale for the ultimate decision.

The first step in this process is to better understand why the business unit is in the redirection quadrant. This means that the strategic human resource manager needs to determine the causes of poor organizational readiness and the likelihood that the competitive situation and, consequently, growth expectations will change.

To tackle the first question, an analysis similar to that undertaken to determine the cause of poor organizational readiness in development should be initiated. Checklist 4, which assesses the business unit's ability to improve organizational readiness given the required knowledge, skills, and abilities, and Checklist 5, which evaluates the cost effectiveness of such an investment in human capital, provide good places to start. If it is not possible to sufficiently improve the level of organizational readiness so that competitive advantage is secure, a turnaround strategy is not a feasible option. Likewise, if an investment in improved organizational readiness is not cost effective, turnaround is not a desirable strategic human resource management choice.

The second issue to be considered is an assessment of the competitive situation. Whether the low growth expectations are the result of a temporary business cycle or a permanent change in industry attractiveness or competitive position needs to be determined first. The information generated in Checklist 6, which outlines the essential elements of an industry analysis, provides a good start. Particular attention should be paid to issues that trigger changes in industry structure.

If low growth expectations are temporary, it might be wise to conduct an evaluation similar to that for business units in the development quadrant. If low growth expectations reflect a declining industry condition, then exit strategies need to be considered. The more investments in improved organizational readiness appear both feasible and desirable, the more freedom a business unit has in selecting an appropriate exit strategy. Assuming a leadership position during industry decline can be an attractive option if the corresponding pay back is expected to be high and the evolutionary process slow. Identifying an attractive niche and positioning the business unit in a way that enhances organizational synergy and companywide competencies can provide a graceful and strategically attractive exit. A harvest strategy is an option only for business units able to develop a strong enough competitive advantage to survive neglect. Therefore, harvest options are unlikely to be feasible without some investment in improved organizational readiness.

Quick exit may be an attractive option if the business unit's human resource capital can be readily redirected toward other, more competitive business units. A firm's previous choices regarding fit and flexibility—see checklists eight and nine—strongly influence whether or not redeployment of a business unit's human resources is practical.

If turnaround is a feasible and desirable strategy, the benefits of achieving revitalization need to be assessed in the context of other opportunities for investment. Checklist 14 points out a number of important elements in this decision.

Checklist 14
Assessing the Relative Benefits of Revitalization

1. Will turnaround or revitalization of this business unit provide a more abundant return than investment in business units currently in the development quadrant?

2. Will turnaround or revitalization of this business unit provide a more abundant return than investment in business units currently in the expansion quadrant?

3. Will the time horizon for a return on investment for turnaround or revitalization of this business unit exceed the time horizon for return on investment of business units in the development quadrant?

4. Will the time horizon for a return on investment for turnaround or revitalization of this business unit exceed the time horizon for return on investment of business units in the expansion quadrant?

5. Does turnaround or revitalization of this business unit offer potential synergies that will lead to new sources of competitive advantage across the business portfolio?

6. Does turnaround or revitalization of this business unit increase or reduce the potential for means-ends reversal within the organization?

7. Does turnaround or revitalization of this business unit offer the potential to capitalize on existing organizational strengths?

8. Does turnaround or revitalization of this business unit offer the potential to eliminate some existing organizational weaknesses?

9. Is turnaround or revitalization of this business unit consistent with the organization culture?

10. Does turnaround or revitalization of this business unit reflect a desirable position on the fit versus flexibility continuum?

These benefits must be weighed against the potential risk that the investment will fail and become a cash trap and against the lost opportunities that come from using scarce organizational resources.

It is equally important to determine any exit costs. While the cost-benefit ratio for a turnaround or revitalization strategy may not be less than one, it may be more attractive than the cost-benefit ratio associated with exit. Both internally derived exit costs, such as high turnover or the costs of settling labor contracts, and externally related costs, such as gaps in the value chain or reduced distribution outlets, should be identified and assessed.

ACHIEVING STRATEGIC HUMAN RESOURCE MANAGEMENT

We propose a broader perspective of strategic human resource management than has typically been offered in the literature or in practice. Previous efforts have captured some of the important relationships among key activities but have ignored the truly multidimensional nature of this process. This can in part be attributed to the relatively recent interest in meshing two areas that have historically developed independent of one another.

Related to this has been the temptation of researchers and managers in one field to gain only a superficial understanding of the other field before attempting to integrate the two. This at best produces inadequate conceptualization of strategic human resource management possibilities and does a disservice to the slighted field, be it strategic management or human resources management. Greater cross-fertilization of ideas seems justified and provides managers who attempt this integrative venture a better understanding of two complex processes.

This book does not argue that all firms should adopt a strategic human resources management perspective. Rather, it highlights some of the advantages and disadvantages of integrating human resource management within the strategic management process. Further, we hope that a useful blueprint has been provided to those who wish to attempt an integration of human resource management and competitive strategy.

If a firm elects not to adopt a strategic human resource perspective, it must solve human resource problems through human resource means and by implication must solve competitive problems with other types of resources. Such a viewpoint may, over time, deplete the human resources of the firm. From this approach, human resources are seen as constraints on business policy.

If a strategic human resource management perspective is adopted, then human resource considerations must be intimately linked with strategic choices. This view assumes that human resources are critical to achieving competitive success. There are opportunity costs associated this view, however. A firm's outlook often becomes more inwardly focused, making it more difficult to accurately predict and interpret environmental events. Further, if human resource considerations are used to determine a strategic position, a firm may become less competitive than those with greater internal flexibility. Finally, linking human resources management intimately with strategic management may tend to overemphasize human resource matters in strategy formulation. Excessive attention may prove to be as detrimental as the prior neglect. To limit these negative effects, a reciprocal interdependence is most appropriate.

There is little empirical evidence to date to suggest that strategic human resource management directly influences organizational performance or competitive advantage. However, there is much anecdotal evidence to suggest that such a relationship does exist and will become increasingly important in a global marketplace. Increasing attention needs to be paid to organizational performance issues in order to provide the necessary support or disconfirmation. We believe, however, that strategic human resource management can provide a significant, and particularly difficult to imitate, source of competitive advantage.

NOTE

1. Adapted from M. Porter, *Competitive Strategy* (New York: Free Press, 1980).

Selected Bibliography

Ansoff, H. I. 1988. *The New Corporate Strategy*. New York: Wiley.

Baird, L., I. Meshoulam, and G. DeGive. (September-October 1983). Meshing human resources planning with strategic business planning: A model approach. *Personnel* 60(5): 14–25.

Cascio, W. 1987a. *Applied Psychology in Personnel Management*. 3d ed. Englewood Cliffs, N.J.: Prentice-Hall.

Cascio, W. 1987b. *Costing Human Resources: The Financial Impact of Behavior in Organizations*. Boston, Mass.: PWS-Kent.

Chandler, A. T., Jr. 1962. *Strategy and Structure: Chapters in the History of the American Enterprise*. Cambridge, Mass.: MIT University Press.

Cheek, L. M. 1973. Cost effectiveness comes from the personnel function. *Harvard Business Review* 51(3): 96–105.

Cooper, A. C., and D. Schendel. 1976. Strategic responses to technological threats. 19(1) *Business Horizons* 1–9.

Day, G. S. 1986. *Analysis for Strategic Market Decisions*. St. Paul, Minn.: West.

De Kluyver, C. A. 1977. Innovation and industrial product life cycles. *California Management Review* 20(1): 21–33.

DeSanto, J. F. October 1983. Work force planning and corporate strategy. *Personnel Administrator* 28(10): 33–42.

Deutch, A. Spring 1982. How employee retention strategies can aid productivity. *The Journal of Business Strategy* 2(4): 106–09.

Dimick, D. E. and V. V. Murray. 1978. Correlates of substantive policy decisions in organizations: The case of human resource management. *Academy of Management Journal* 21(4): 611–23.

Dyer, L. Fall 1983. Bringing human resources into the strategy formulation process. *Human Resource Management* 22(3): 257–71.

Dyer, L. Spring 1984. Studying human resource strategy: An approach and an agenda. *Industrial Relations* 23(2): 156–69.

Dyer, L. 1985. Strategic human resources management and planning. In *Research in Personnel and Human Resources Management*, eds. K. M. Rowland and G. R. Ferris, 1–30. Greenwich, Conn.: JAI Press.

Ellis, R. J. Winter 1982. Improving management response in turbulent times. *Sloan Management Review* 23(2): 3–12.

Flamholtz, E. April 1971. A model for human resource valuation: A stochastic process with service rewards. *The Accounting Review* 46(2): 253–67.

Fombrun, C. Summer 1982. Environmental trends create new pressures on human resources. *The Journal of Business Strategy.* 3(1): 61–69.

Frantzreb, R. B., L. T Landau, and D. P. Lundberg. June 1977 The valuation of human resources. *Business Horizons* 20(3): 73–80.

Galbraith, J. R. and R. J. Kazanjian. 1986 *Strategy Implementation: Structure, Systems and Process.* 2d ed. St. Paul: West.

Galosy, J. R. September-October 1983. Meshing human resources planning with strategic business planning: One company's experience. *Personnel* 60(5): 26–35.

Gerstein, M. and H. Reisman. Winter 1983. Strategic selection: Matching executives to business conditions. *Sloan Management Review* 24(2): 1–18.

Gutteridge, T. and F. L. Otte. 1983. *Organizational Career Development: State of Practice.* Washington, D.C.: ASTD Press.

Harvey, L. J. October 1983. "Effective planning for human resource development. *Personnel Administrator* 28(10): 45–52.

Hayes, R. H. and S. C. Wheelwright. March-April 1979. The dynamics of process-product life cycles. *Harvard Business Review* 57(2): 127–36.

Hrebiniak, L. G. and W. F. Joyce. 1984. *Implementing Strategy.* New York: Macmillan.

Hofer, C. W. and D. Schendel. 1978. *Strategy Formulation: Analytical Concepts.* St. Paul: West.

Kozlowski, S. W. J. 1984. Technological innovation and strategic HRM: Facing the challenge of change. In Eds. R. S. Schuler and S. A. Youngblood, pp. 72–81. *Readings in Personnel and Human Resource Management.* 2d ed. St. Paul: West,

Lawrence, P. 1984 Executive summary—The history of human resource management in America. Human resource management future conference, Harvard Business School, May 9–11.

Lenz, R. T. 1981. Determinants of organizational performance: An interdisciplinary review. *Strategic Management Journal* 2(2): 131–54.

Leontiades, M. Fall 1982. Choosing the right manager to fit the strategy. *The Journal of Business Strategy* 2(2): 58–69.

Lengnick-Hall, C. A. 1988. Fit and misfit: How to achieve efficiency and innovation. *Organization Development Journal* 6(2): 67–74.

Lengnick-Hall C. A. and M. L. Lengnick-Hall. 1988. Strategic human resources management: A review of the literature and a proposed typology. *Academy of Management Review* 13(3): 454–70.

Lengnick-Hall, C. A. and R. R. McDaniel, Jr. 1984. Scanning policies, structure and adaptability in human service systems. *American Business Review* 2(1): 12–23.

Lindroth, J. April 1982. How to beat the coming labor shortage. *Personnel Journal* 6(4): 268–72.

Lorange, P., M. F. S. Morton, and S. Ghoshal. 1986. *Strategic Control.* St. Paul: West.

MacMillan, I. C. and P. E. Jones. 1986. *Strategy Formulation: Power and Politics.* 2d ed. St. Paul: West.

MacMillan, I. C. and R. S. Schuler. 1985. Gaining a competitive edge through human resources. *Personnel* 62(4): 24–29.

Maier, H. 1982. Innovation, efficiency, and the quantitative and qualitative demand for human resources. *Technological Forecasting and Social Change* 21: 15–31.

Migliore, R. H. Summer 1982. Linking strategy, performance and pay. *The Journal of Business Strategy* 3(1): 90–94.

Miles, R. E. and C. C. Snow. 1984 Fit, failure and the hall of fame. In *Strategy and Organization*, eds. G. Carroll and D. Vogel. Boston: Pitman.

Miles, R. E., C. C. Snow, A. D. Meyer, and H. J. Coleman, Jr. 1978. Organization strategy, structure and process. *Academy of Management Review* (9): 546–662.

Milkovich, G. T. and J. M. Newman. 1987. *Compensation.* 2d ed. Dallas: Business Publications.

Mintzberg, H. 1988. Opening up the definition of strategy. In *The Strategy Process*, pp. 13–20. Englewood Cliffs, N.J: Prentice Hall.

Olian, J. D. and S. L. Rynes. 1984. Organizational staffing: Integrating practice with strategy. *Industrial Relations* 23(2): 170–83.

Perry, L. T. 1986. Least-cost alternatives to layoffs in declining industries. *Organizational Dynamics* 14(4): 48–61.

Pitts, R. A. and C. C. Snow. 1986. *Strategies for Competitive Success.* New York: Wiley.

Porter, M. E. 1980. *Competitive Strategy.* New York: Free Press.

Porter, M. E. 1985. *Competitive Advantage.* New York: Free Press.

Reypert, L. S. 1981. Successsdion planning in the ministry of transportation and communications, province of Ontario. *Human Resource Planning* 4(3): 151–56.

Rowland, K. M. and S. L. Summers. 1984. Human resource planning: A second look. *Personnel Administrator* 26(12): 73–80.

Rumelt, R. P. 1974. *Strategy, Structure and Economic Performance in Large American Industrial Corporations.* Boston: Harvard Graduate School of Business Administration.

Russ, C. F., Jr. 1982. Manpower planning systems: Part II. *Personnel Journal* 61(2): 119–23.

Schlesinger, L. A. 1984. Linking human resource management and business strategy. Human resource management future conference, Harvard Business School, May 9–11.

Schuler, R. S. and S. E. Jackson. 1987. Linking competitive strategies with human resource management practices. *Academy of Management Executive* 1(3): 207–19.

Schuler, R. S. and I. C. MacMillan. 1984. Gaining competitive advantage through human resource management practices. *Human Resource Management* 23(3): 241–56.

Schuler, R. S. and J. W. Walker. (in press) Don't waste time on planning—act: The development of human resource strategy. *Organizational Dynamics*.

Smith, E. C. August 1982. Strategic business planning and human resources: Part I. *Personnel Journal* 61(8): 606–10.

Smith, E. C. September 1982. Strategic business planning and human resources: Part II. *Personnel Journal* 61(9): 680–82.

Stumpf, S. A. and N. M. Hanrahan. 1984. Designing organizational career management practices to fit strategic management objectives. In *Readings in Personnel and Human Resource Management*. 2d ed. Eds. R. S. Schuler and S. A. Youngblood. St. Paul: West.

Sweet, J. Summer 1982. How manpower development can support your strategic plan. *The Journal of Business Strategy* 3(1): 77–81.

Tichy, N. M., C. J. Fombrun, and M. A. Devanna. Winter 1982. Strategic human resource management. *Sloan Management Review* 23(2): 47–61.

Walton, R. E. 1984. From control to commitment: Transforming work force management in the United States. Seventy-fifth anniversary colloquium on technology and productivity, Harvard Business School, March 27–29.

Warner, M. 1984. New technology, work organizations, and industrial relations. *Omega* 12(3): 203–10.

Wils, T. and L. Dyer. August 1984. Relating business strategy to human resource strategy: Some preliminary evidence. Paper presented at the forty-fourth annual meeting of the Academy of Management, Boston.

Zedeck, S., and W. F. Cascio. 1984. Psychological issues in personnel decisions. *Annual Review of Psychology* 35: 461–518.

Index

About the Authors

CYNTHIA A. LENGNICK-HALL is Associate Professor of Strategic Management at Wichita State University. She has published articles in such journals as *Academy of Management Review*, *Journal of Management*, and *Organization Studies*.

MARK L. LENGNICK-HALL is Assistant Professor of Human Resources at Wichita State University. His articles have appeared in such publications as *Academy of Management Review*, *Personnel Psychology*, and *Personnel Journal*.